I0902396

IMAGES of Rail

Boston & Maine in the 19th Century

IMAGES
of Rail

BOSTON & MAINE IN THE 19TH CENTURY

Bruce D. Heald, Ph.D.

ARCADIA
PUBLISHING

ISBN 978-0-7385-0546-6

Published by Arcadia Publishing
Charleston, South Carolina

Printed in the United States of America

Library of Congress Catalog Card Number: 00111688

For all general information contact Arcadia Publishing at:
Telephone 843-853-2070
Fax 843-853-0044
E-mail sales@arcadiapublishing.com
For customer service and orders:
Toll-Free 1-888-313-2665

Visit us on the Internet at www.arcadiapublishing.com

To the Boston & Maine Railroad Historical Society, Center for Lowell History, Lowell, Massachusetts, for the use of their extensive archives so that we may enjoy and preserve the rich heritage of the Boston and Maine Railroad Company.

Author's note: The groups of numbers seen in many captions refer to the wheel arrangement of the steam locomotive. For example, 4-4-0 means that there are four pilot wheels in the front, four driving wheels, and no trailing wheels. By comparison, a 4-6-2 type has four pilot wheels under the front of the boiler, six driving wheels, and two trailing wheels under the firebox.

Contents

Acknowledgments

I would like to thank the following individuals, companies, and societies that have made this history and material possible for publication: Stephen Boothroyd; Peter Barney; Francis B.C. Bradlee; the Boston & Maine Railroad Historical Society of Lowell, Massachusetts; the R.E. Chaffin collection; David Dickinson; the Essex Institute of Salem, Massachusetts; William T. Fletcher; Walter R. Fogg; M.W. Fowler; John Goodwin; the Arthur J. Grant collection; the Ralph Hanson collection; Charles J. Kennedy; Edward C. Kirkland; Ron LeBlond; Walter E. Lenk; Chet Lord; the Maine Central Railroad; Herbert Marsh; the Kenneth F. McCall estate; Kathryn Melanson; James Nigzus; Rick Nowell; C. David Perry; the Railway & Locomotive Historical Society collection; F.W. Smith; G.P. Starbuck; Edward Strobridge; L. Ashton Thorp; Raymond E. Tobey; Ralph S. Wallace; the Wolfeboro Historical Society; and Forrester Wyman.

INTRODUCTION

The earliest date in the development of the Boston & Maine (officially the Boston and Maine Rail Road) is 1833, when the line was chartered under the name Andover & Wilmington Railroad. It was an 8-mile line in Massachusetts intended to connect the town of Andover with Boston over the tracks of the Boston & Lowell Railroad. It is recorded that this line was opened in 1836, its major stockholder being the Andover Academy and Theological Seminary. Soon after this line was completed, plans for another were developed to extend to Haverhill, Massachusetts, via Portsmouth, New Hampshire, and finally to the Maine state line. The line to Haverhill was completed in 1837, but an extension to New Hampshire and Maine never materialized.

In 1835, the Boston & Maine acquired a New Hampshire charter and incorporated it as a separate New Hampshire entity called the Boston & Maine. Shortly thereafter, a charter in the state of Maine was procured for the rest of the planned extension to be known as the Maine, New Hampshire & Massachusetts Railroad. This strategy of incorporating separately in all three states soon proved to be crucial in the future development of the Boston & Maine line.

In 1842, this line, located in all three northern states of New England, merged into one (the Boston and Maine Rail Road) while retaining its separate charters in all three states—New Hampshire, Massachusetts, and Maine. Not being content to use the tracks of the Boston & Lowell, the Boston & Maine began developing its own lines to Boston in 1845. Within two years, it gained access to Portland, Maine, by jointly leasing the Portland, Saco & Portsmouth Railroad with the Eastern Railroad, a line that had been the Boston & Maine's most active competitor.

Although the Boston & Maine was considered to be one of the most conservative railroads during the 19th century, it was certainly one of the most aggressive. A major objective was to concentrate on its quality service, facilities, and an image of stability and fair prices. In the 1880s, the Boston & Maine became a dominant rail system in the Northeast. One of its major investments was the acquisition of the 1884 lease of the Eastern Railroad, which was facing bankruptcy at that time. The original strategy of incorporating separately in three states enabled the Boston & Maine to take control and gain a favorable position. Thus, the Boston & Maine signed a 54-year lease for the Eastern Railroad Company, thereby allowing the Boston & Maine to consolidate the line completely in its ownership in 1890.

The year 1884 witnessed the leasing of several smaller independent railroads, such as the Worcester, Nashua & Rochester line. This acquisition added little to the Boston & Maine except protection for its Portsmouth traffic. In 1887, the Boston & Maine successfully negotiated the lease of the Boston & Lowell Railroad and its associated lines. At the time, the Boston & Lowell was under the leadership of Charles S. Mellen, who later became president of the New York, New Haven & Hartford Railroad. The line had formed a massive system of railroads in New England. In March 1887, however, the New Hampshire Supreme Court ruled against the Boston & Lowell in reference to a lawsuit concerning the railroad's lease of the Northern

Railroad. The result of this ruling was "to dismember the Boston & Lowell system and to force the constituent lines to seek affiliation with the B & M."

In 1893, A. Alexander McLeod assumed the presidency of the Boston & Maine and quickly managed to lease the Connecticut River Railroad, a line that was coveted by the New York, New Haven & Hartford Railroad and J.P. Morgan. Morgan stabilized the situation by imposing a settlement between the Boston & Maine and the New York, New Haven & Hartford lines. The settlement also removed McLeod from his presidency of the Boston & Maine, and Lucius Tuttle (formerly of the New York, New Haven & Hartford Railroad) became the new president. Before the end of the 19th century, Tuttle was able to lease two major lines: the 424-mile Concord & Montreal Railroad in 1895 and the 478-mile Fitchburg system in 1900. With these acquisitions, the Boston & Maine dynasty was able to compete more effectively with other major railroad systems in the Northeast.

At the start of the 20th century, the Boston & Maine operated on 2,324 miles of track—a product of consolidating 47 major and minor independent lines in central and northern New England. It should be remembered, however, that the company only owned 519 miles of that track; the rest of it was leased.

In this book, it is the intent of the author to illustrate the growth and magnitude of this influential rail system in the Northeast. Through the generosity of the Boston & Maine Railroad Historical Society in Lowell and its intensive collection of rare photographs and documents (most of which have never been published), I am privileged to present this first volume, *Boston & Maine in the 19th Century*. A companion volume is entitled *Boston & Maine in the 20th Century*.

—Bruce D. Heald, Ph.D.

One

The Advent of the Railroad in Northern New England

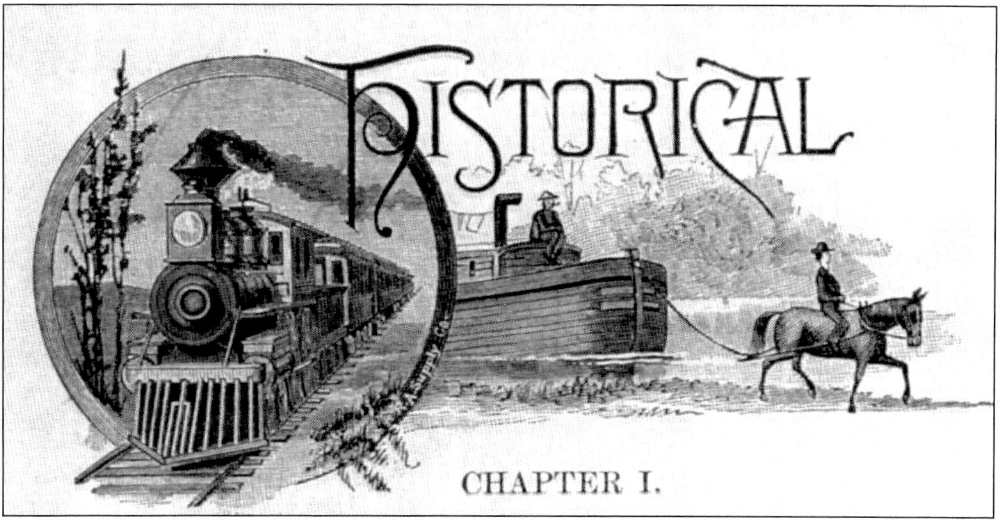

The Successor. The successor to the stagecoach was the steam railroad. New England may be considered a pioneer of steam for transportation. The first application of steam to locomotion was made on the Connecticut River by a Mr. Morey of Orford, New Hampshire, whose experiments predate those of Robert Fulton. The first steam engine was built by Nehemiah S. Bean in Gilmanton, New Hampshire. Sylvester March of Campton, New Hampshire, invented the cogwheel railroad system and built the Mount Washington Railroad.

The coming of the railroads took place in the first half of the 19th century. Roads were not welcome by all the people, as evidenced by a resolution passed at the annual town meeting in Dorchester in 1842: "that our Representatives to the Legislature be instructed to use his endeavor to prevent, if possible, so great a calamity to our farms as must be the location of any railroad passing through." The Boston & Lowell was indeed a pioneer in the growth of the railroad industry and rail transportation in New England.

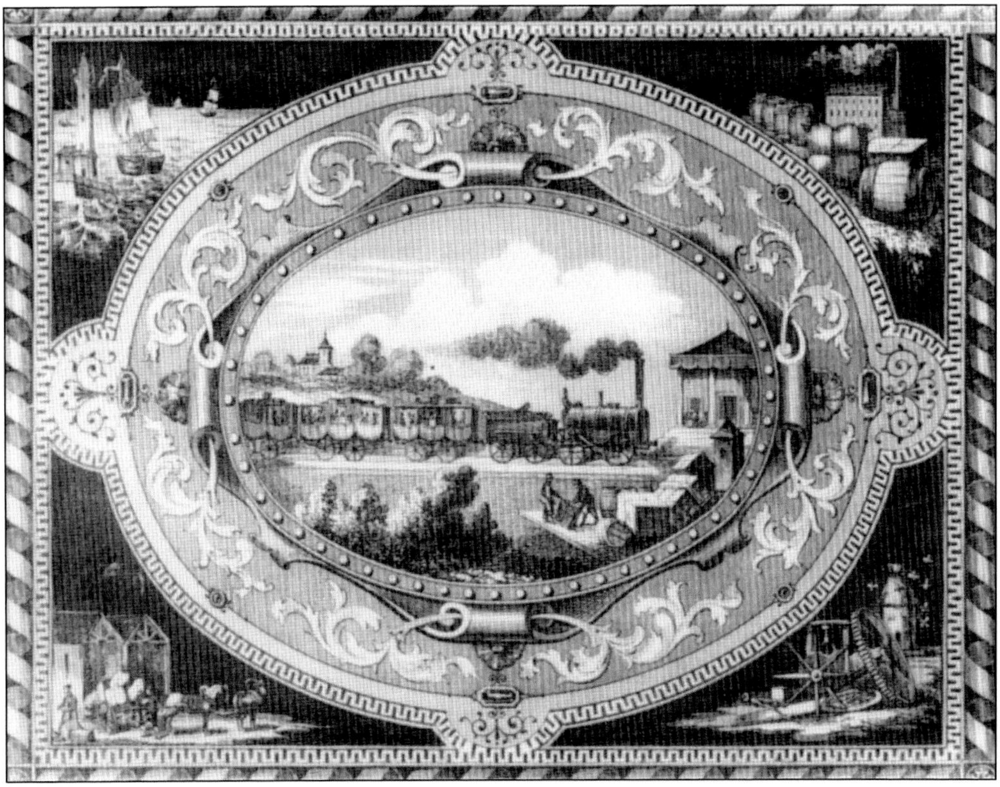

THE ORIGINAL TRAIN, BOSTON & LOWELL RAILROAD, 1835. In the early 1800s, growth of the textile business and an increasing population brought about the need for better transportation of raw material to New England's manufacturing center. In 1830, a project was proposed to build a railroad between Boston and Lowell, a distance of 26 miles. On June 24, 1835, the Boston & Lowell Railroad was opened for service.

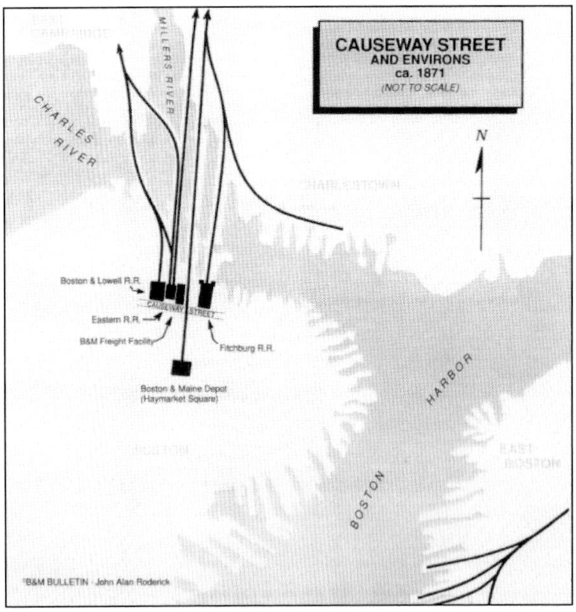

A MAP OF THE CAUSEWAY STREET TERMINALS, BOSTON, MASSACHUSETTS, C. 1871. Shown on this map, from west to east, are the Boston & Lowell's freight and passenger depots, the Eastern Railroad passenger depot, the Boston & Maine freight depot, and the Fitchburg Railroad passenger depot. The Boston & Maine's Haymarket Square depot stood in the middle of what used to be a millpond. The Lowell, Eastern, and Fitchburg depots occupied land just north of the old island causeway. Gradually, more land was filled in toward the Charles River as the need for more track space increased.

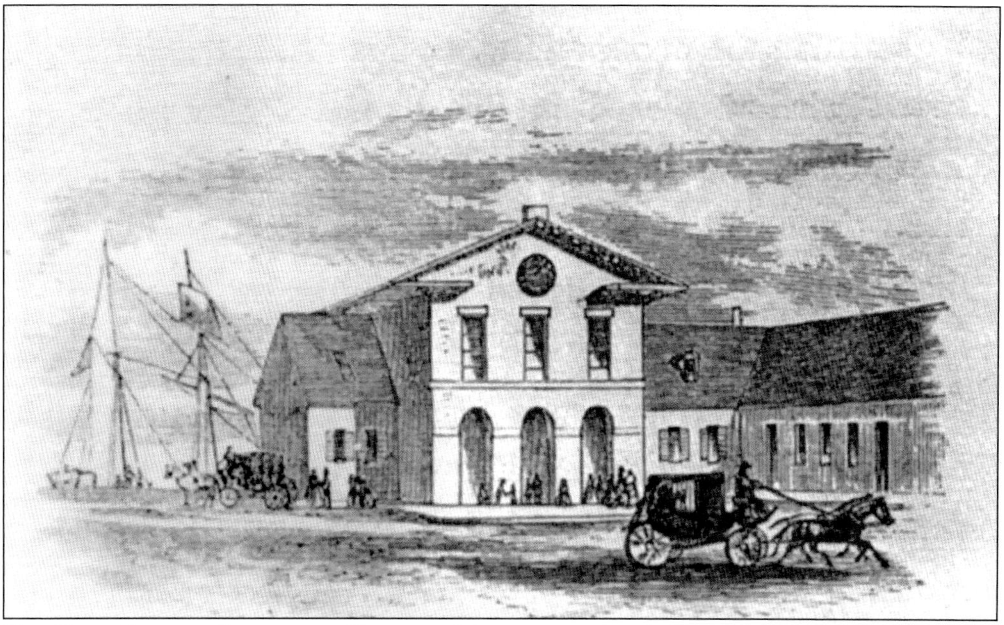

THE FIRST LOWELL STATION IN BOSTON, MASSACHUSETTS, 1835. The first passenger station in Boston was a small one-story brick building on the corner of Leverett and Brighton Streets in the North End. At first the cars did not run into it, but stopped at East Cambridge until the bridge was built. The building may have been designed by Richard Upjohn; however, more serious evidence indicates that it was designed by George M. Dexter, who also designed the Fitchburg Railroad depot.

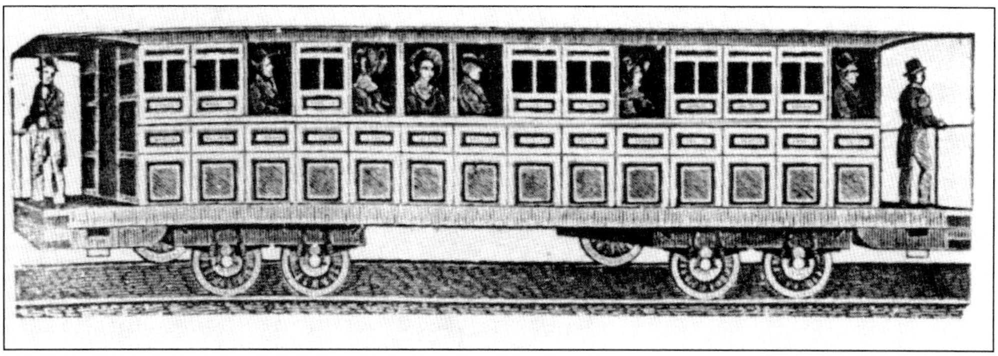

THE PASSENGER CAR USED ON THE NEW ENGLAND RAILROADS, C. 1840. The first type of passenger car on the Lowell road resembled an ordinary stagecoach mounted on a frame with wheels adapted to the rails. Each was divided into three compartments, with doors on the sides. The passengers sat back-to-back, as was customary in England. A short chain of three links coupled the cars, which were neither heated nor lighted.

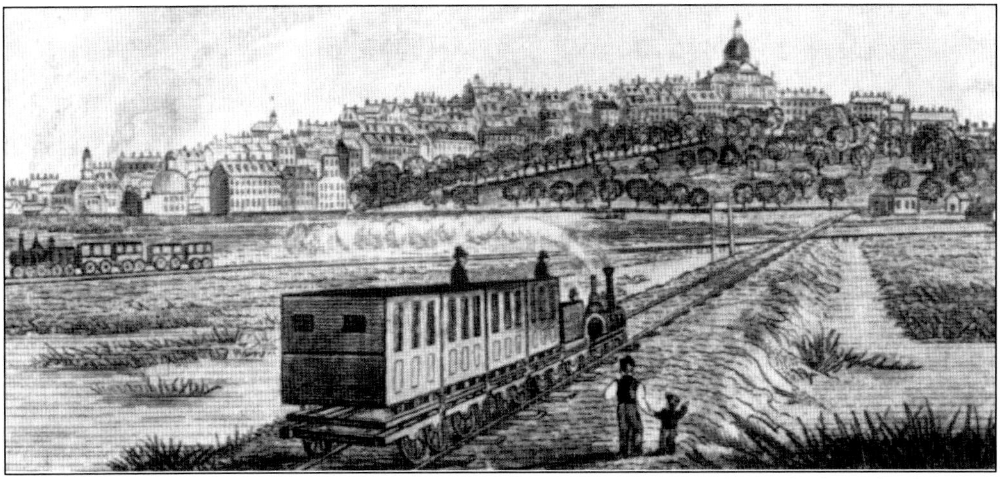

THE STATE'S FIRST RAILROAD. Within a few years, train tracks were being laid north of Boston into New Hampshire and west to the Berkshires.

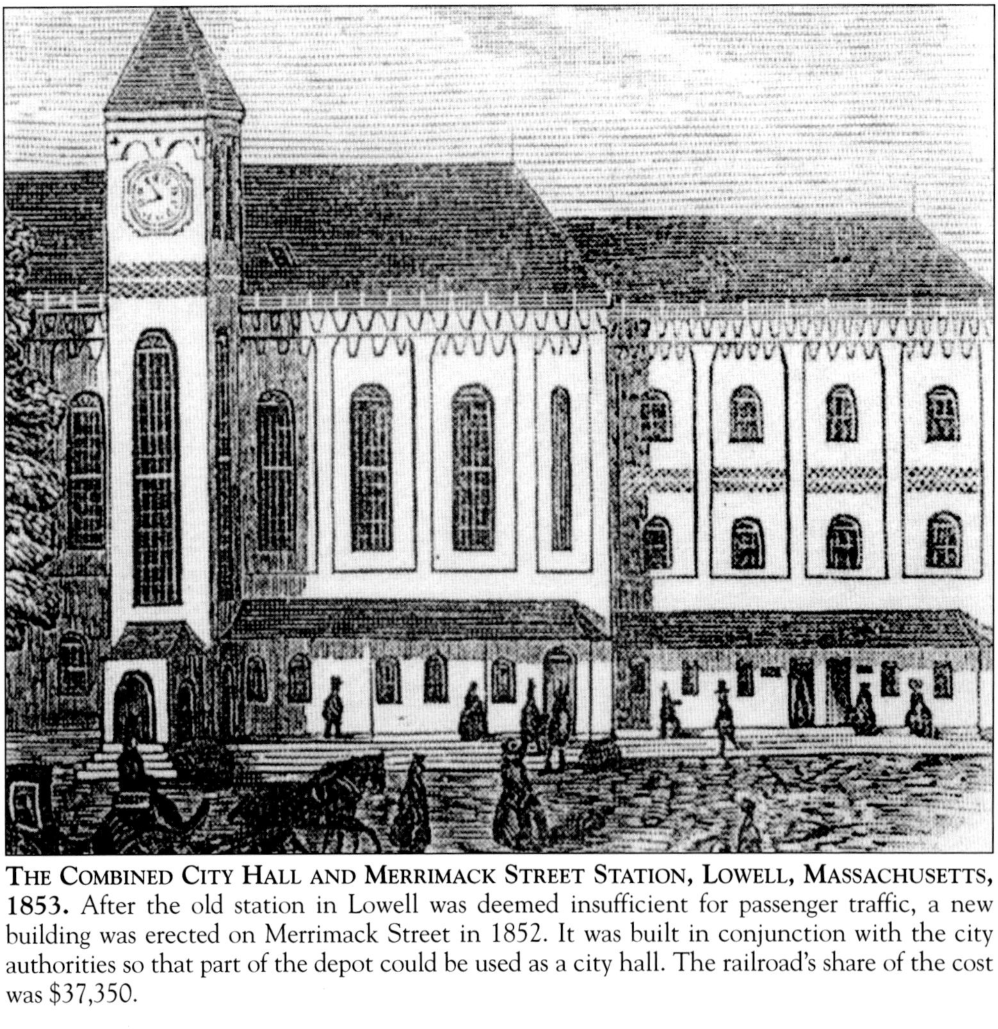

THE COMBINED CITY HALL AND MERRIMACK STREET STATION, LOWELL, MASSACHUSETTS, 1853. After the old station in Lowell was deemed insufficient for passenger traffic, a new building was erected on Merrimack Street in 1852. It was built in conjunction with the city authorities so that part of the depot could be used as a city hall. The railroad's share of the cost was $37,350.

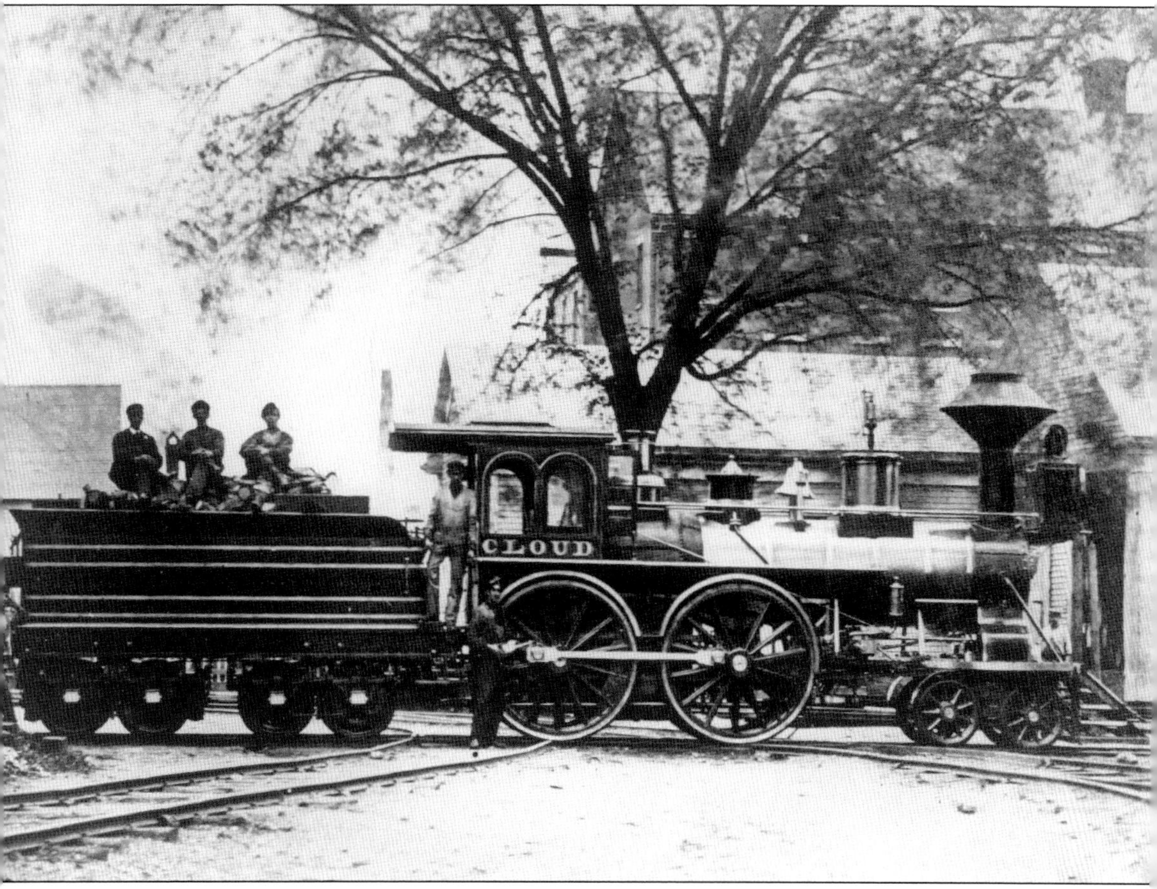

THE LOCOMOTIVE "CLOUD." This engine was built by the Lowell Machine Shops in 1853 and was broken up for junk a year later. The Boston & Lowell was considered the first and principal link to what was known as "the Great Northern Route." From Lowell, the line was continued by the Nashua & Lowell Railroad. This line then extended by the Concord Railroad along the Merrimack Valley to Concord, New Hampshire, and then by the Northern Railroad to the Connecticut River in Lebanon. There, it crossed the Connecticut River and united with the Vermont Central Railroad at the mouth of the White River. From there it went to Burlington, Vermont, 245 miles from Boston, and extended into New York by the Champlain and Montreal Railroad to the St. Lawrence near Montreal, 326 miles from Boston.

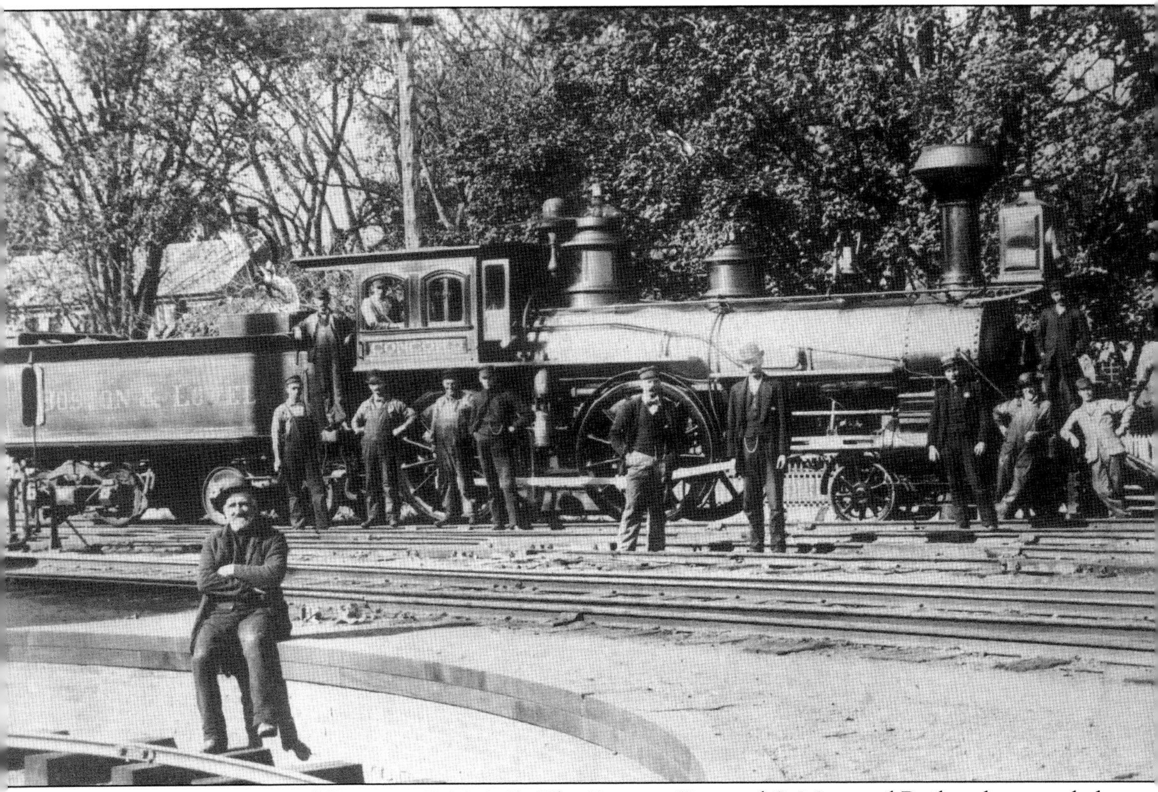

THE LOCOMOTIVE "CONCORD" (4-4-0). The Boston, Concord & Montreal Railroad proceeded from Concord, New Hampshire, through the White Mountains, and connected with the Grand Trunk and Portland & Ogdensburg Railroads. In the mid-1880s, there were two other railroads connected with this general line leading westward from Concord: the Concord and Claremont and Contoocook Valley Railroads. These lines formed an overall length of 632 miles, of which the Boston & Lowell was the main trunk and principal link.

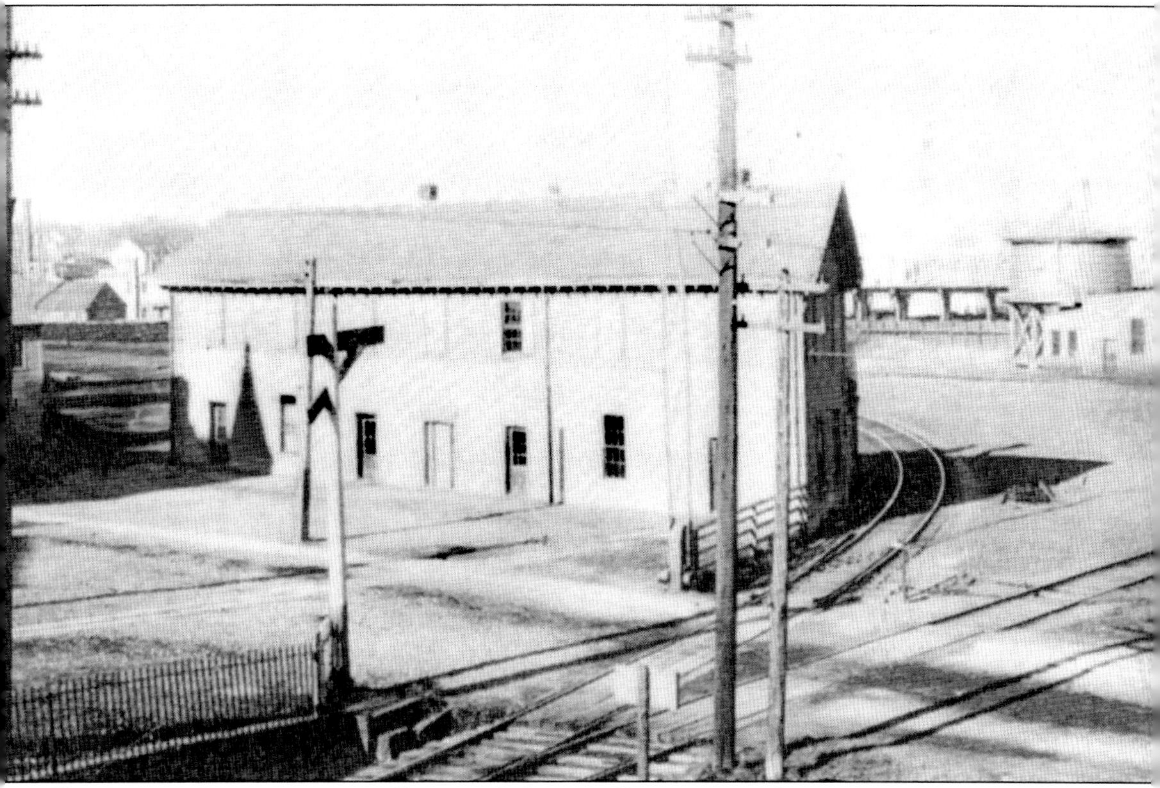

THE LOWELL STATION FOR THE BOSTON & LOWELL RAILROAD IN SALEM, MASSACHUSETTS, 1850–1892. All the outward and inward trains connected at Lowell, with trains proceeding over these lines: Nashua & Lowell; Wilton; Concord; New Hampshire Central; Northern; Vermont Central; Concord and Claremont; Contoocook Valley; Boston, Concord & Montreal; and the Connecticut and Passumpsic Rivers Railroad.

In 1869, the Boston & Lowell Railroad received a Massachusetts charter for the Great Northern Railroad Company to include the Boston & Lowell, the Nashua & Lowell, the Concord, and the Northern Railroads. This marked the beginning of the effort to create a system connecting Boston with the St. Lawrence valley. The Boston & Lowell fight lasted until 1887, when it leased itself to the Boston & Maine. In 1874, the New Hampshire General Court authorized the Nashua & Lowell and the Boston & Lowell to become one corporation. In that same year, the Boston & Lowell acquired the Northern and the Boston, Concord & Montreal lines. A group of Concord Railroad stockholders soon acquired controlling interest in the Boston, Concord & Montreal. They then asked Boston & Lowell to release the Boston, Concord & Montreal from the lease. In 1887, the New Hampshire Supreme Court ordered the Boston & Lowell to stop managing the Boston, Concord & Montreal line.

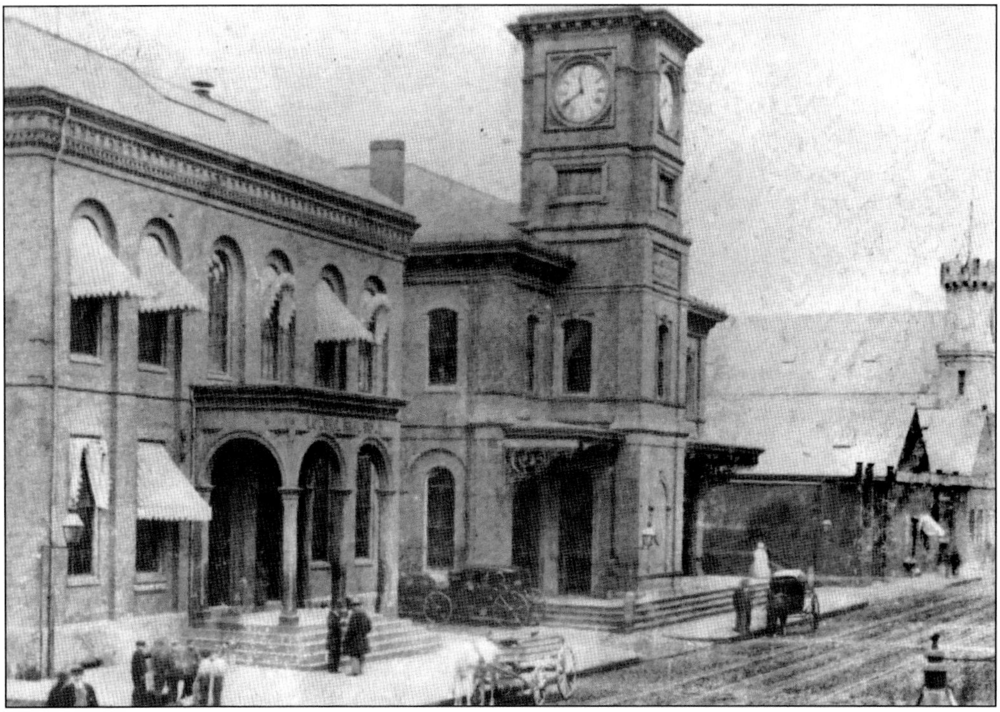

The Lowell, Eastern, and Fitchburg Stations on Causeway Street in Boston, Massachusetts (1852–1873), c. 1870. The second and third outward and inward trains connected at Lowell, with trains proceeding over the Stony Brook Railroad to Groton. From there, trains went in one direction over the Peterboro and Shirley Railroad and in another direction over the Fitchburg, Vermont and Massachusetts, Cheshire, Sullivan, Rutland, and Burlington Railroads. This was known as "the Great Northern Route" to Canada. The complex shown here also included the Worcester & Nashua, Western, Norwich & Worcester, and Providence & Worcester Railroads. The station is believed to have been located at 70 Causeway Street in Boston.

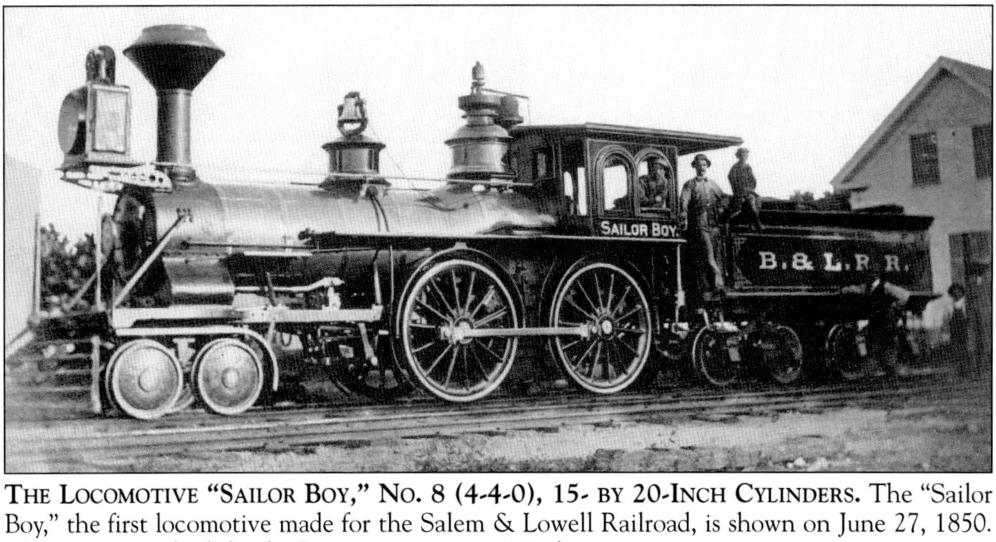

The Locomotive "Sailor Boy," No. 8 (4-4-0), 15- by 20-Inch Cylinders. The "Sailor Boy," the first locomotive made for the Salem & Lowell Railroad, is shown on June 27, 1850. The engine was built by the Boston Locomotive Works.

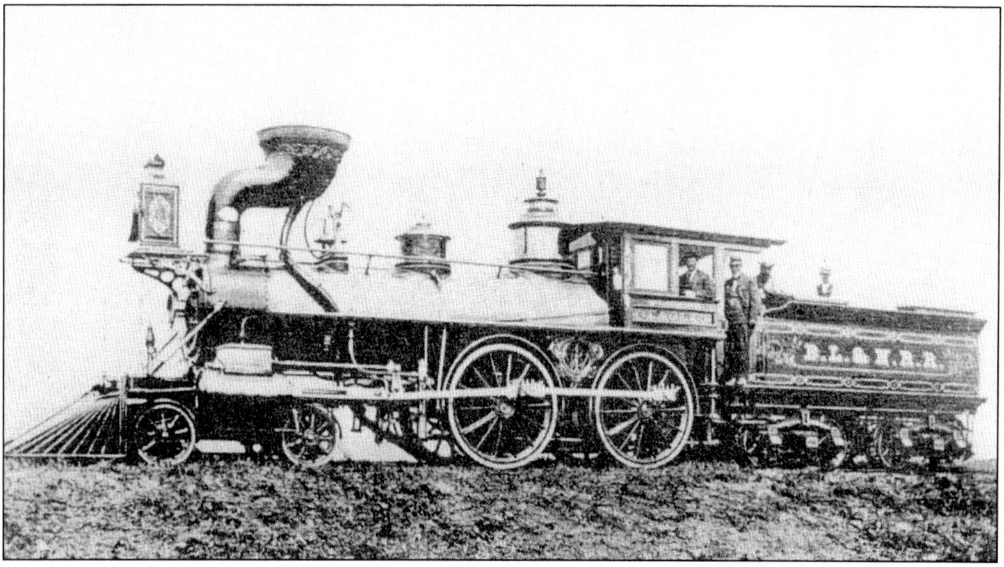

The Locomotive "Eagle," the Boston, Lowell & Nashua Railroad. The "Eagle" is shown here in 1870.

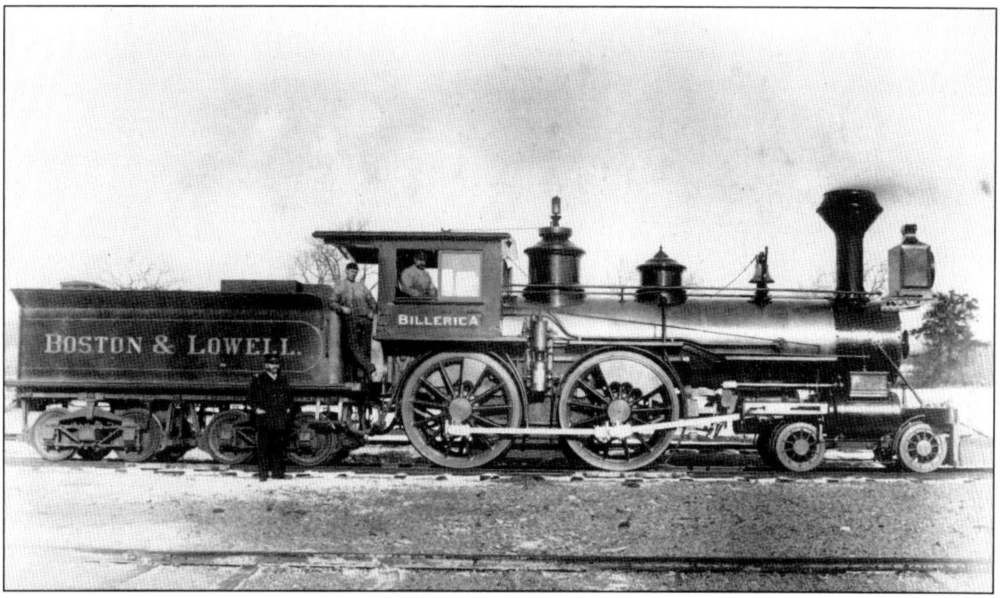

Locomotive No. 20, "Billerica" (4-4-0), 16- by 24-Inch Cylinders, 1869. Built by William Mason, this locomotive later became the property of the Boston & Maine as No. 320. It was finally scrapped in 1904.

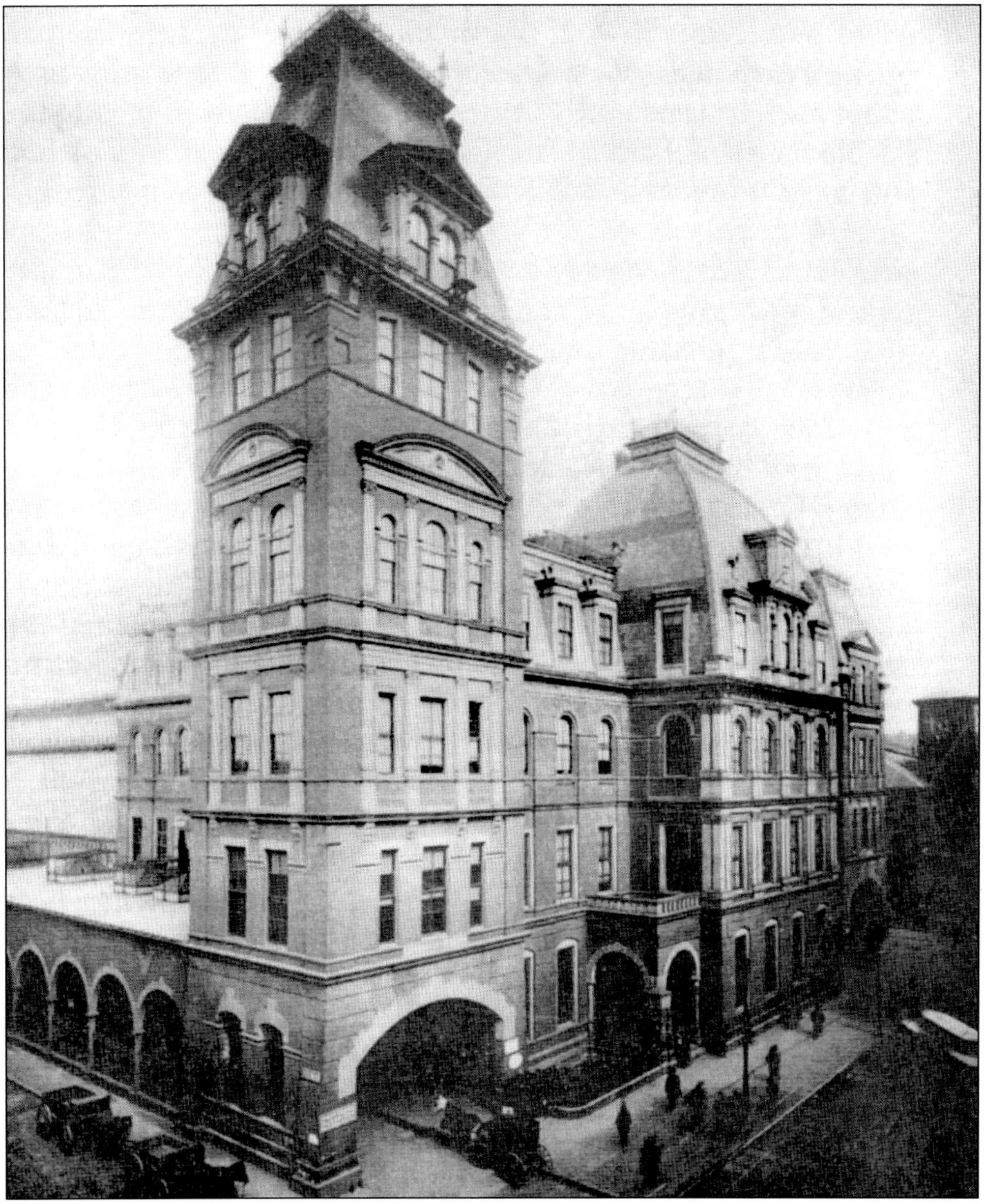

THE THIRD BOSTON STATION, 1873. When the need for a new passenger station in Boston became imperative, a terminus was built at 92 Causeway Street. It was constructed on the site of the 1857 station, which was torn down in December 1873 when the new building was completed. This edifice, which was later encompassed into the North Union Station, covered a total area of 3.25 acres, 2 acres of which were devoted to the train shed. The passenger depot had a frontage of 205 feet on Causeway Street and was about 700 feet long. The general offices of the company were housed within this building. In addition to the main line, the roads operated by the Boston & Lowell around that time consisted of the following: Boston to Nashua, Mystic River Branch, Lexington Branch, Woburn Branch, Stoneham Branch, Lowell and Lawrence Railroad, Salem and Lowell Railroad, Stony Brook Railroad, and the Wilton Railroad. These amounted to a total track mileage of 135 miles.

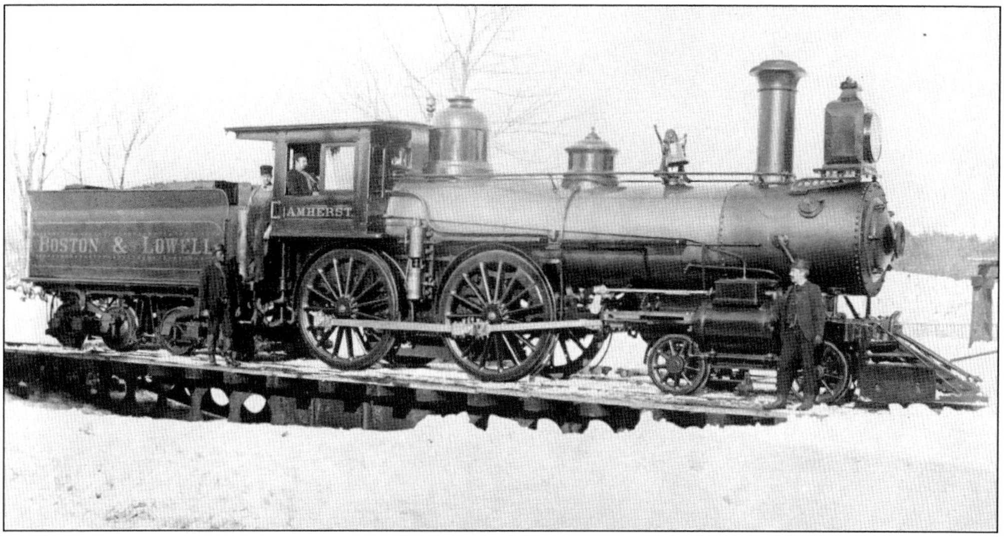

The Locomotive "Amherst," No. 24 (4-4-0), 16- by 24-Inch Cylinders. Built by William Mason in 1872, this locomotive later became B & M No. 324. It was finally scrapped in 1898. Fifty passenger trains departed and arrived daily at Boston's Lowell Station in 1873.

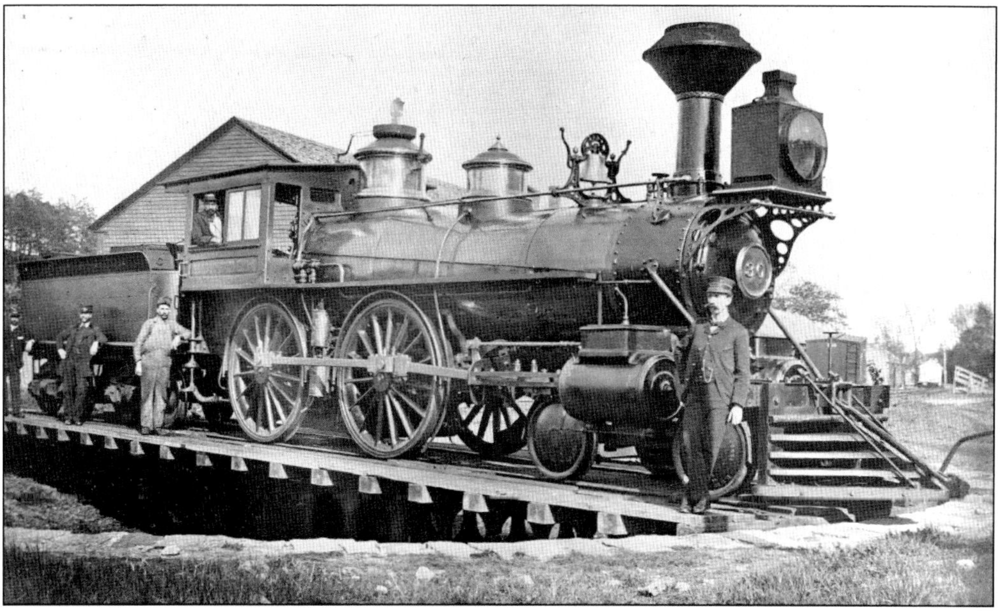

Locomotive No. 30, "Suffolk," (4-4-0), 17- by 24-Inch Cylinders, Built by William Mason, 1873. This locomotive later became the property of the Boston & Maine as No. 330, the "General Garfield." In August 1880, the directors of the Lowell road entered into a contract with the directors of the Concord Railroad of New Hampshire by which the two properties were to be merged as one. On March 1, 1883, the contract was terminated by mutual consent. In time, many financial difficulties burdened the company, and the directors of the Boston & Lowell accordingly proposed a lease of their system to the directors of the Boston & Maine. The lease was ratified by the stockholders of both parties and took effect in June 1887 but dated back to April.

BOSTON TO WINNIPESAUKEE AND WHITE MOUNTAINS.

THROUGH SCHEDULE, IN EFFECT JUNE 28, 1886.

Miles.	STATIONS.	No. 51 Local.	No. 29 Mail.	No. 53 Mont'l Exp.	No. 75 Mt. Exp.	No. 145 Mont'l Exp.	No. 189 Local.	No. 285 Mont'l Exp.
		A.M.	A.M.	A.M.	A.M.	P.M.	P.M.	P.M.
....	Lv. Boston ....B. & L. R.R.	......	7.30	8.30	9.30	1.00	3.00	7.00
....	" Salem .... " "	......	......	7.50	9.10	12.40	......	5.50
....	" Lawrence (via Lowell) " "	......	......	8.15	9.30	12.05	3.15	6.40
26	" Lowell .... " "	......	8.30	9.20	10.14	1.48	3.53	7.48
40	" Nashua Junction... " "	......	9.00	9.46	10.40	2.13	4.20	8.20
57	" Manchester.......Concord R.R.	......	9.48	10.16	11.10	2.43	5.02	8.54
75	Ar. Concord .... " "	......	10.30	10.50	11.40	3.12	5.42	9.25
....	Lv. Concord............B. & L. R.R.	6.55	11.00	10.55	11.42	3.17	5.50	9.30
84	" Canterbury .... " "	7.14	11.21	......	......	......	*6.17	*
88	" Northfield.......... " "	7.22	11.28	......	......	......	*6.24	*
93	" Tilton .... " "	7.32	11.39	11.27	......	3.50	6.35	10.11
97	" East Tilton......... " "	7.39	11.47	......	......	......	*6.43	*
102	" Laconia .... " "	7.49	11.58	11.43	12.25	4.08	6.55	10.30
104	" Lake Village....... " "	7.54	12.03	11.50	......	4.12	6.59	10.35
109	" Weirs .... " "	8.03	12.13	12.00	12.36	4.23	7.09	10.46
119	Ar. Centre Harbor..........Steamer	......	......	1.00	......	5.10	......	......
125	" Wolfboro'............ "	10.10	......	3.05	......	7.00	......	......
113	Lv. Meredith ....B. & L. R.R.	8.10	12.21	12.08	......	4.32	7.16	10.55
121	" Ashland........... " "	8.28	12.38	12.28	......	4.51	7.34	11.14
126	Ar. Plymouth .... " "	8.38	12.50	12.40	1.05	5.02	7.45	11.26
....	Lv. Plymouth ....B. & L. R.R.	8.50	......	......	1.38	5.20	P.M.	......
128	Ar. Livermore Falls.... " "	8.55	......	......	1.51	5.26	......	......
130	" Blairs .... " "	9.05	......	......	1.55	5.30	......	......
134	" Campton Village... " "	9.14	......	......	2.03	5.38	......	......
135	" Thornton........... " "	9.22	......	......	2.07	5.42	......	......
140	" West Thornton .... " "	9.38	......	......	2.18	5.53	......	......
143	" Woodstock .... " "	9.49	......	......	2.25	6.00	......	......
147	" North Woodstock.. " "	10.00	......	......	2.35	6.10	......	......
154	" Flume House ....Stage	11.45	......	......	3.50	7.40	......	......
159	Ar. Profile House............ "	12.45	......	......	4.50	8.40	......	......
126	Lv. Plymouth ....B. & L. R.R.	8.48	1.40	1.15	1.35	5.17	......	11.36
131	Ar. Quincy .... " "	8.59	1.52	......	......	......	......	......
134	" Rumney........... " "	9.04	1.57	......	......	*	......	*
137	" West Rumney...... " "	9.11	2.04	......	......	......	......	*
142	" Wentworth......... " "	9.20	2.15	......	......	......	......	*
146	" Warren........... " "	9.28	2.23	1.50	......	5.50	......	12.23
155	" East Haverhill ..... " "	9.48	2.45	......	......	......	......	*
160	" Haverhill........... " "	9.58	2.55	2.16	......	*6.18	......	*
163	" North Haverhill.... " "	10.05	3.03	......	......	*	......	*
....	" White Mt. Transfer " "	......	3.11	......	2.50	6.32	......	......
168	" Woodsville......... " "	10.15	3.15	2.30	......	6.38	......	‡1.20
....	Lv. Woodsville......... " "	10.40	4.00		......	......	......	‡7.05
173	Ar. Bath............... " "	10.57	4.13	P.M.	......	*6.42	......	7.16
178	" Lisbon............ " "	11.10	4.27	......	3.15	6.53	......	7.28
184	" North Lisbon ...... " "	11.23	4.42	......	......	......	......	7.41
189	" Littleton .... " "	11.35	4.54	......	3.37	7.14	......	7.52
195	" Wing Road......... " "	11.50	5.10	......	3.50	7.25	......	8.05
199	Ar. Bethlehem Junc.... " "	12.04	5.26	......	4.04	7.37	......	8.17
201	Ar. Maplewood......P. & F. N. R.R.	12.15	5.40	......	4.16	7.50	......	8.32
202	" Bethlehem ...... " " "	12.20	5.45	......	4.21	7.55	......	8.37
209	" Profile House... " " "	2.18	6.05	......	4.40	8.13	......	8.55
203	Ar. Twin Mt. House....B. & L. R.R.	12.15	5.38	......	4.16	7.48	......	8.31
207	" White Mt. House... " "	12.23	5.48	......	......	......	......	8.43
208	" Fabyan's........... " "	12.25	5.50	......	4.28	8.00	......	8.45
209	" Mt. Pleasant House " "	12.35	5.55	......	4.35	8.05	......	9.25
213	" Crawford House...P. & O. R.R.	......	6.00	......	5.00	8.30	......	9.20
217	Ar. Summit Mt. Wash...Mt. W. Ry	......	......	......	6.30	......	......	11.00
195	Lv. Wing Road ....B. & L. R.R.	11.55	5.15	......	4.00	7.27	......	8.28
200	Ar. Whitefield.......... " "	12.08	5.28	......	4.13	7.36	......	8.43
210	" Jefferson...........W. & J. R.R.	12.30	5.55	......	4.40	8.00	......	9.10
202	" Scott's ....B. & L. R.R.	12.14	5.34	......	4.19	7.42	......	
204	" Dalton............. " "	12.18	5.37	......	4.23	7.46	......	......
206	" South Lancaster... " "	12.23	5.43	......	4.29	7.50	......	......
211	" Lancaster.......... " "	12.35	5.55	......	4.40	8.00	......	......
217	" Guildhall.......... " "	......	6.50	......	6.50	......	......	......
221	Ar. Groveton .... " "	......	7.00	......	7.00	......	......	......
		P.M.	P.M.		P.M.	P.M.		A.M.

A BOSTON & LOWELL RAILROAD SCHEDULE, BOSTON TO WINNIPESAUKEE AND THE WHITE MOUNTAINS, 1886. This early schedule was provided to passengers en route to the White Mountains. It shows the times, mail runs, local stops, and the distance from Boston for each station.

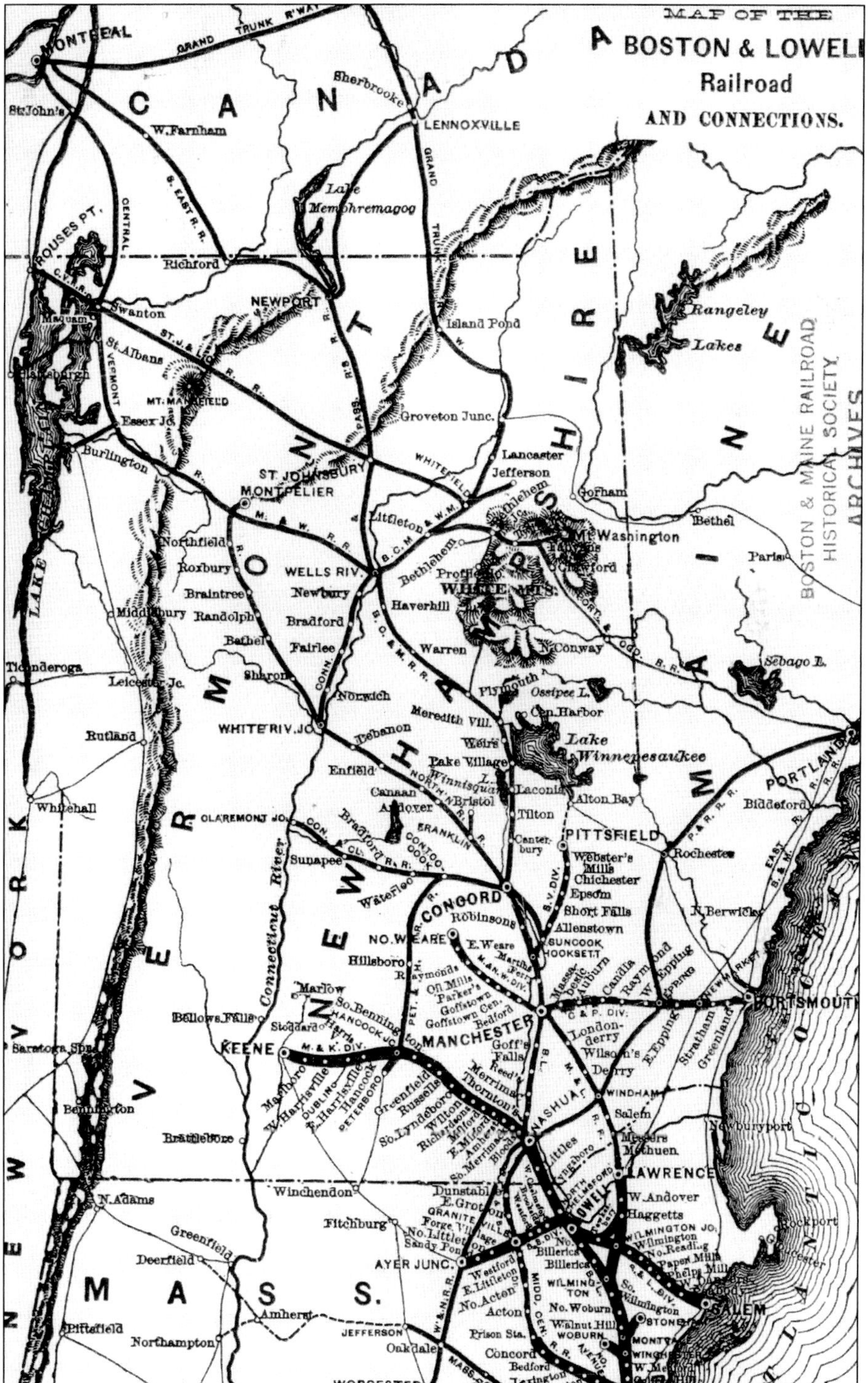

A Map of the Boston & Lowell Railroad and Connections. This early map indicates the major routes of the Boston & Lowell line and its principal connections with the smaller independent railroads.

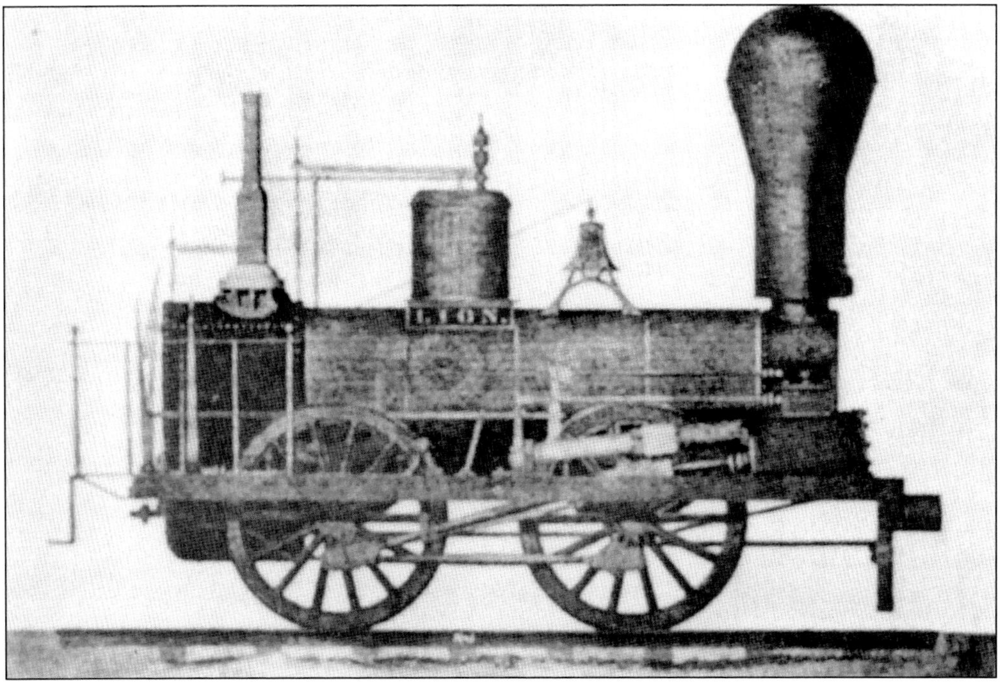

THE LOCOMOTIVE "LION," NASHUA & LOWELL RAILROAD, 1844. The Nashua & Lowell Railroad was a double-track line extending from Lowell, Massachusetts, to Nashua, New Hampshire, for 14.5 miles, with 5.25 miles in New Hampshire. It was chartered in New Hampshire in 1835, and its Massachusetts charter dates from 1836. The two roads were consolidated in 1838, the year that the road was opened to Nashua. As soon as 1844, disputes arose between the Boston & Lowell and the Boston & Maine as to which line's cars and engines could occupy certain tracks at Wilmington.

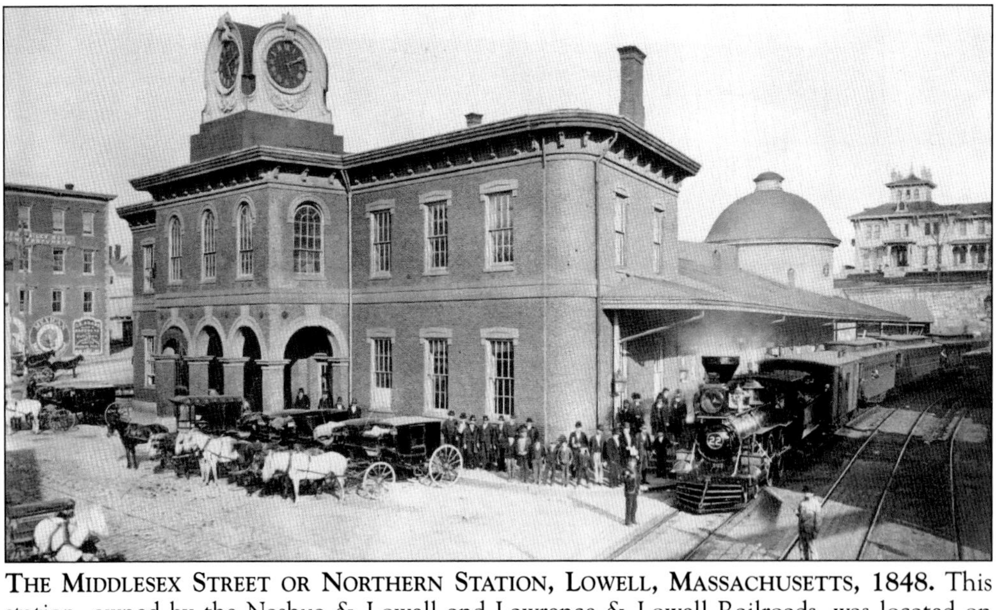

THE MIDDLESEX STREET OR NORTHERN STATION, LOWELL, MASSACHUSETTS, 1848. This station, owned by the Nashua & Lowell and Lawrence & Lowell Railroads, was located on Middlesex Street and was generally known as "the Northern Depot."

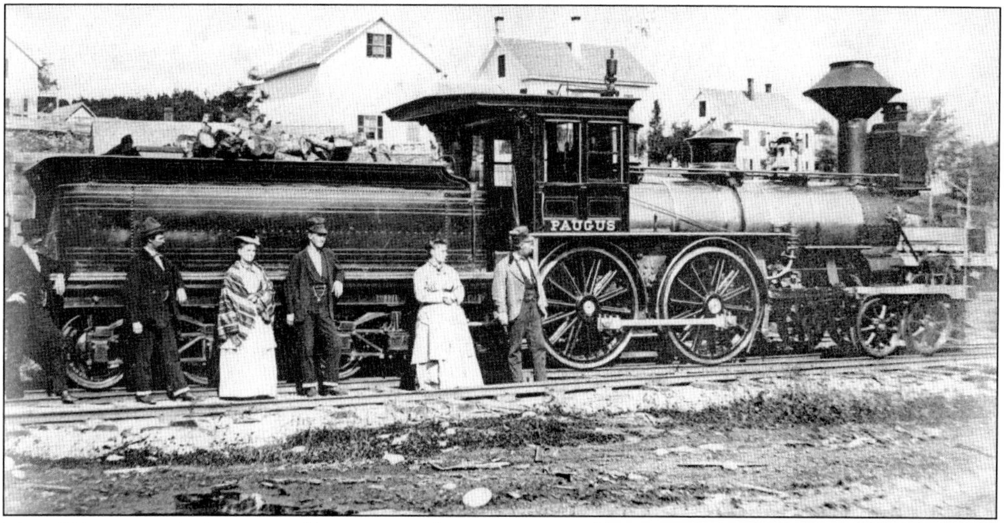

THE NASHUA & LOWELL RAILROAD LOCOMOTIVE "PAUGUS" (4-4-0), 14- BY 18-INCH CYLINDERS. This engine was built by Hinkley & Drury in 1848. The Nashua & Lowell Railroad—a double-track line extending from Lowell, Massachusetts, to Nashua, New Hampshire—was chartered in New Hampshire in 1835. From the beginning, the road was quite prosperous, and the second track was laid in 1846. The independent operation of the railroad ended in 1857, when the company entered into an operating contract with the Boston & Lowell for three years and two months.

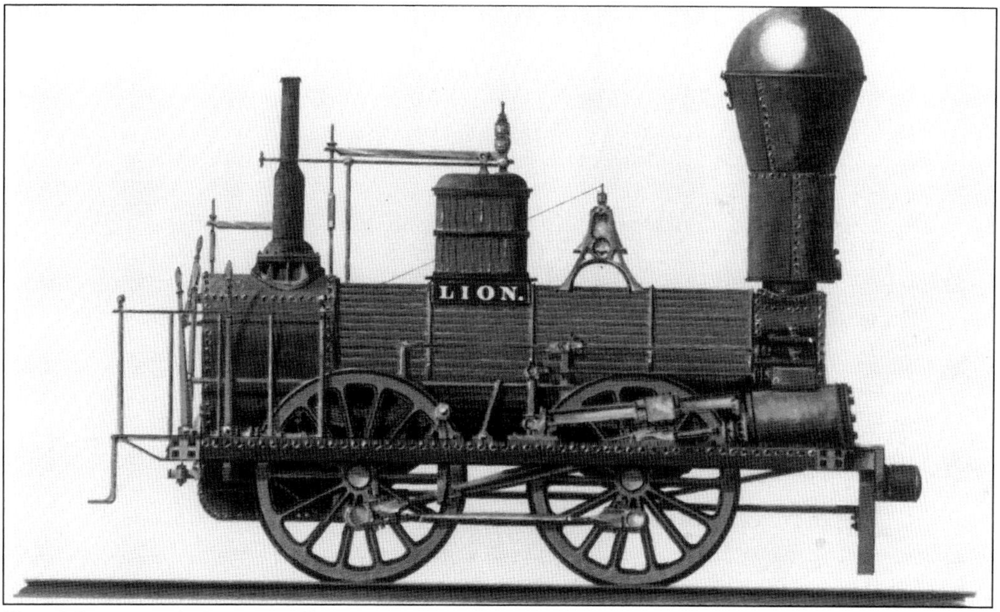

THE NASHUA & LOWELL RAILROAD LOCOMOTIVE "LION," 1844. In 1878, the lease of the Nashua & Lowell Railroad to the Boston & Lowell Railroad expired. Failing to agree on new terms, the company (and with it the Stony Brook, Wilton, and Peterboro Railroads) was independently operated. The independent operation of the line without the cooperation of the Boston & Lowell proved impracticable and, on October 1, 1880, it was leased to the Boston & Lowell Railroad for 99 years. In 1887, the 99-year lease was assigned to the Boston & Maine by the Boston & Lowell Railroad.

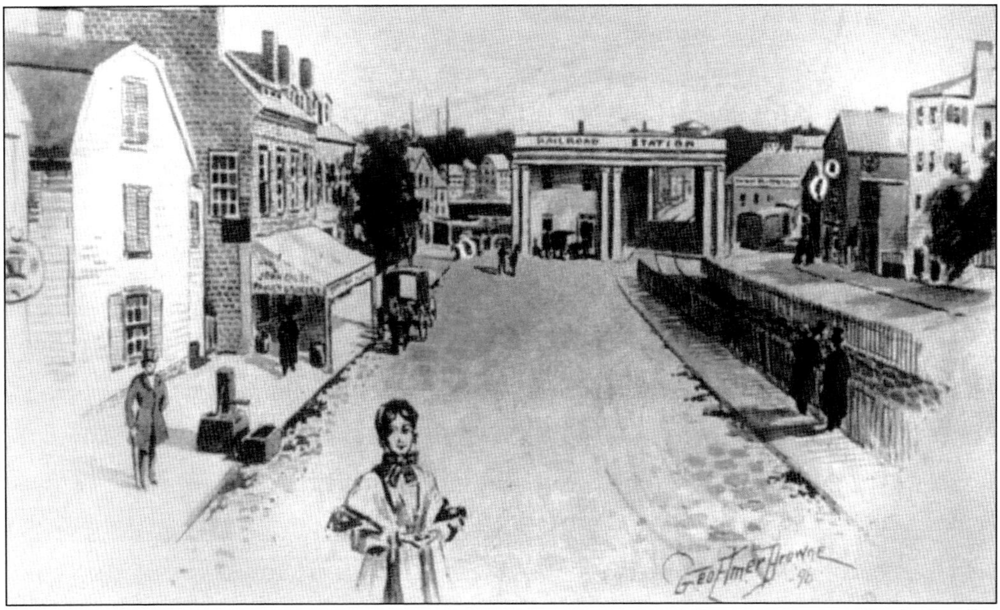

The First Railroad Station at Salem, Massachusetts. This station was built for the Eastern Railroad Company in 1838. As early as 1832, there was a project for a railroad between Boston and the eastern points. On April 14, 1836, an act to incorporate the Eastern Railroad Company was signed by Gov. Edward Everett. Originally, the plan of the projectors was to build a line extending to Salem only, but the legislature would not grant a charter unless they agreed to extend the road to the New Hampshire line. As it was quite impossible to accomplish this through private capital alone, the legislature passed the "Act to aid the Construction of the Eastern Railroad" on April 18, 1837. By the spring of 1838, work had progressed so far that it was certain the road would be open to travel as far as Salem. This illustration is from a drawing by George Elmer Browne after a daguerreotype now owned by the Essex Institute.

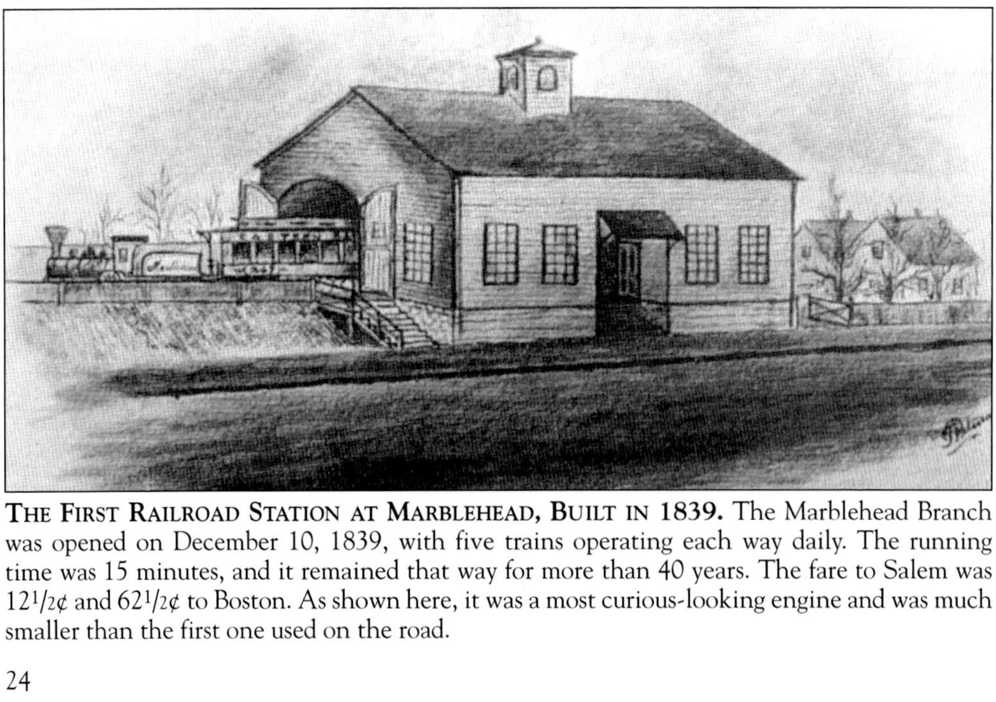

The First Railroad Station at Marblehead, Built in 1839. The Marblehead Branch was opened on December 10, 1839, with five trains operating each way daily. The running time was 15 minutes, and it remained that way for more than 40 years. The fare to Salem was $12^{1}/_{2}$¢ and $62^{1}/_{2}$¢ to Boston. As shown here, it was a most curious-looking engine and was much smaller than the first one used on the road.

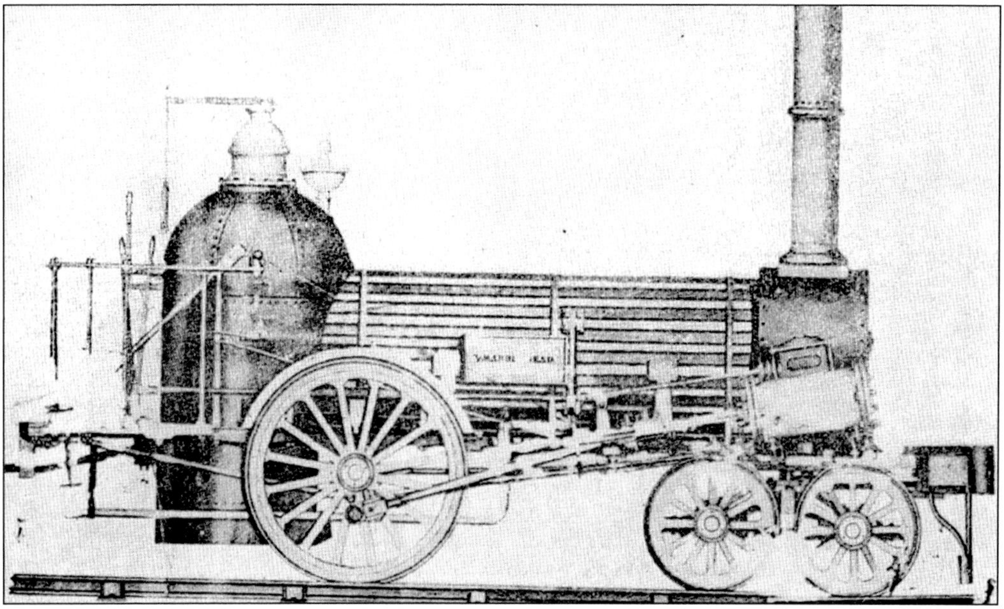

EASTERN RAILROAD NO. 5, "MARBLEHEAD." This locomotive was built by William Norris in Philadelphia in 1839. Its total weight was only 18,000 pounds, and the diameter of the single driver was but 4.5 feet. This picture is from an imperfect but unique lithograph by J.T. Bowen of Philadelphia.

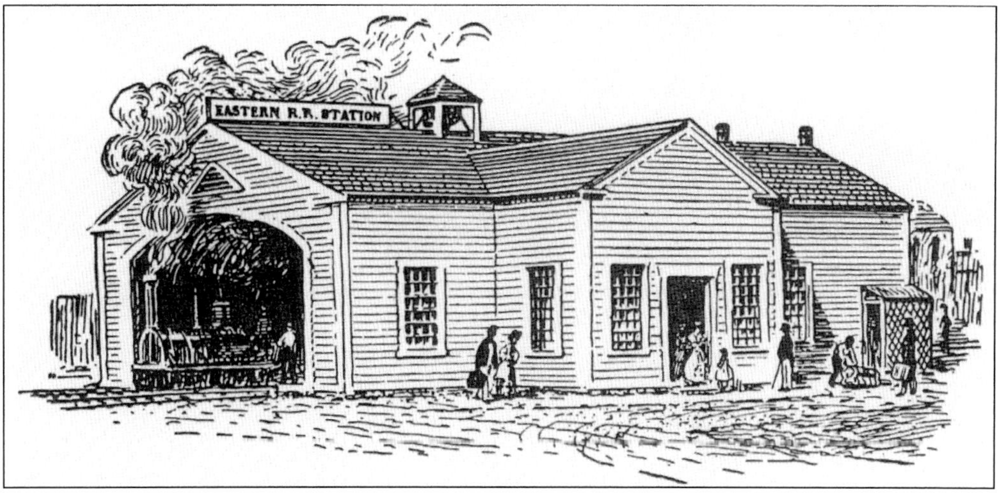

THE FIRST RAILROAD STATION AT NEWBURYPORT, BUILT IN 1840. On September 23, 1838, a meeting of the Eastern Railroad stockholders authorized the directors to complete a road to Newburyport, Massachusetts, and the New Hampshire state line. From the first, Portsmouth had been intended as the terminus of the Eastern Railroad, but owing to the different state laws, it was thought best to make a separate company to the part of the line in New Hampshire. Accordingly, the Eastern Railroad Company of New Hampshire had been incorporated by an act of legislature on June 18, 1836. The act authorized the construction of a road running in a generally northerly direction from the Massachusetts line to the town of Portsmouth and the Maine state line, there connecting with the Portland, Saco & Portsmouth Railroad. The first passenger station erected in Newburyport was a one-story building situated on Washington Street. This sketch was taken from Currier's *History of Newburyport*.

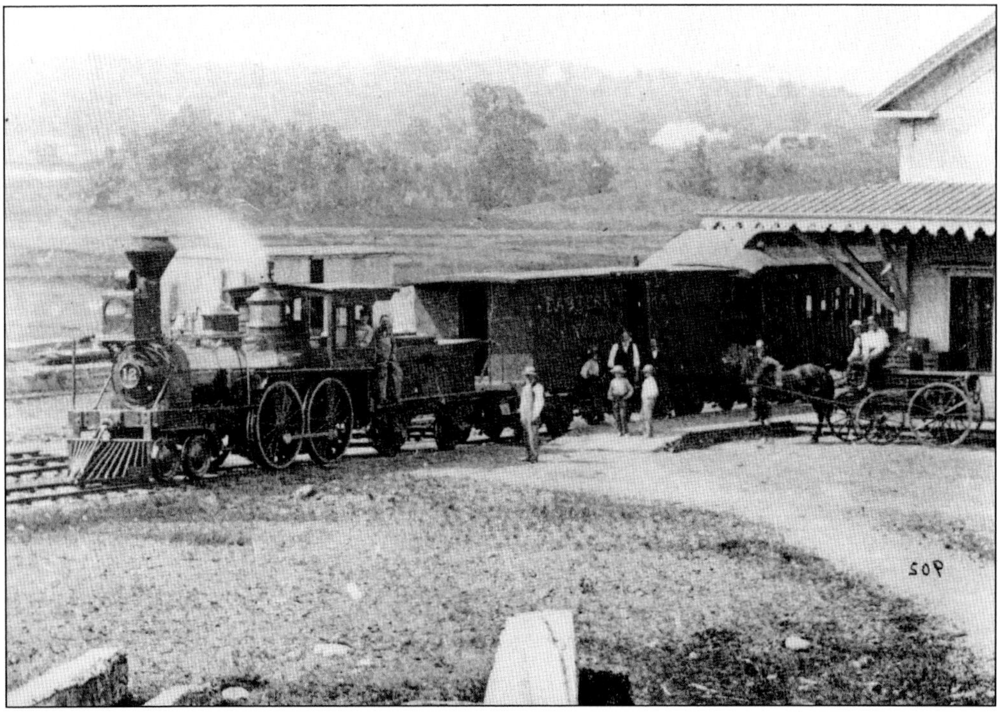

EASTERN RAILROAD LOCOMOTIVE NO. 12, "ROUGH AND READY" (4-4-0), 14- BY 18-INCH CYLINDERS. This locomotive was built by the Taunton Locomotive Works in 1847.

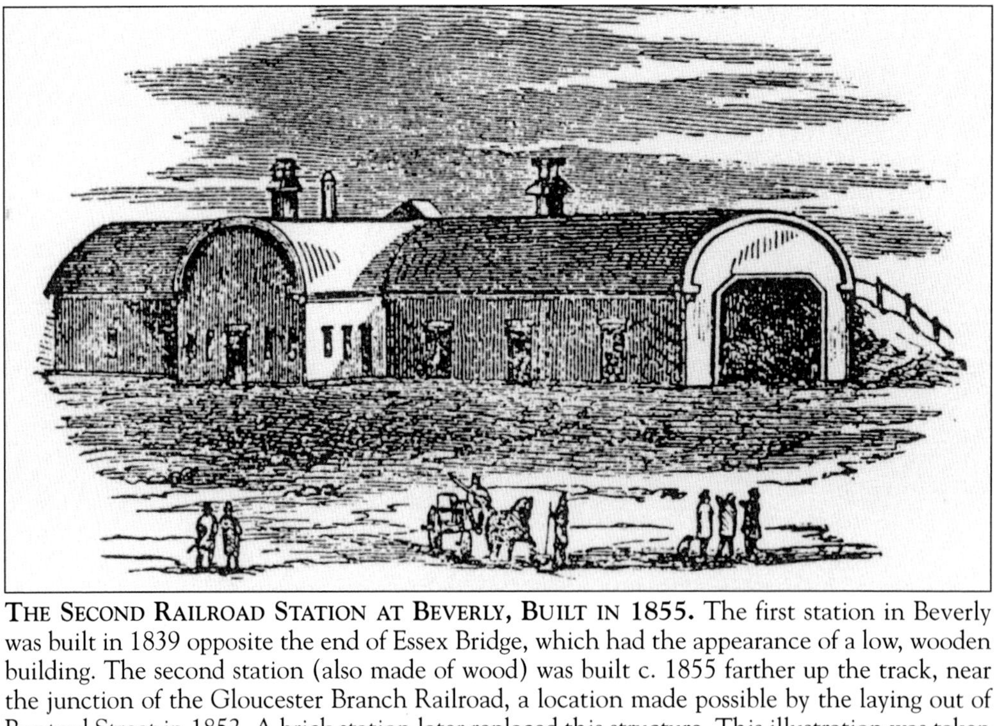

THE SECOND RAILROAD STATION AT BEVERLY, BUILT IN 1855. The first station in Beverly was built in 1839 opposite the end of Essex Bridge, which had the appearance of a low, wooden building. The second station (also made of wood) was built c. 1855 farther up the track, near the junction of the Gloucester Branch Railroad, a location made possible by the laying out of Rantoul Street in 1852. A brick station later replaced this structure. This illustration was taken from a woodcut in *The Traveller's Guide* (1857).

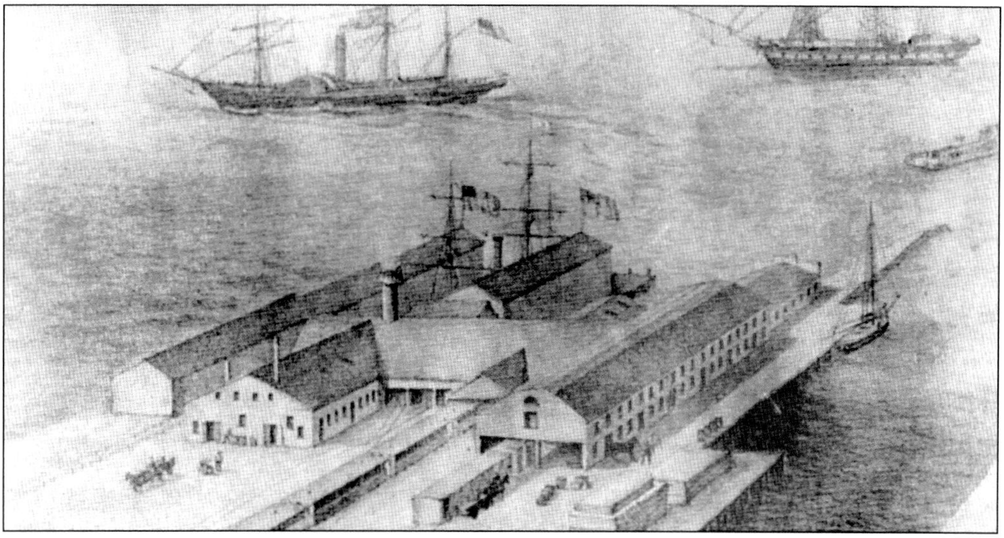

THE RAILROAD STATION AT EAST BOSTON, BUILT IN 1842. This station replaced the second station, which had been destroyed by fire. In 1841, the stockholders authorized various improvements, including the construction of a new depot at East Boston. The stockholders also decided to establish a double-track line from East Boston to Chelsea (and a line between Lynn and Salem) and planned to open the Portland, Saco & Portsmouth Railroad to Portland. The directors thought that "trains coming from such a distance might, very likely, be occasionally delayed and so upset the arrangement of the time table."

On January 25, 1842, the new East Boston depot was used for the first time and burned down that evening. It was replaced the next year by a less pretentious structure, which was given up almost entirely to freight purposes. This image is taken from a lithograph of Boston in 1848, patterned after a drawing by E. Whitefield.

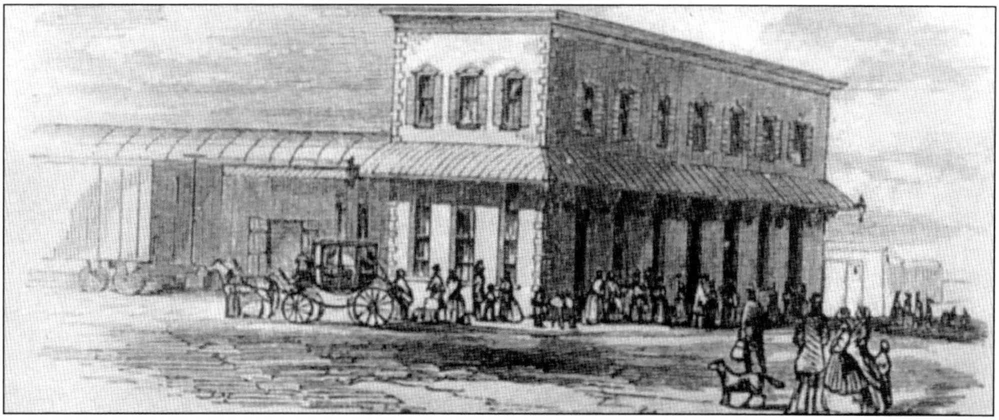

THE FIRST EASTERN STATION ON CAUSEWAY STREET, BOSTON, MASSACHUSETTS. This station, built in 1854, was destroyed by fire in 1862. The trains first ran into Causeway Street Station on April 10, 1854. The depot itself was a temporary wooden one-story building, for it was hoped that in time a Union Station could be built for the use of the Eastern and Boston & Lowell Railroads. This new terminus was so small that the locomotives drawing the trains did not enter it at all. About a half mile outside the station, the engine would be detached and switched off and the cars would be rolled into the station on their own momentum. Strangely, the practice continued for many years. This illustration is taken from an engraving in Midgley's *Sights in Boston* (1857).

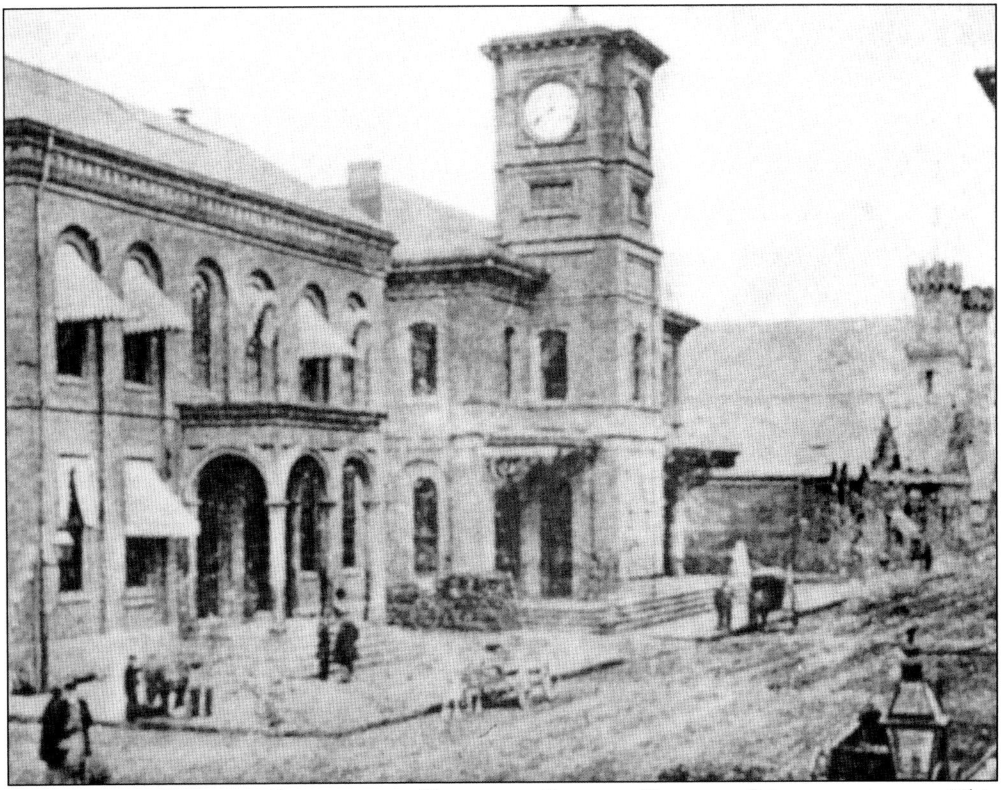

THE SECOND EASTERN STATION ON CAUSEWAY STREET, BOSTON, MASSACHUSETTS. This structure was built in 1862. Also visible here is the Lowell Station (left) and the Fitchburg Station (far right), known as "the Castle." This image was taken from a photograph made before 1870.

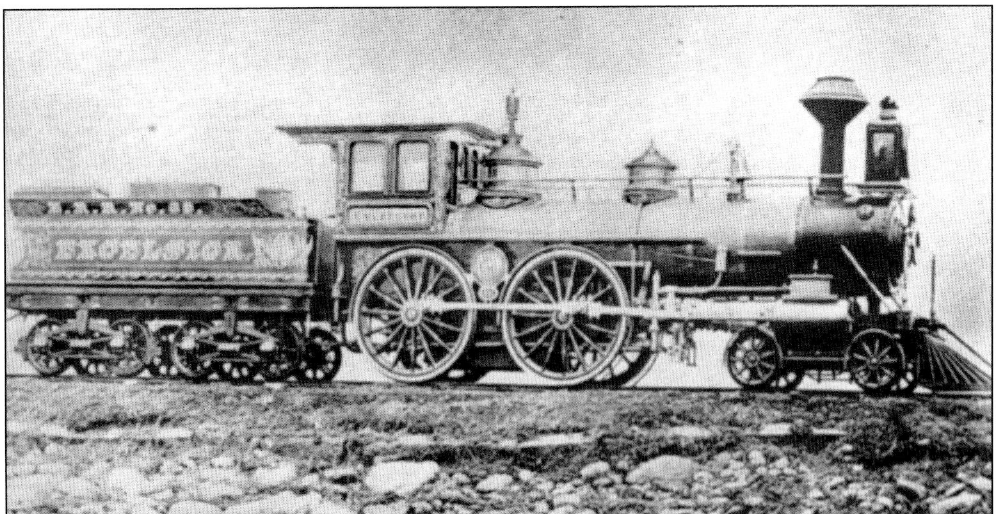

EASTERN RAILROAD NO. 39, "EXCELSIOR," BUILT AT THE EASTERN RAILROAD SHOPS IN 1867. This locomotive was considered one of the handsomest and fastest engines run on the old Eastern Railroad at the time.

SAUGUS BRANCH RAILROAD.

ARRANGEMENT COMMENCING

MONDAY, OCTOBER 16, 1854.

Passenger Trains will leave WEST LYNN for BOSTON & MAINE RAIL ROAD STATION, in Haymarket Square, through Saugus, Cliftondale, East Malden, Maplewood, Malden Center, and Edgeworth, as follows:

TRAINS FOR BOSTON---LEAVE

Lynn - - - -	7,30	9,35	1,45	4,40
East Saugus -	7,34	9,39	1,48	4,44
Saugus Center	7,38	9,43	1,52	4,49
Cliftondale - -	7,43	9,48	1,57	4,54
East Malden -	7,47	9,52	2,00	4,57
Maplewood -	7,50	9,55	2,04	5,00
Malden Center	7,54	10,00	2,09	5,05
Edgeworth - -	7,58	10,03	2,13	5,08

TRAINS FROM BOSTON---LEAVE

BOSTON - - - - - - - - -	8,30	12,00	3,00	6,00
EDGEWORTH - - - - - -	8,40	12,10	3,10	6,10
MALDEN CENTER - - - -	8,43	12,13	3,13	6,13
MAPLEWOOD - - - - - -	8,48	12,18	3,18	6,18
EAST MALDEN - - - - -	8,53	12,23	3,23	6,23
CLIFTONDALE - - - - -	8,58	12,28	3,28	6,28
SAUGUS CENTER - - - -	9,02	12,32	3,32	6,32
EAST SAUGUS - - - - -	9,06	12,36	3,36	6,36

The Train on Saturdays, leaving Lynn at 8 P.M., & Boston at 10 P.M., will be discontinued.

ANDREWS BREED, Supt.

Lynn, Oct. 10, 1854.

W. W Kellogg, Printer, Typographic Hall, Over Depot, Lynn.

THE SAUGUS BRANCH RAILROAD TIMETABLE FOR MONDAY, OCTOBER 16, 1854. The Saugus Branch was opened for travel on February 1, 1853. Its eastern terminus was Lynn Common, for its track did not join the main line of the Eastern at West Lynn. At its other end, it connected with the Boston & Maine (main line) at Malden, Massachusetts. The only intermediate stations at the beginning were East Saugus, Saugus, and a few others. The Eastern Railroad soon began to complain that the Saugus Branch benefitted no one but its bitter enemy, the Boston & Maine, and that it was forced to keep up separate rolling stock that could be of little use on other parts of its system. The company therefore petitioned the legislature for permission to consolidate the Saugus Branch Railroad Company with their own corporation, while at the same time discontinuing the connection of the branch with the Boston & Maine at Malden. The Saugus Branch was one of the few fortunate investments of the Eastern, for it opened large tracts of land that were soon built up with suburban residences.

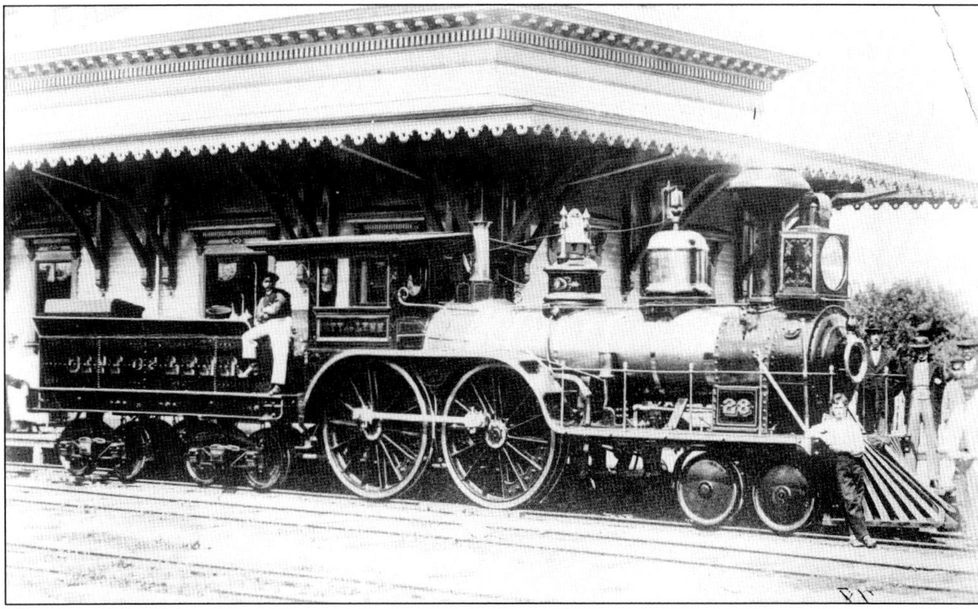

EASTERN RAILROAD NO. 28, "CITY OF LYNN" (4-4-0), BUILT BY THE TAUNTON LOCOMOTIVE WORKS. After touring-Canada and the United States, the Prince of Wales (afterwards Edward VII) left Boston at 8:45 A.M. on Saturday, October 20, 1860, for Portland, Maine, passing through Salem over the Eastern Railroad. From Portland, he would embark for England. The "City of Lynn" preceded the royal train 2 miles in advance. The locomotive attached to the train was the "Cape Ann," No. 6, which had been put in thorough order, ornamented, and surrounded with flags, wreaths, and other decorations. The event was a tremendous success, for a crowd of some 10,000 people gathered near the station to see the prince.

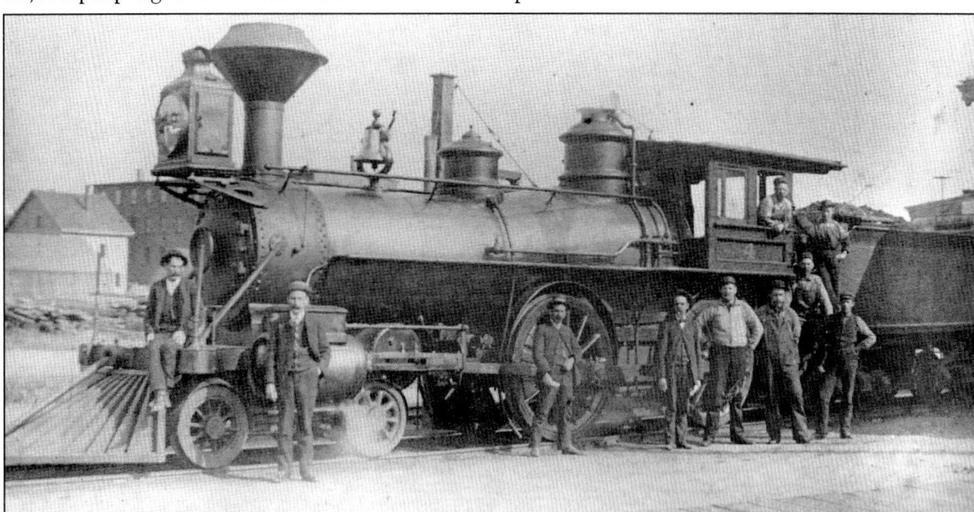

EASTERN RAILROAD NO. 4 (4-4-0), 17- BY 24-INCH CYLINDERS. This engine was built by the Rhode Island Locomotive Works in 1882 and was later rebuilt by the Boston & Maine in 1901. In its campaigns against the Eastern Railroad, the Boston & Maine always had the advantage of a superior location. With unusual sagacity, it adopted a policy of low fares and thus built up a populous and dependent suburban territory. The Boston & Maine carried more passengers than any other railroad in New England and occasionally more than any in the nation.

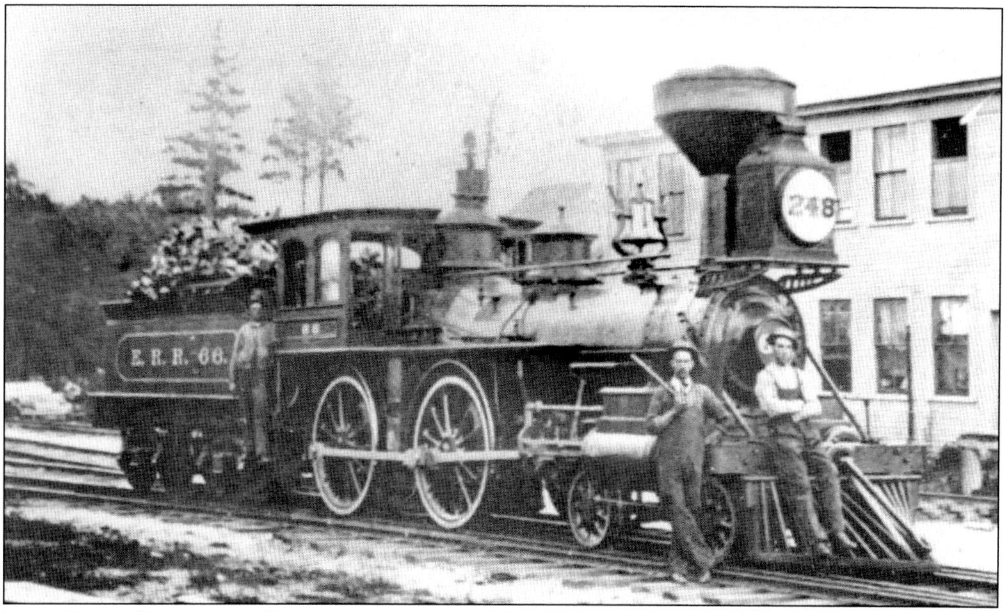

The First Train at Wolfeboro Falls. The first train to arrive in Wolfeboro Falls on opening day, August 19, 1872, was Eastern Railroad No. 66, a wood burner built by Hinkley & Williams in 1871. In addition to outside investments, the Eastern had at this time guaranteed bonds of the Great Falls and Conway Railroad of New Hampshire. In 1865, the Portsmouth, Great Falls and Conway Railroad was incorporated with the power to purchase both the Great Falls and Conway Road as well as the South Berwick Branch.

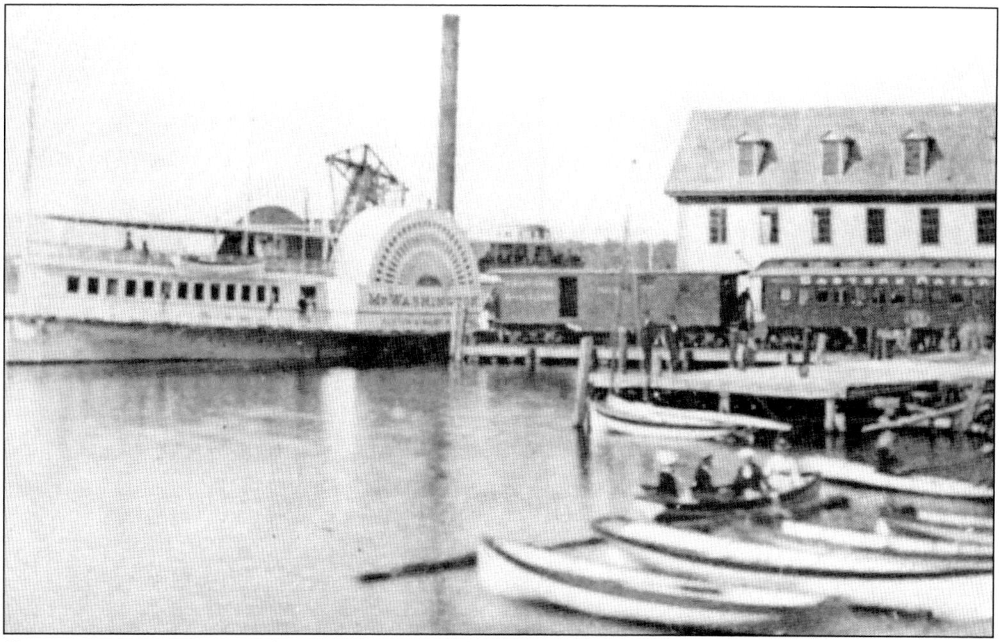

The Wolfeboro Dock Station, 1880. The Eastern Railroad train connected here with the Boston & Maine steamer *Mount Washington*. The large Boston & Maine building in the rear burned in 1899. This dock was a junction for three railroad companies: the Boston & Maine; the Boston, Concord & Montreal; and the Eastern.

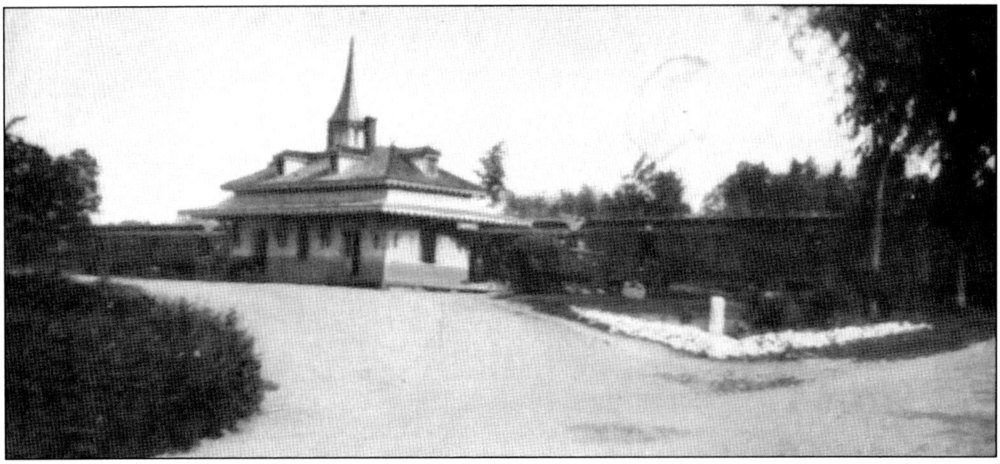

The Eastern Railroad Station, Ossipee, New Hampshire. The intention of the Eastern Railroad investment was to construct a road from Union Village to West Ossipee, New Hampshire, thus opening a new route for tourist travel to the White Mountains. In June 1871, rails between Union Village and West Ossipee were laid, and passenger trains commenced running to West Ossipee a month later.

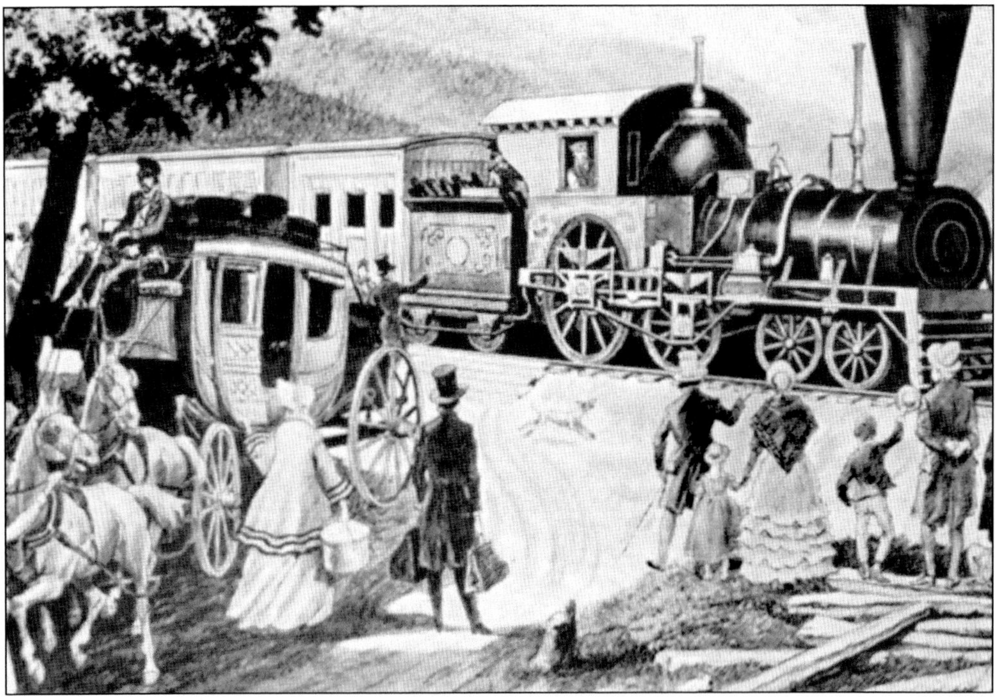

The Stagecoach Meeting the Railroad. From Ossipee, it was proposed that traveling over the 17 miles to Conway should be done by stagecoach. It was soon decided, however, that such an arrangement would imply that the whole railroad scheme was a failure. The building of the railroad soon put the stagecoach out of business, as travel in those days was done at the speed of 20 or 30 mph. Imagine the arrival of such an early train. One observer noted, "The engine came up in grand style, and when opposite our village, gave one of its most savage yells, frightening men, women, and children considerably." In 1865, the total railroad mileage in New Hampshire was 667 miles.

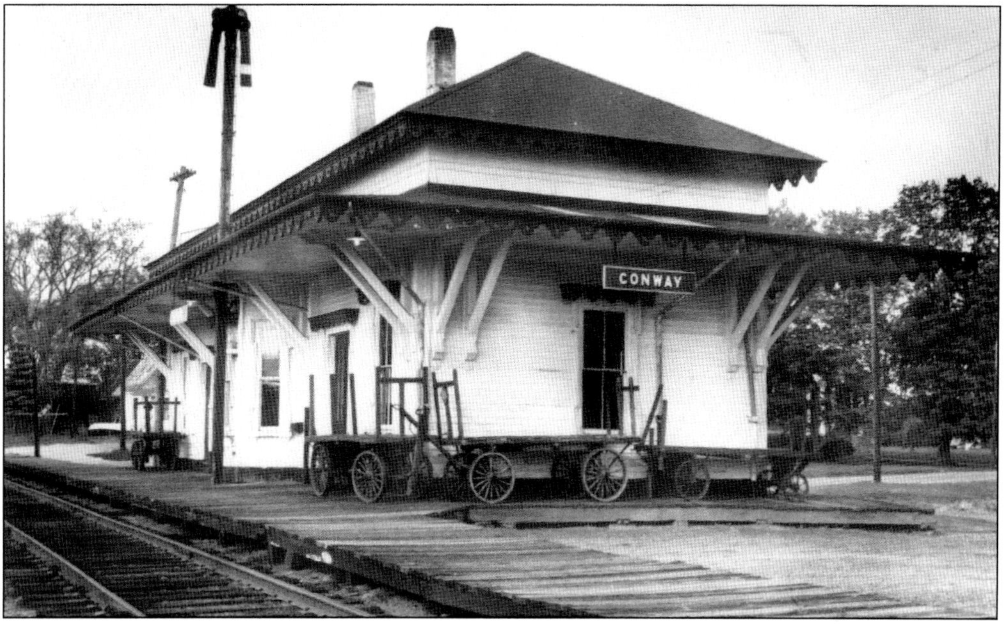

THE CONWAY CENTRE RAILROAD STATION, CONWAY, NEW HAMPSHIRE. The extension to the Conways was undertaken and completed in September 1874 so that connections were established with the Portland & Ogdensburg Railroad in North Conway, 71 miles from Conway Junction.

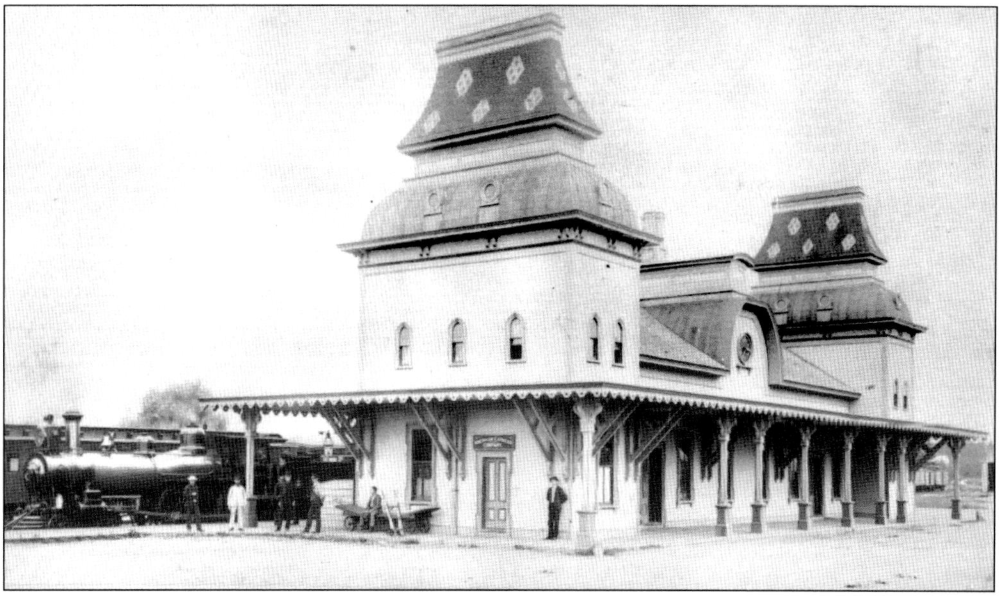

THE NORTH CONWAY STATION, NORTH CONWAY, NEW HAMPSHIRE, 1878. From this grand Victorian depot on Main Street, rail service continued north through Crawford Notch to Fabyan's at the base of Mount Washington. The Eastern Railroad felt that if the line could be extended to North Conway, nearly all the mountain travel could be secured. Connection could be made there with the Portland & Ogdensburg Railroad to obtain a reasonable part of the travel and freight from Montreal, the Canadas, and the Great Lakes region, as it would afford a route to Boston shorter by 27 miles than that of the Boston & Maine.

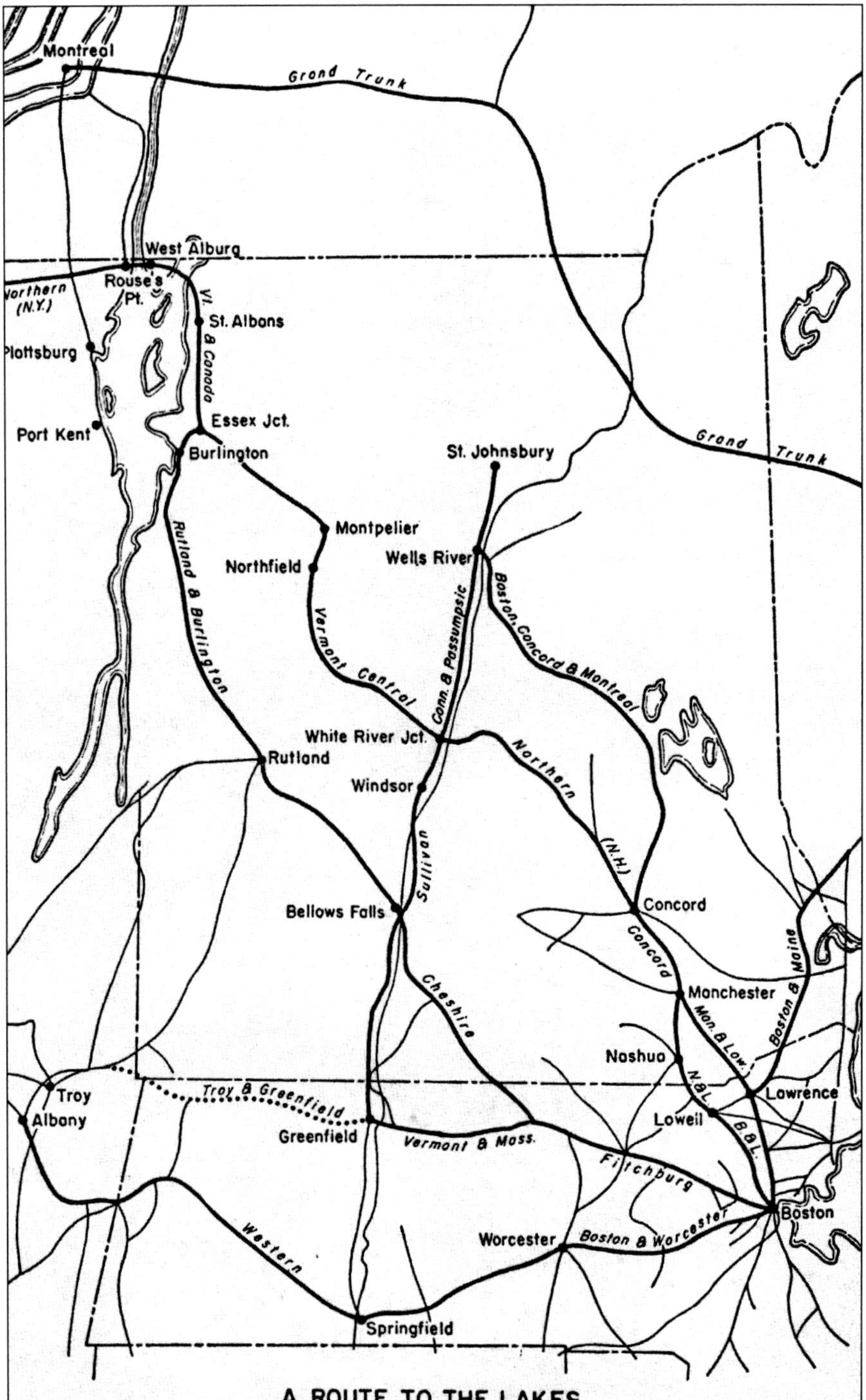

A Route to the Lakes. The development of railroads changed the shape of our towns and cities. They cut a swath through older road systems, and railroad depots became new centers of local commerce, manufacturing, and domicile. Some communities withered when bypassed by the rail system, but others flourished when rail service arrived.

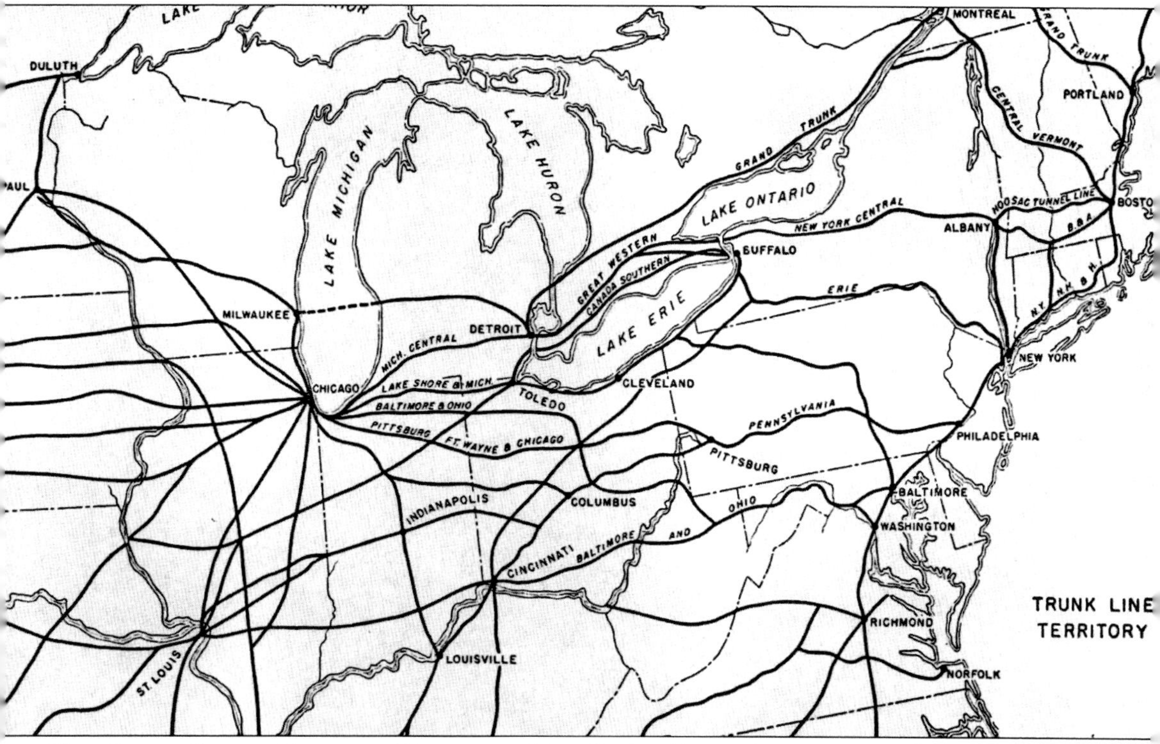

THE GRAND TRUNK RAILROAD TERRITORY. New England lay at the outermost edge of Grand Trunk Railroad territory, which stretched from the Great Lakes and the St. Lawrence to the Potomac and the Ohio and from the Mississippi to the Atlantic coastline. Before the great east-west railroads had been constructed and the area had been named for the existing trunk lines, water transportation dominated its commerce. It had now become imperative that a link be made with these water lines in order to protect the commerce and industrial growth of New England.

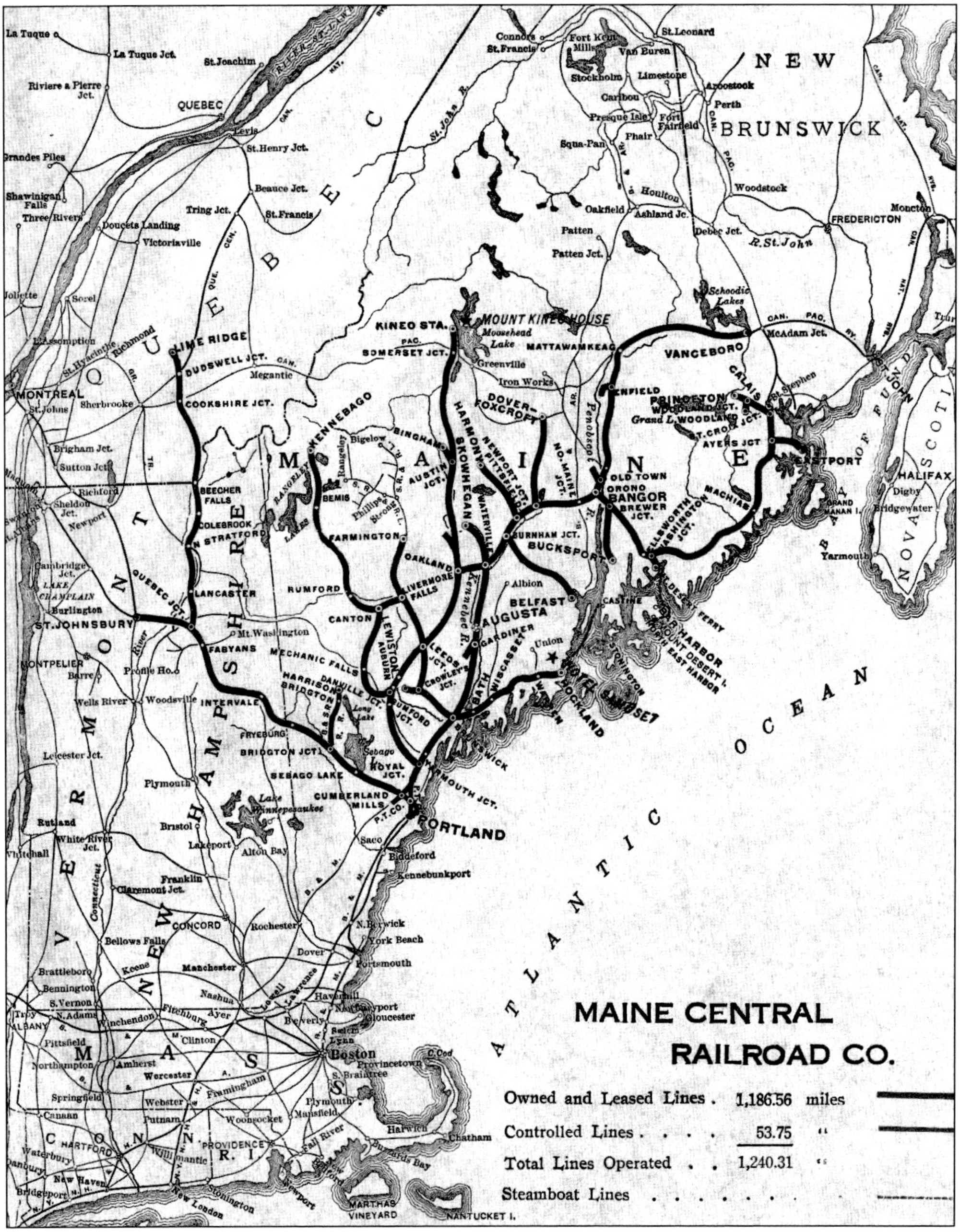

A Maine Central Railroad Company Map. The Maine Central Railroad was formed in 1862 by the consolidation of the two railroads (Penobscot & Kennebec and the Androscoggin & Kennebec). It connected Portland and Bangor by way of Lewiston and Waterville. This broad-gauge route reached Portland, Maine, over the tracks of the Grand Trunk and transferred its passengers and commodities to the Portland, Saco & Portsmouth Railroad. At this time, the Maine Central was one of the seven largest railroad systems in the nation; it was certainly the greatest in New England. By the late 1970s, the Central had dropped its leases in southwestern Vermont and returned, though only for a brief time, the Ogdensburg and Lake Champlain to its owners.

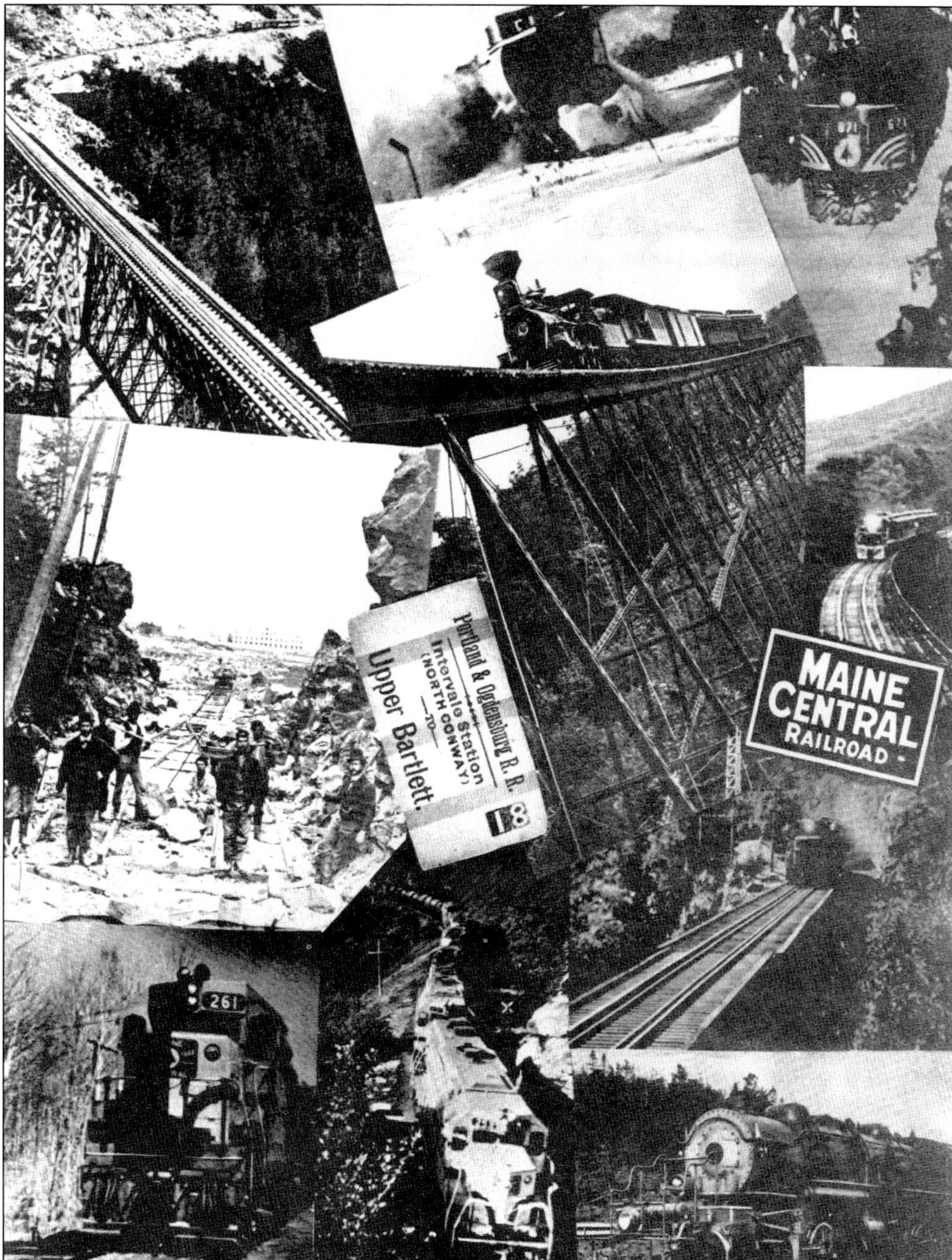

A Poster for the Maine Central Railroad Company and the Ogdensburg Railroad. In 1875, the Maine Central Railroad Company entered the Conways and passed through the White Mountains through Crawford Notch via the Ogdensburg Railroad. Shortly after the Civil War, the Portland & Ogdensburg Railroad was chartered to build a line from the coast of Maine to Ogdensburg, New York, on the St. Lawrence River. In 1875, more than 80 miles of track had been opened for passenger and freight service into the White Mountains and through the Crawford Notch gateway of New Hampshire.

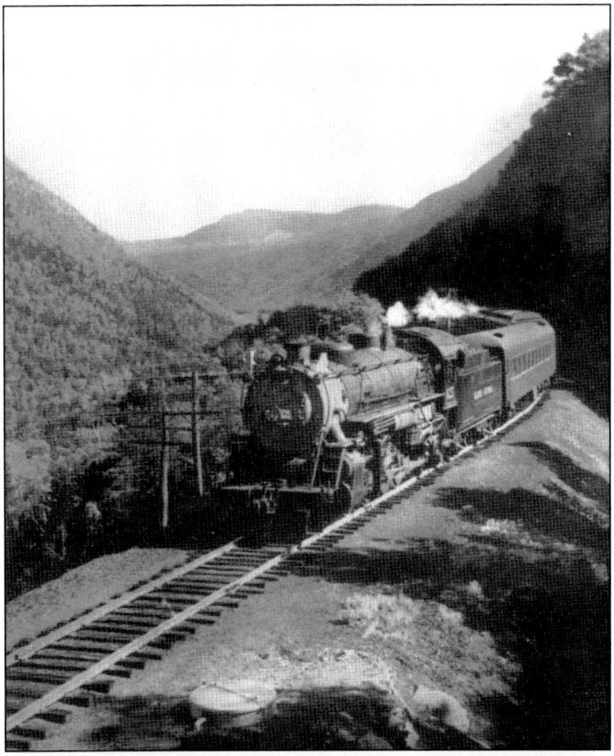

ON THE MOUNTAIN ROUTE OF THE MAINE CENTRAL RAILROAD. One of the most picturesque rides in the east is the trip through Crawford Notch in the White Mountains of New Hampshire. This locomotive, a Mikado (2-8-2), is approaching the Notch Pass.

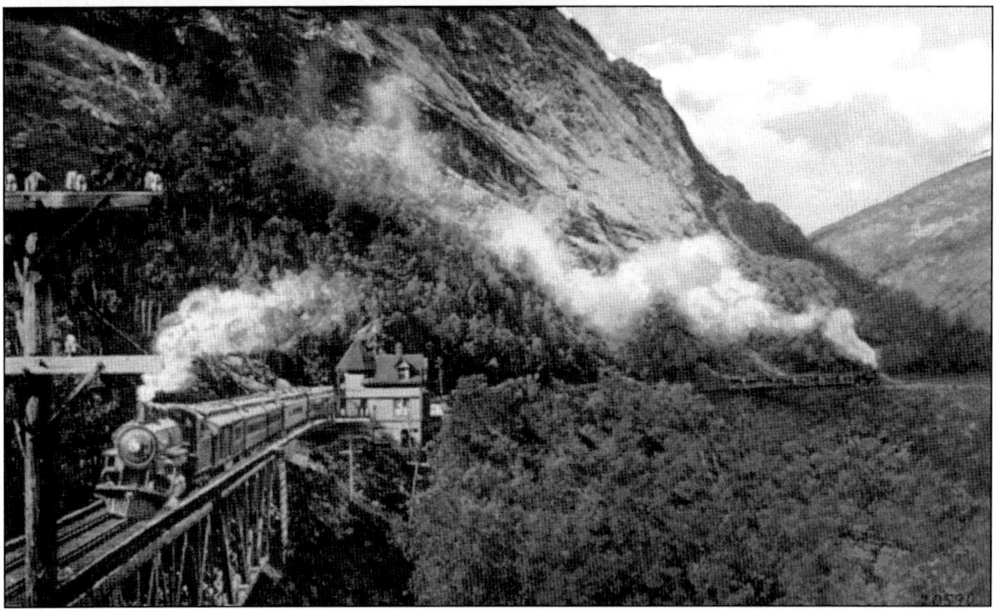

THE WILLEY BROOK BRIDGE AND THE PORTLAND & OGDENSBURG RAILROAD TRAIN. This station burned in 1974. The Willey Brook Bridge and Frankenstein Cliff (with an altitude of 2,150 feet) are considered the major attractions of Crawford Notch. The notch is about 15 miles in length and 2 to 4 miles wide. The rail winds along the mountainside, passing over two deep gorges, spanned by the Willey Brook Bridge and the Frankenstein Trestle, a triumph of engineering skill.

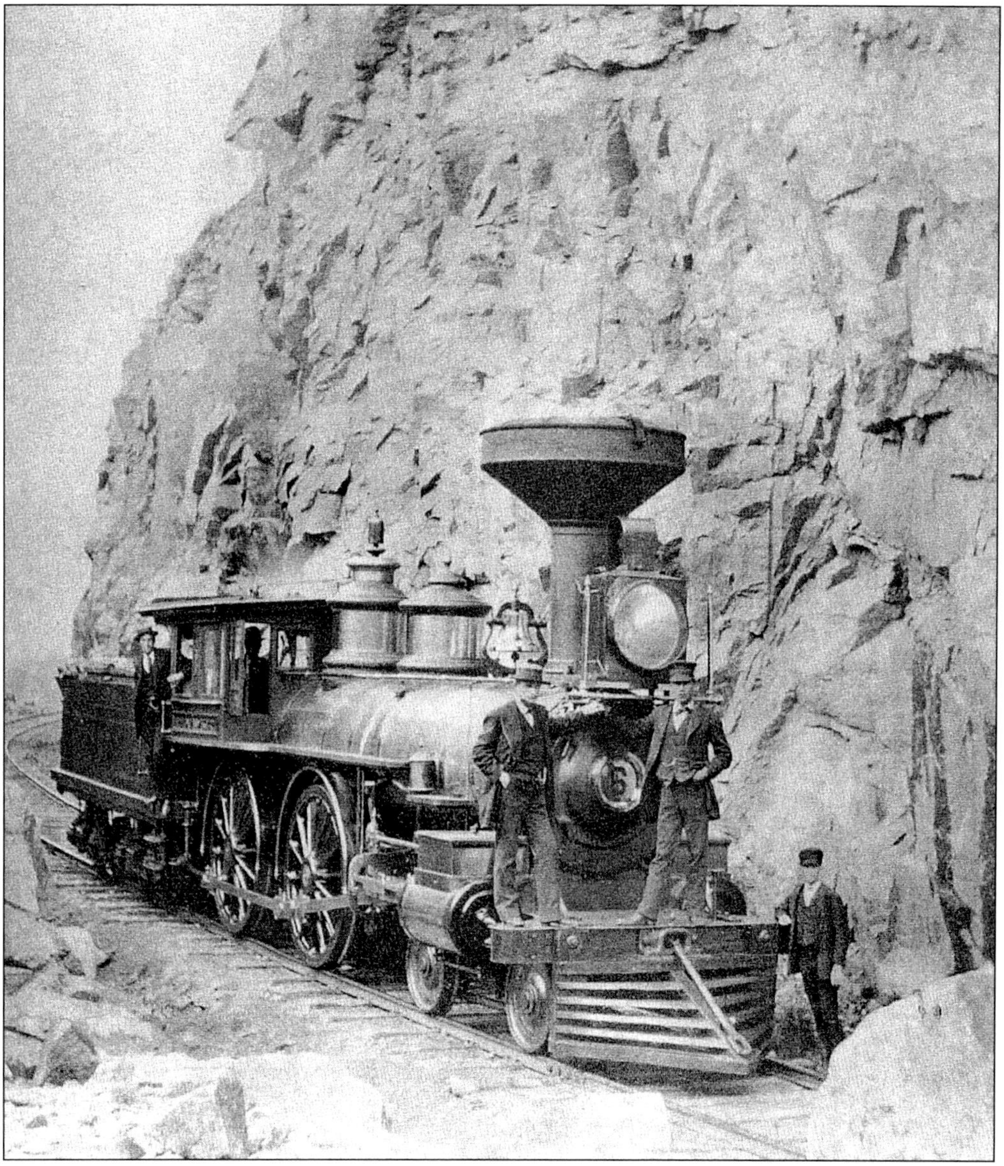

THE "MOUNTAINEER" IN THE CRAWFORD NOTCH PASS, 1875. The 27-mile ride from North Conway to the Crawford House took about an hour and a half. According to early town reports, the first produce carried over this road was a barrel of rum from Portland to Lancaster, a gift to anyone who could get it through the notch. Captain Rosebrook accomplished the feat, although nearly all of the contents were consumed en route by "those who helped manage the affair." In 1875, the Eastern Railroad purchased controlling interest in the Maine Central, but went bankrupt in the process. In 1876, it went into receivership and, in 1883, the Boston & Maine leased the Eastern Railroad.

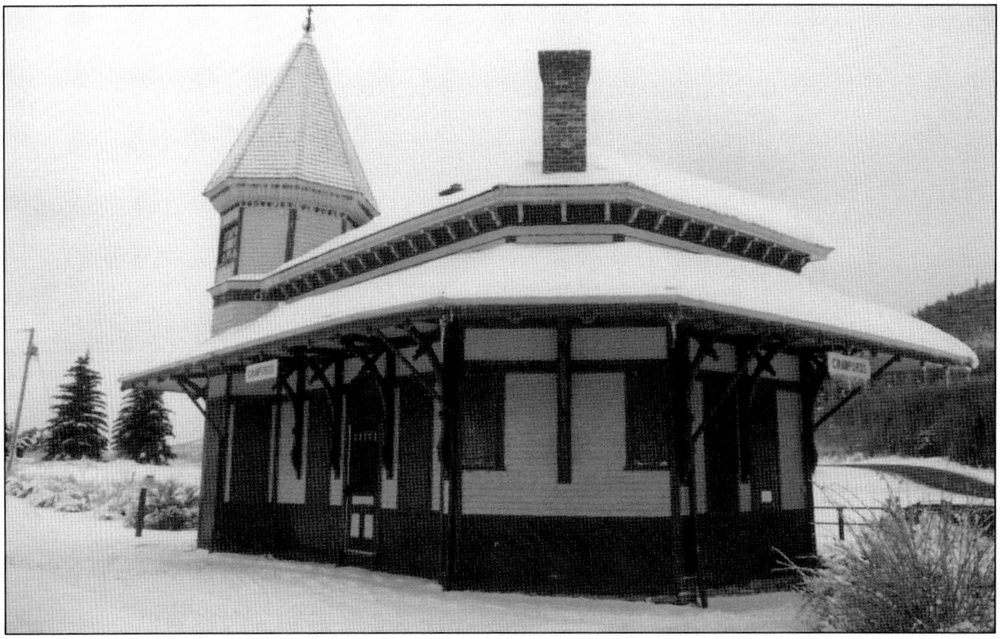

THE CRAWFORD RAILROAD STATION. This station on the Maine Central Railroad takes its name from nearby Crawford Notch and resort.

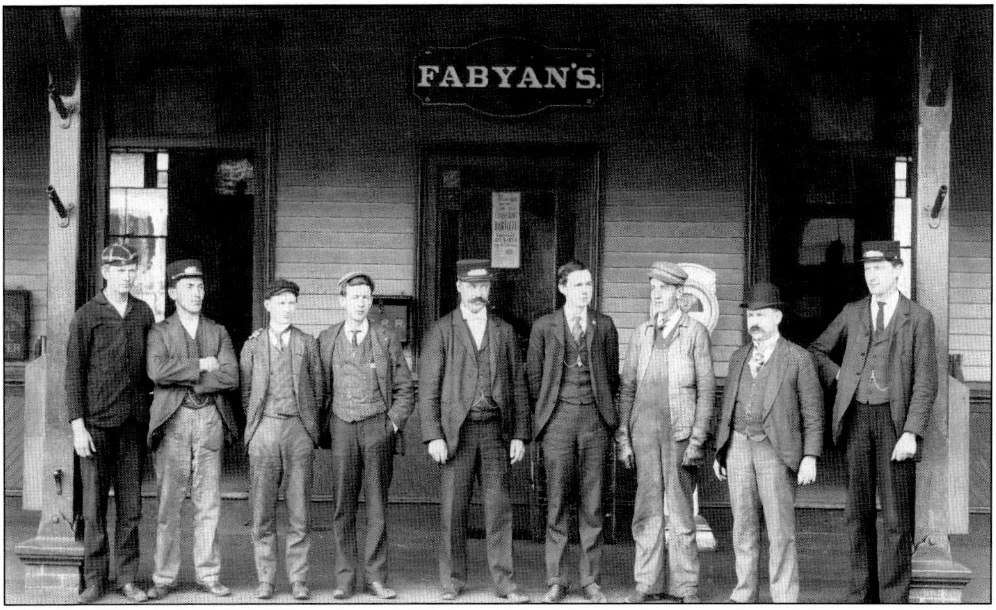

FABYAN'S STATION, 1900, THE MAINE CENTRAL RAILROAD MOUNTAIN DIVISION. Pictured from left to right are John Green (switchman for the west end of the yard), Ed Bartlett (baggagemaster), Earnest Emery (night operator), Willey Cane (expressman), James J. Parks (station agent), Fred Learnerd (switchman for the east end of the yard), Frank Gallagher (ticket agent), and Hugh Chisholm (assistant baggagemaster). This station, the most important railroad point in the mountain region, is 208 miles from Boston. All Boston and New York express trains ran to and from this station, as did the Mount Washington trains, for the Crawford House and through Crawford Notch.

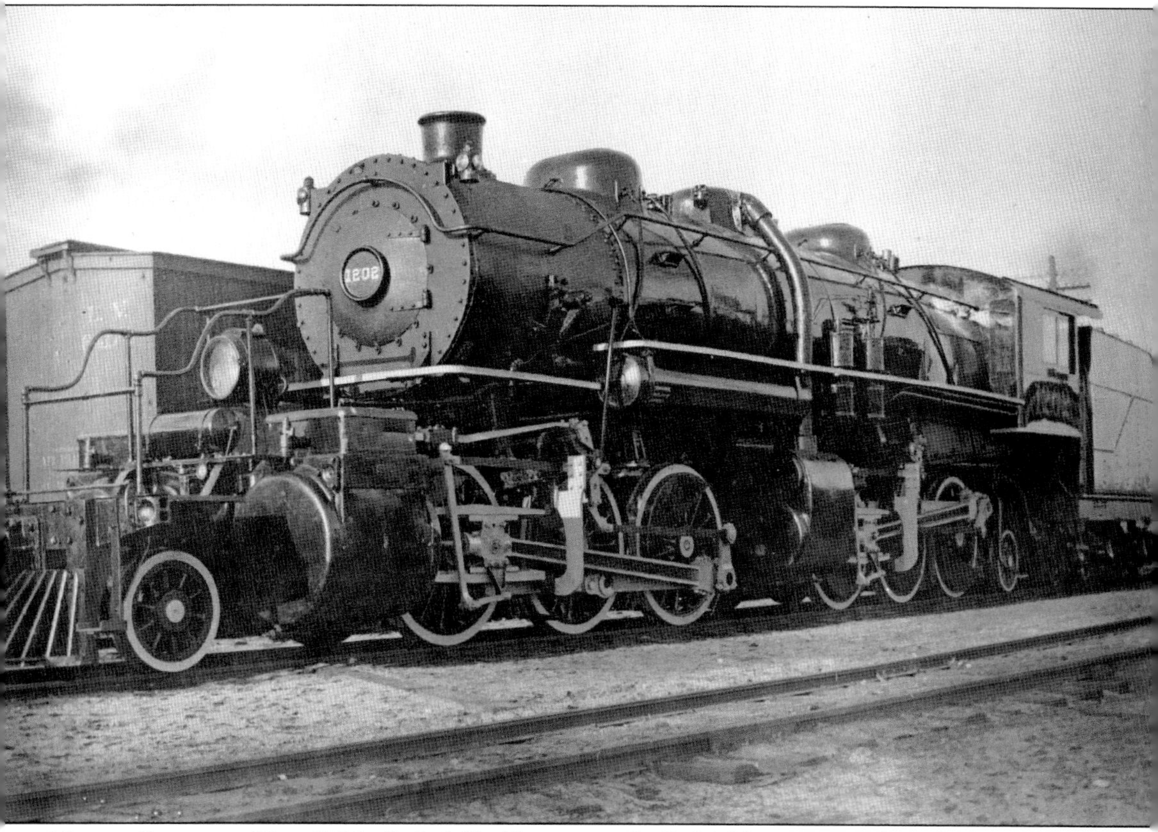

MAINE CENTRAL NO. 1202 (2-6-6-2), FORMERLY B & M NO. 1293. This photograph shows an excellent view of the "cowcatcher" mounted to the front of the locomotive. The first cowcatcher and pilot wheels were used in 1833, fitted to the "John Bull" by the Camden & Amboy Railroad. Starting around 1835, the cowcatcher was adopted by many railroads. A well-made cowcatcher could throw a 2,000-pound buffalo some 30 feet.

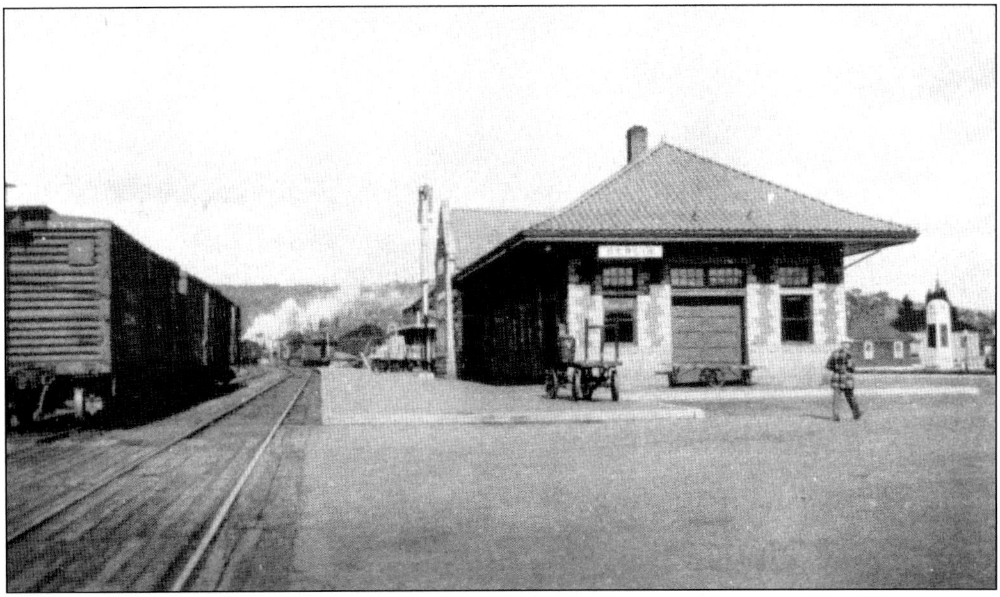

THE CANADIAN NATIONAL, GRAND TRUNK RAILROAD DEPOT AT BERLIN, NEW HAMPSHIRE. The Atlantic and St. Lawrence Railroad, predecessor to the Grand Trunk line, was chartered in the 1840s to cut across a section of the northern New Hampshire through Berlin and establish a depot on the Atlantic seaboard in Portland, Maine. This project was the brainstorm of John A. Poor of Portland. The line was built under both American and Canadian charters and was open for service in July 1853.

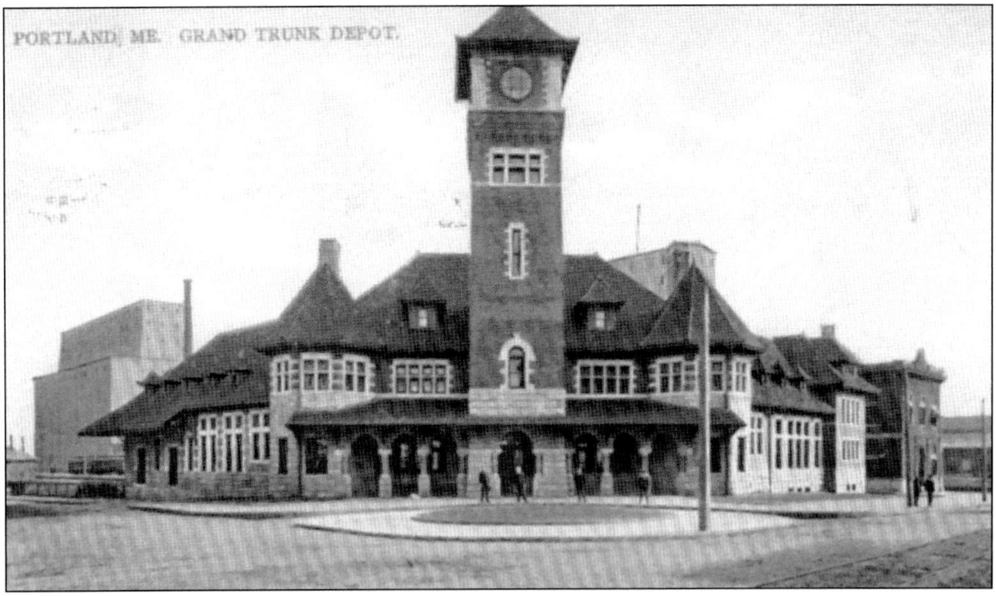

THE GRAND TRUNK RAILROAD DEPOT, PORTLAND, MAINE. In 1853, the old fort site assumed a new and international importance. That year, the Atlantic and St. Lawrence Railroad (subsequently leased to the Grand Trunk Railway Company of Canada and now forming a part of the Canadian National Railway) was completed between Portland and Montreal. This station was the third depot to serve the Grand Trunk in Portland. In 1903, it replaced an older covered station on India Street.

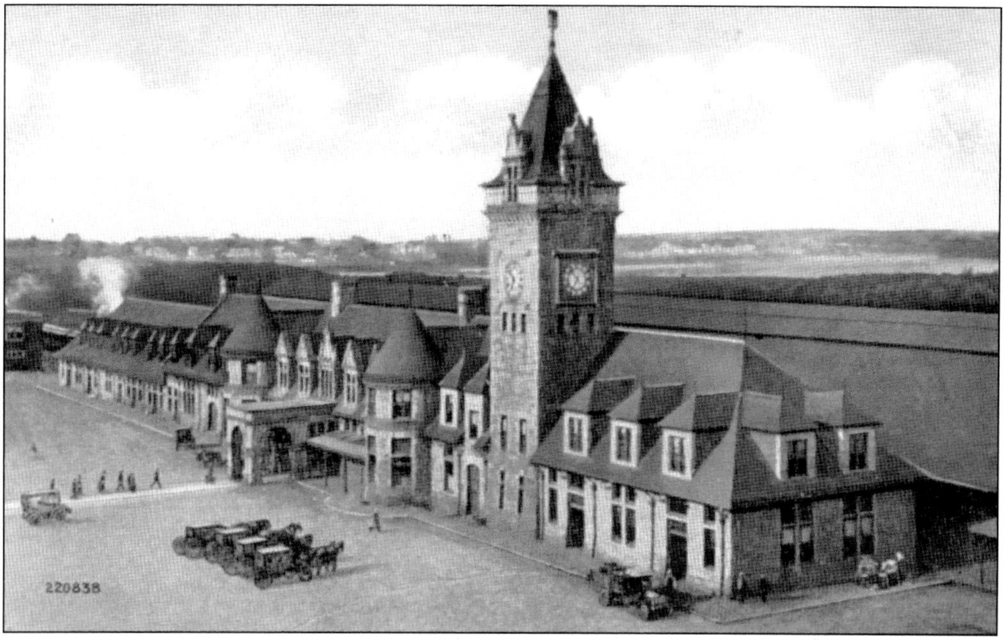

UNION STATION, PORTLAND, MAINE, 1888. This Victorian station was constructed of brick and rough granite, its facade surmounted by an illuminated clock tower. East of the station, the railway's two huge grain elevators raised their gaunt shapes above yards and wharves. In 1850, increased trade and the projected railway to Canada seemed to demand more ample transportation and better terminal facilities than were possible before the new station, which at that time bordered the water.

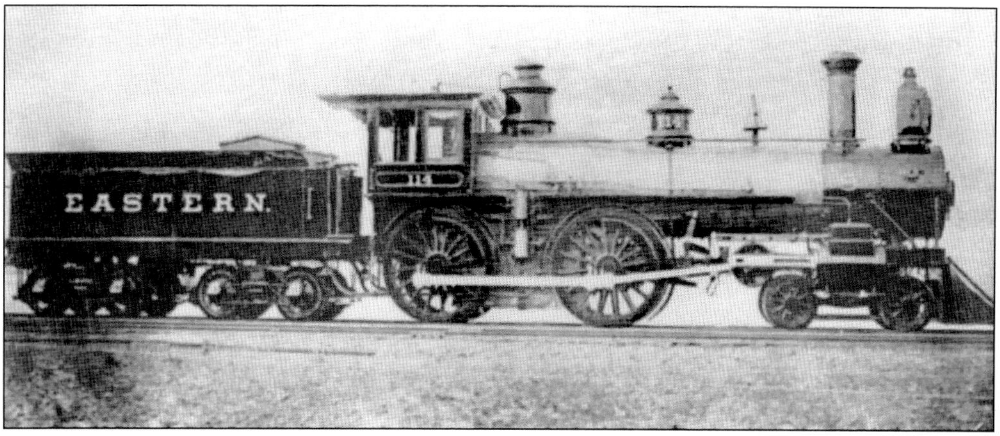

THE LAST EASTERN RAILROAD LOCOMOTIVE. This engine was the last one built for the Eastern Railroad before consolidation with the Boston & Maine in 1884. In November 1874, an arrangement was entered into between the Eastern Railroad and the Boston & Maine that stopped this ruinous competition, but relations between the two roads were never very friendly.

In 1884, a new 54-year lease that conformed to the opinion of the Massachusetts Supreme Court was agreed upon by the directors and approved by the stockholders of both the Eastern and the Boston & Maine. On December 2, 1884, the property was handed over to the lessee. The Eastern Railroad, after an existence of over 46 years, ceased to operate as an independent road. It was run until 1910 as the Eastern Division of the Boston & Maine with a separate organization and its own superintendent, staff, and rules.

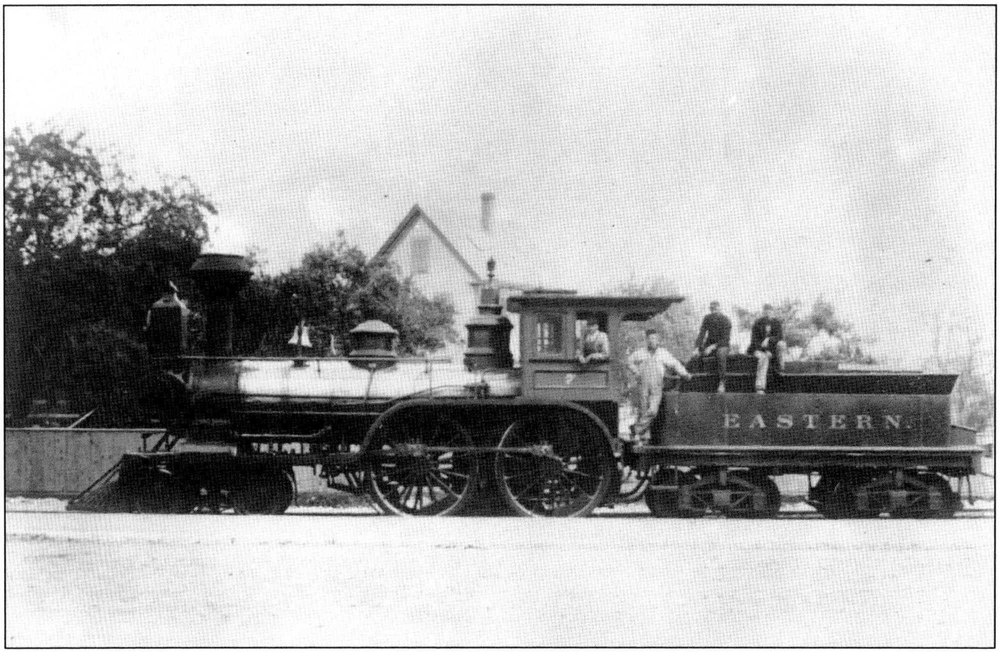

EASTERN RAILROAD LOCOMOTIVE NO. 7 (4-4-0), 15- BY 22-INCH CYLINDERS. This engine was built by the Boston Locomotive Works in 1858. Engineer Charles Fowler is shown standing in the gangway.

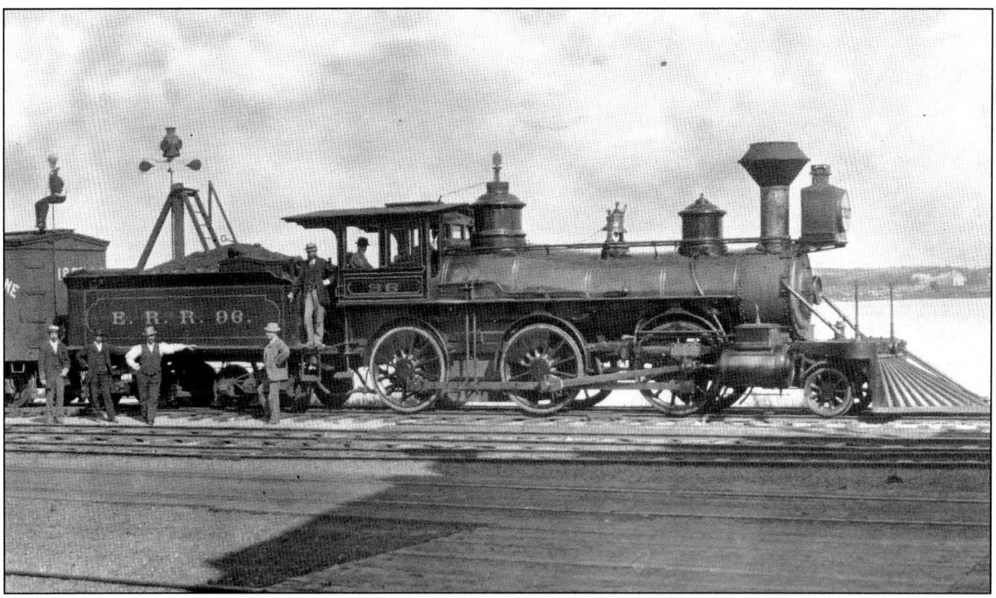

EASTERN RAILROAD LOCOMOTIVE NO. 96 (2-6-0). The Rhode Island Locomotive Works built this engine in 1878.

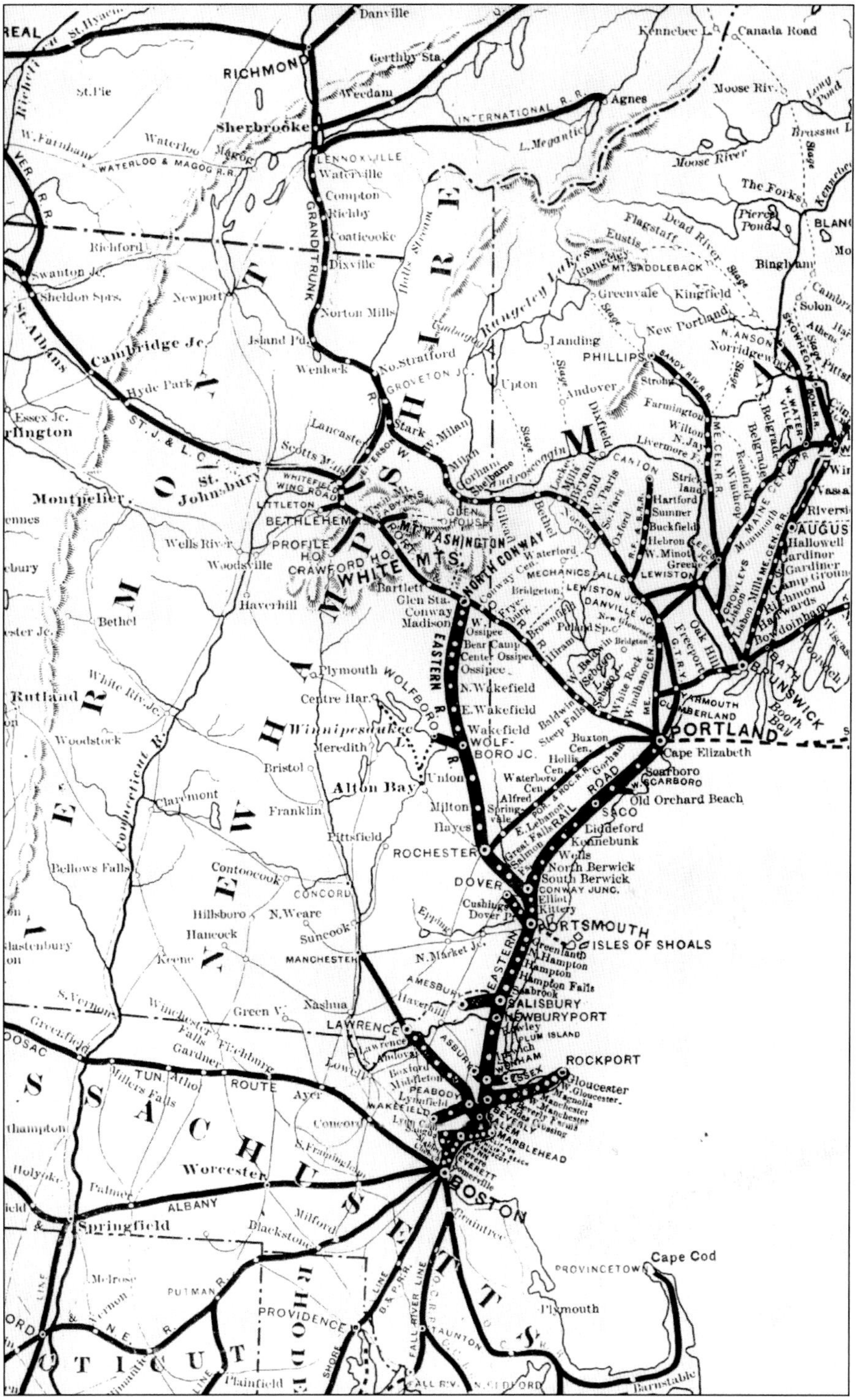

A MAP OF THE EASTERN RAILROAD COMPANY AND CONNECTIONS. This map indicates the major routes of the Eastern Railroad Company and its principal connections with smaller independent railroad companies in northern New England.

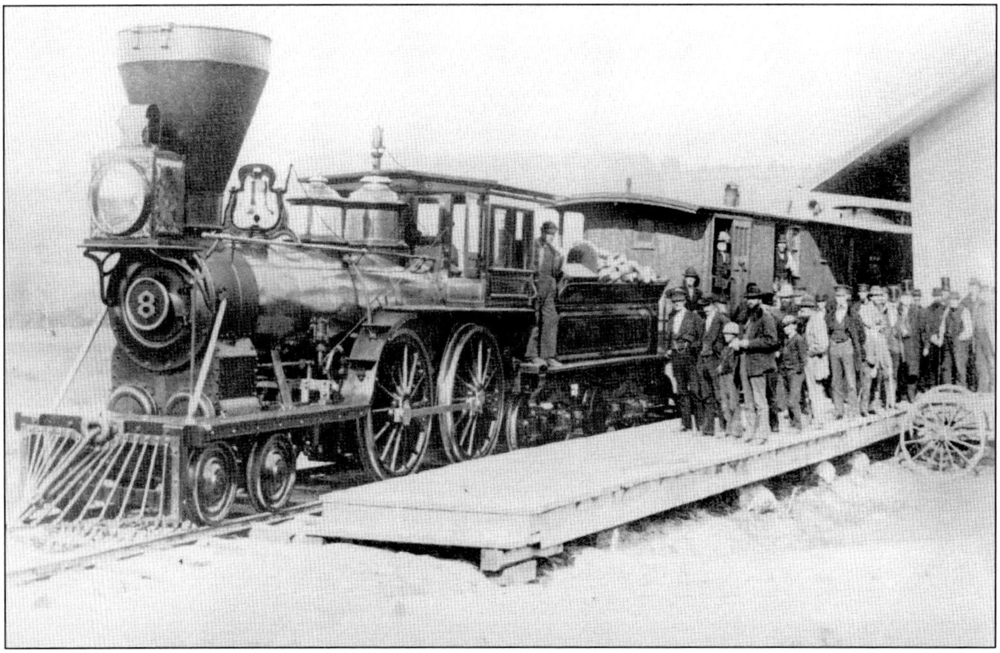

NORTHERN RAILROAD NO. 8, "GRAFTON" (4-4-0), 15- BY 18-INCH CYLINDERS. This engine was built by Hinkley & Drury in 1847. The Northern Railroad was a single-track line from Concord, New Hampshire, to White River Junction, Vermont. It was 69.5 miles in all, with a branch line from Franklin to Bristol, New Hampshire, measuring 13.41 miles. The main line was chartered in 1844 and completed in 1848.

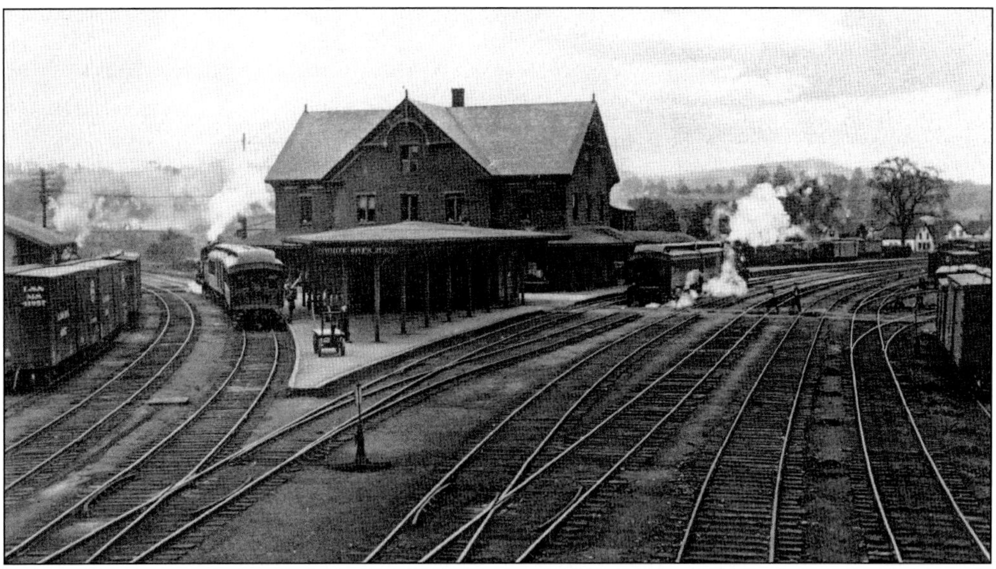

THE PASSENGER STATION AT WHITE RIVER JUNCTION, VERMONT. The Northern Railroad was operated independently until January 1, 1888. It was then operated by the Boston & Maine until leased to the Boston & Lowell under operating contract with a minimum of $199,920 per year. In 1890, the Northern was leased to the Boston & Lowell for 99 years from January 1, 1890, on the basis of 5 percent. Onslow Stearns, president of the Northern Railroad, became governor of New Hampshire, serving until 1871.

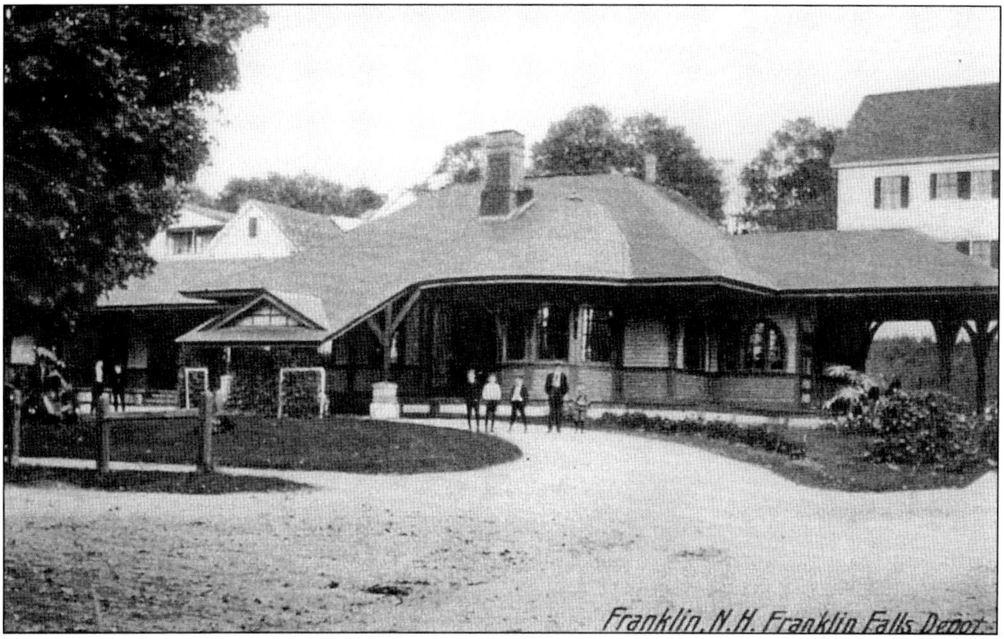

The Franklin Falls Depot, Franklin, New Hampshire. This was originally part of the old Tilton, Franklin & Belmont Railroad.

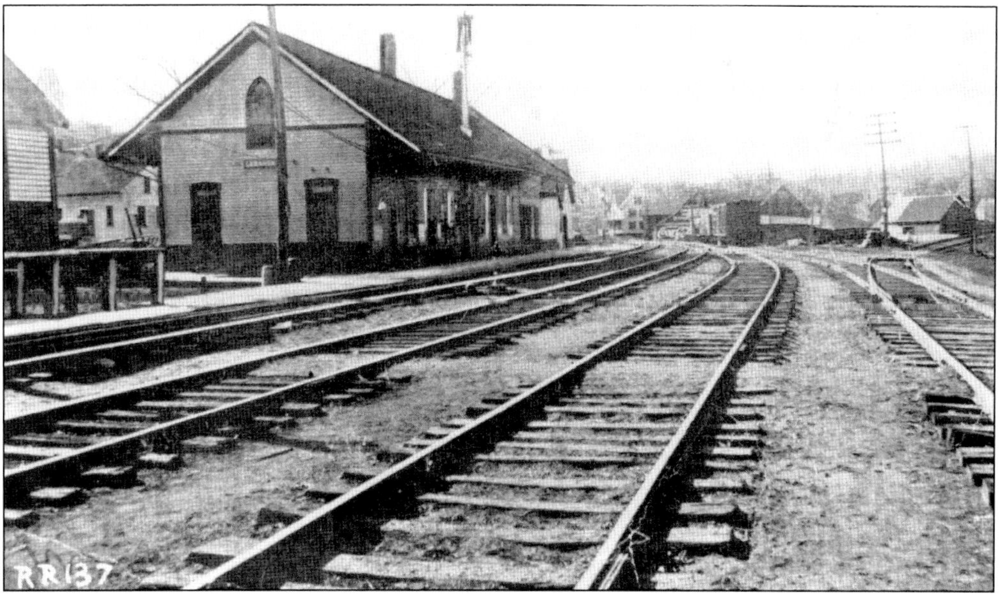

The Lebanon Railroad Station, Lebanon, New Hampshire. On November 17, 1847, the Northern Railroad's first train between Concord and Lebanon arrived amid much fanfare in Lebanon. Daniel Webster gave a speech honoring the occasion.

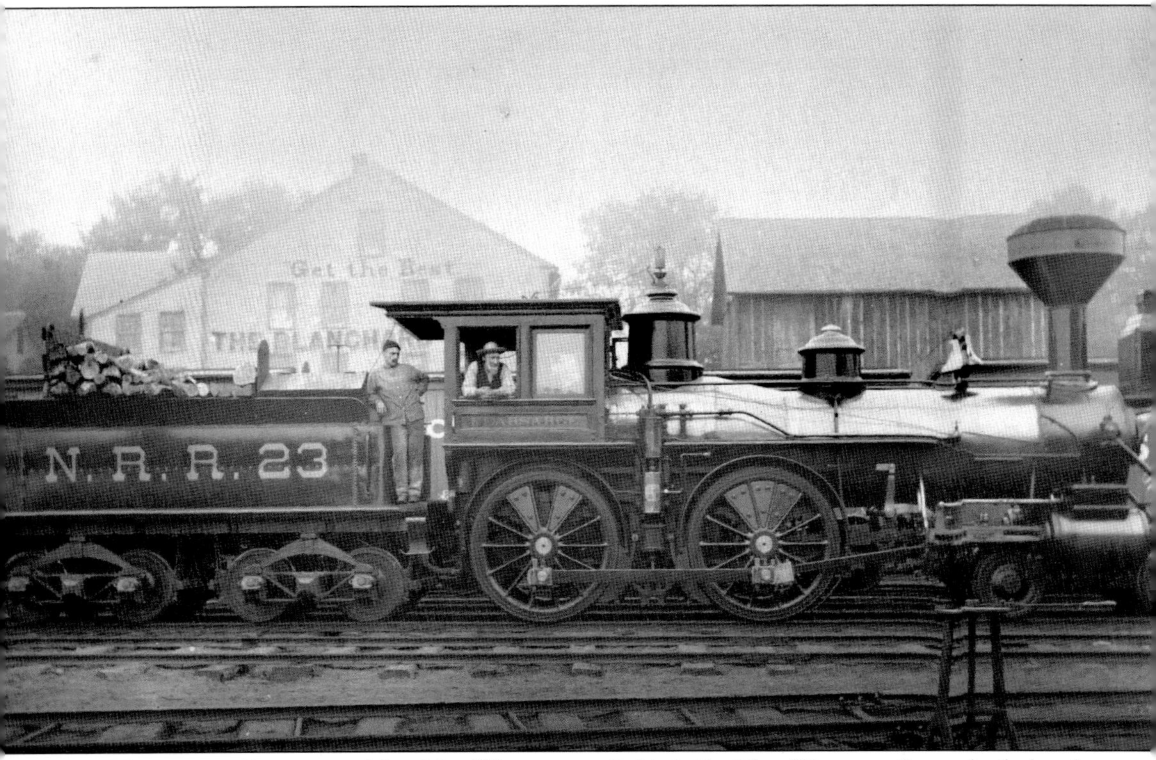

NORTHERN RAILROAD NO. 23, "KEARSARGE" (4-4-0). The "Kearsarge" was built by the Northern Railroad in 1879 and later became the "Warner," No. 291 of the Boston & Maine. Engineer Lucius Groves, pictured here, was killed in the collision at Andover Plains on October 9, 1885. The "Kearsarge" was later rebuilt with a new boiler, and this boiler was applied to the "Blackwater."

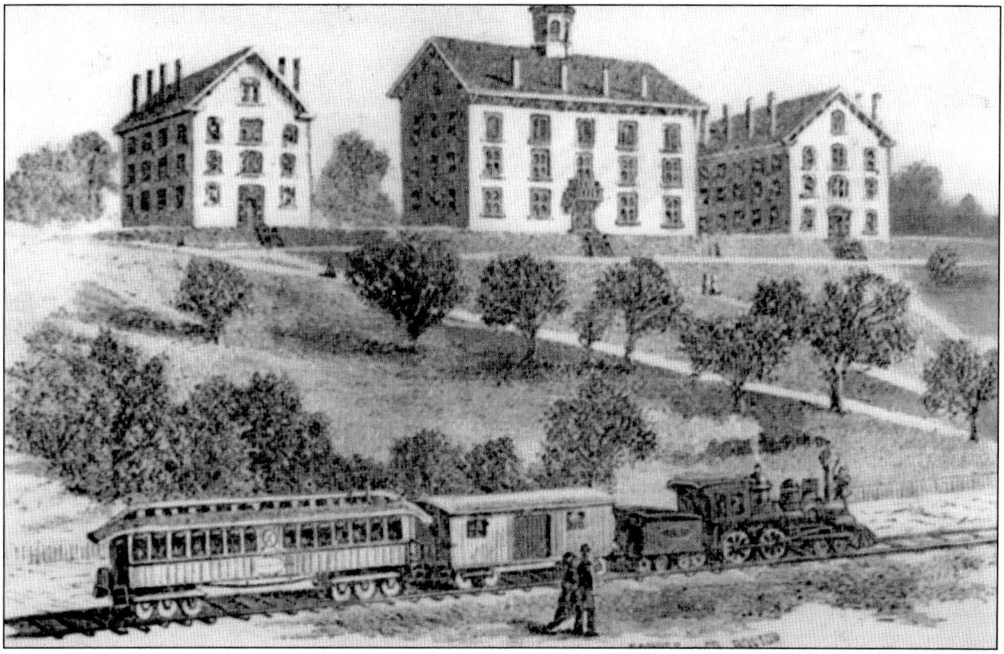

THE FIRST TRAIN IN NEW HAMPSHIRE. Arriving in Nashua in 1838, the first train in New Hampshire signaled a rapid growth in the rail system. New Hampshire made a contribution to railroading in general with the construction of nearly 2,000 locomotives in Manchester.

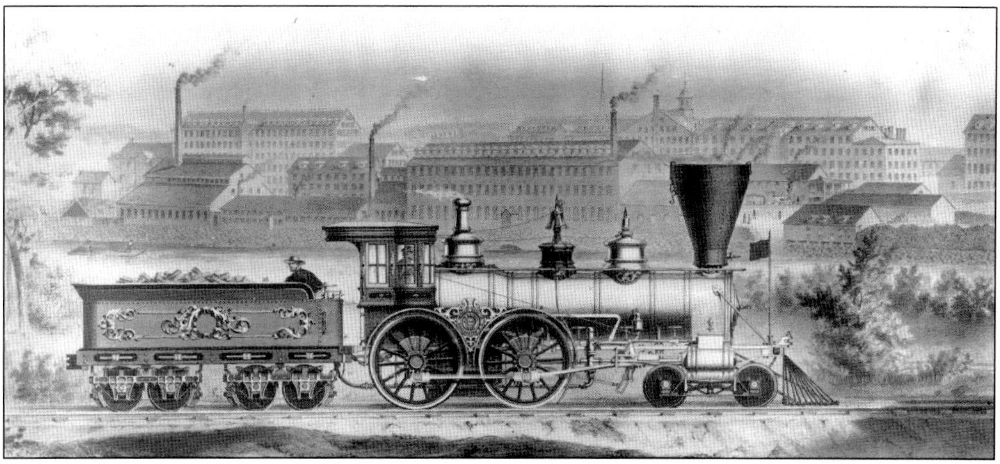

THE AMOSKEAG LOCOMOTIVE WORKS AND "BIG SHOP," 1855. The Amoskeag Manufacturing Company of Manchester, New Hampshire, was one of the largest companies of its kind in the United States. Its charter empowered it to manufacture "woolen, cotton, iron, and other goods." The apparently meaningless Native American name Amoskeag was sent on bales of cotton, sheeting, and the like, to the farthest limits of America. The company was divided into five distinct departments: the Land and Water-Power Company, Amoskeag New Mills, Amoskeag Machine Shop and Locomotive Works, the Amoskeag Batting Mill, and the Hooksett Company. The construction of these works dated from *c.* 1840. The New Hampshire General Court later authorized the Amoskeag Manufacturing Company of Manchester to hold stock in the Concord Railroad.

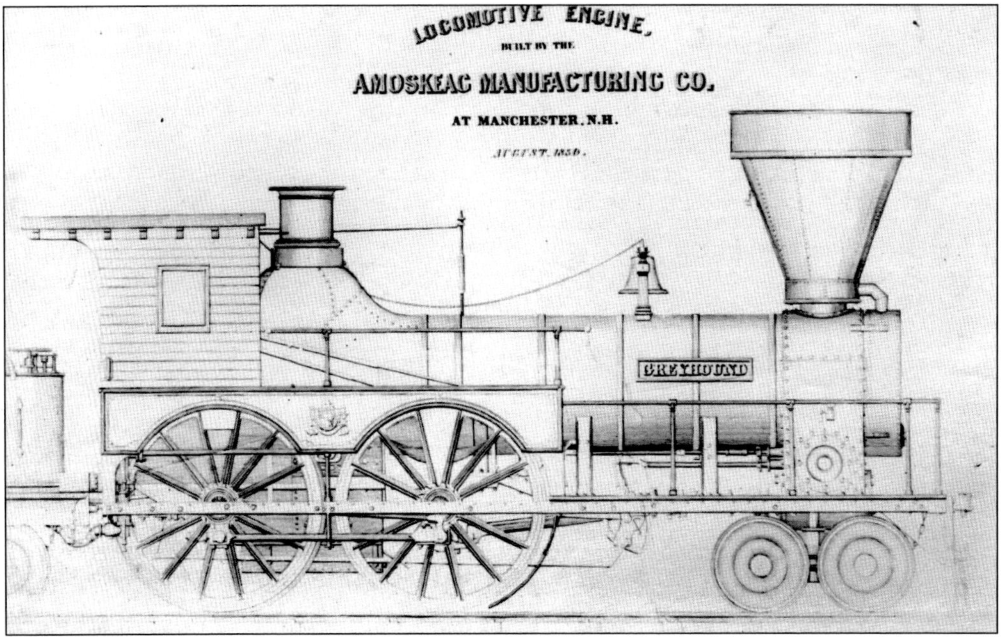

THE LOCOMOTIVE "GREYHOUND" (4-4-0), THE AMOSKEAG MANUFACTURING COMPANY, MANCHESTER, NEW HAMPSHIRE. The building of locomotives was usually connected with the shops devoted to the construction and repair of cotton machinery. Such shops had the equipment, and their workers had the training and skill. Locomotive building at Manchester fell into this category. In 1836, the first 4-4-0 locomotive was developed by Henry R. Campbell of the Philadelphia, Germantown & Norristown Railroad. The eight-wheeler later became a classic design, universally known as the "American" type.

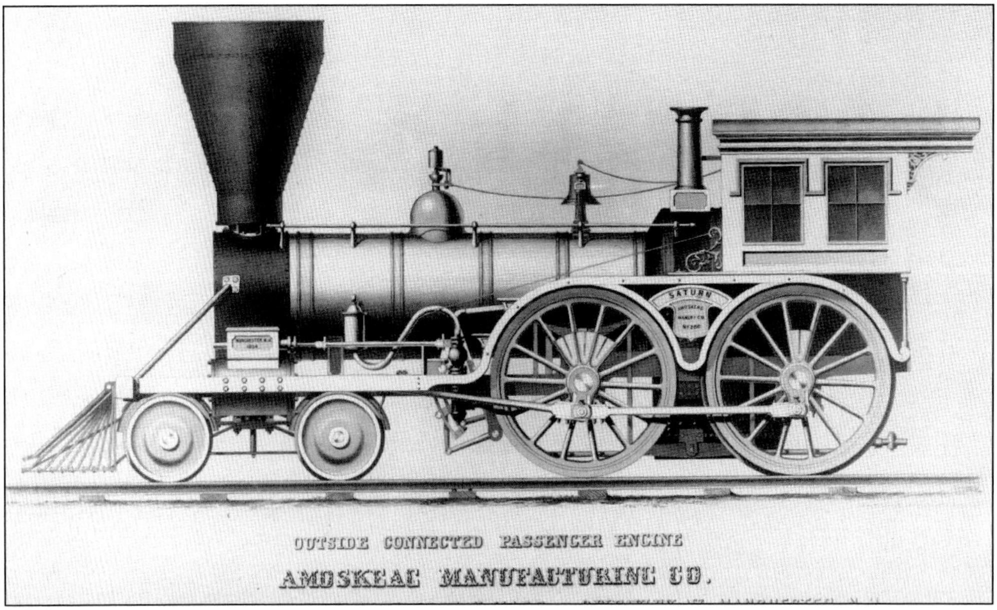

THE AMOSKEAG MANUFACTURING COMPANY. Although the New England locomotives were sold to the transcontinental lines and were shipped to foreign countries, their greatest market was naturally in New England.

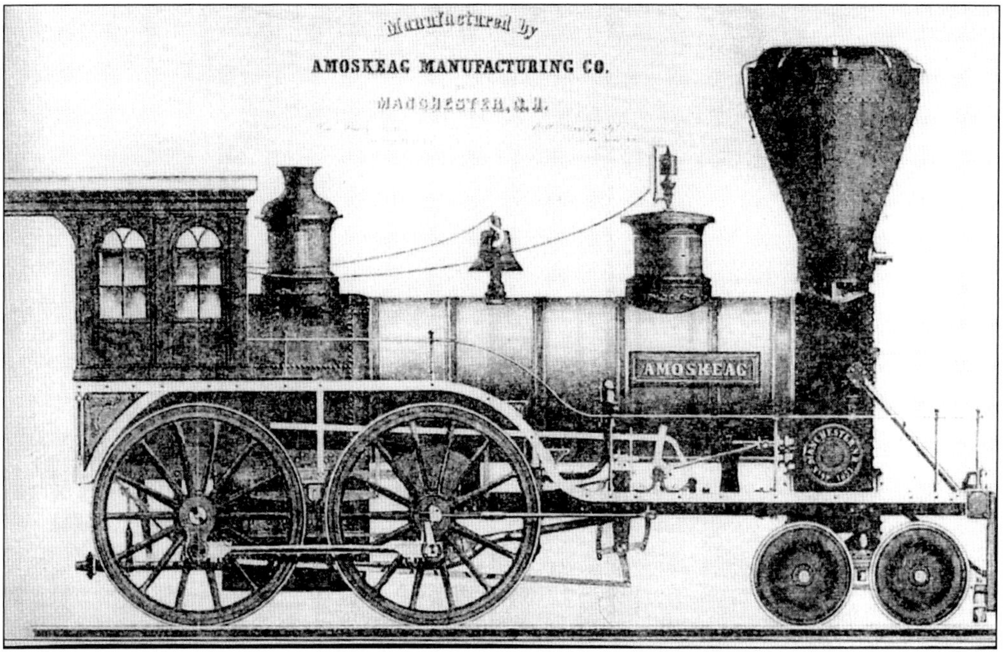

THE LOCOMOTIVE "AMOSKEAG" (4-4-0). The first line reached the capital city of New Hampshire on September 6, 1842, as noted in a Concord Railroad pamphlet: "The locomotive *Amoskeag* with a train of three passenger cars and some baggage, came through from Boston to Concord." Led by Isaac Hill, most of the grantees in the state charter were from Concord. Judge Nathaniel G. Upham was the first superintendent.

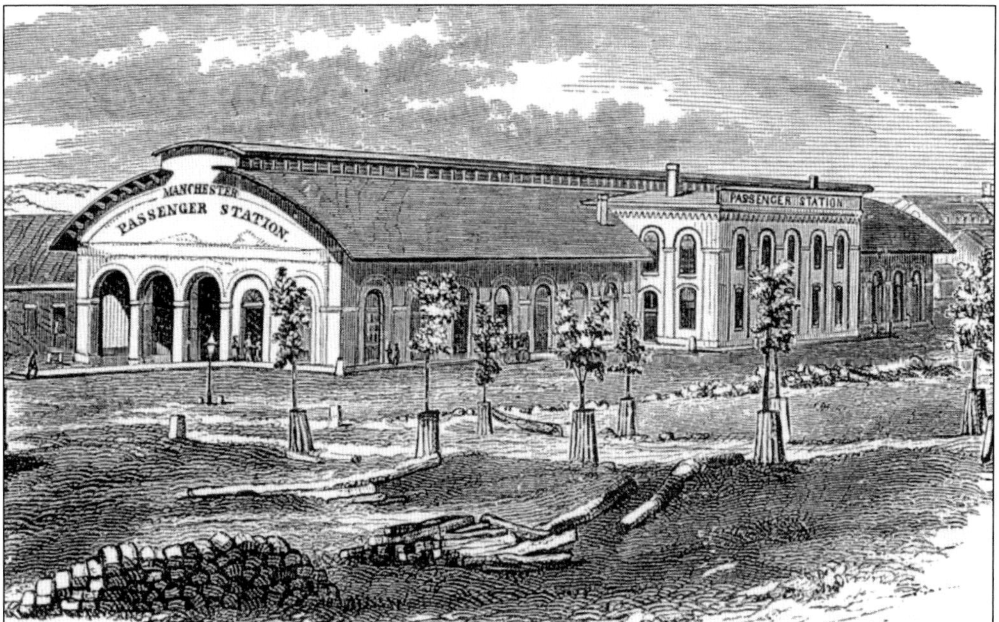

THE OLD RAILROAD PASSENGER STATION IN MANCHESTER, NEW HAMPSHIRE. Built in 1855, this station stood east and north of the Granite Street crossing on what was later a playground for Amoskeag children whose parents worked for the corporation.

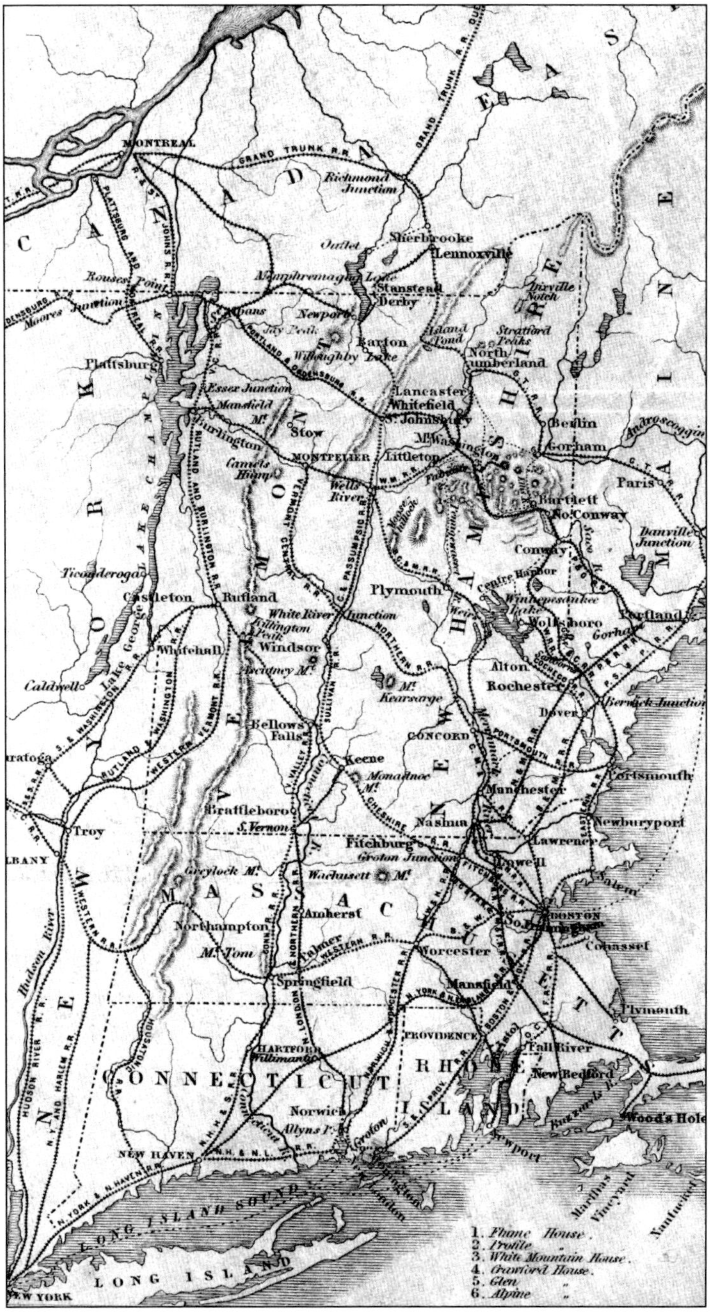

A MAP OF ROUTES TO THE WHITE MOUNTAINS, 1878. This map, taken from Eastman's *White Mountain Guide*, shows the many independent railroad lines throughout New England and eastern New York before the consolidation in the 1890s with the Boston & Maine. During the process of consolidation, virtually all of New Hampshire's railroad corporations disappeared or ceased operating independently. By 1905, the Boston & Maine controlled all but 52 miles of New Hampshire's 1,174 miles of commercial track. These 52 miles belonged to the Grand Trunk Railroad. Some of the old New Hampshire lines maintained their own corporate status following mergers, but management decisions for the state's railroads were coming out of Massachusetts.

Two

Railroad Expansion in Northern New England

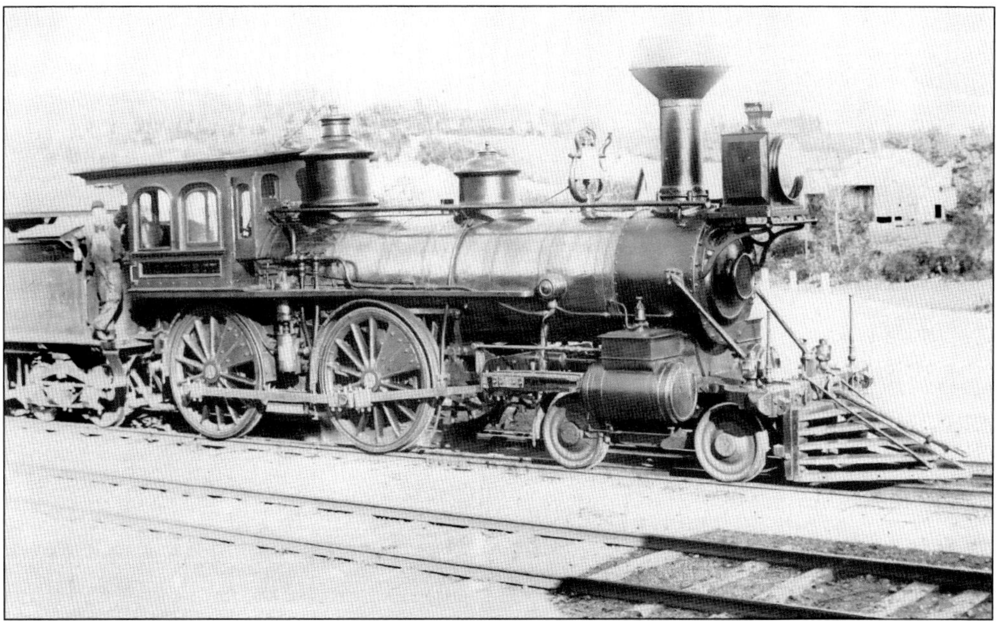

Concord Railroad No. 17, "Hooksett" (4-4-0). This engine was built at the Concord Railroad shop.The Concord Railroad Corporation began as a double-track line from Concord to Nashua, New Hampshire. The charter for the line was granted by the New Hampshire legislature on June 27, 1835. Isaac Hill, U.S. senator and future governor, was one of the early incorporators.

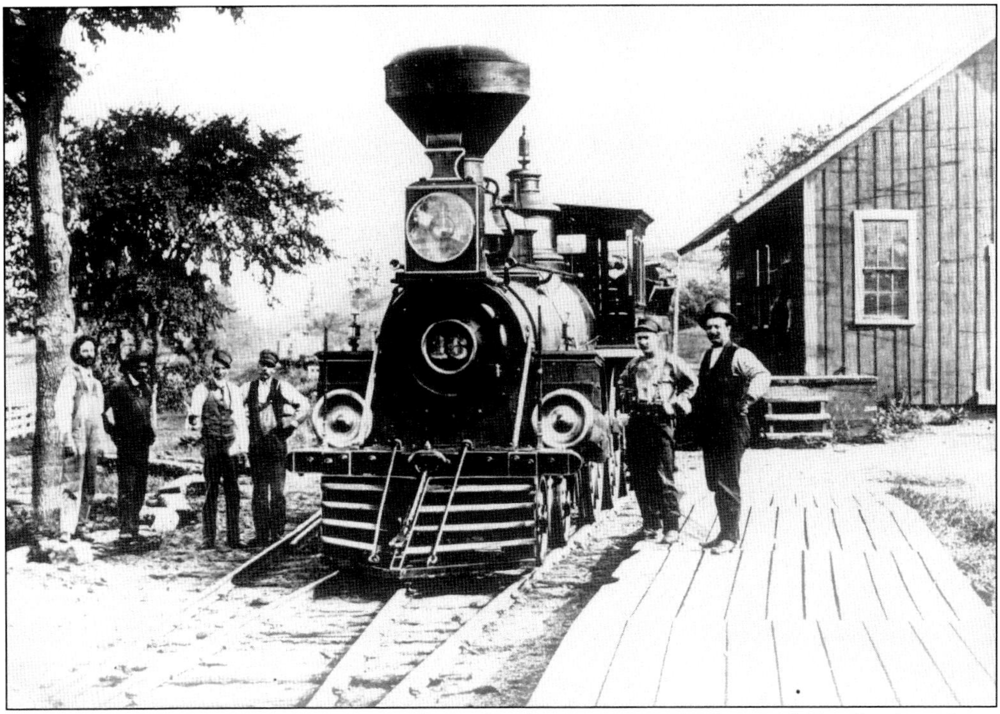

CONCORD RAILROAD NO. 16, "LION" (4-4-0). This engine was built in 1855 by the Amoskeag Manufacturing Company in Manchester, New Hampshire.

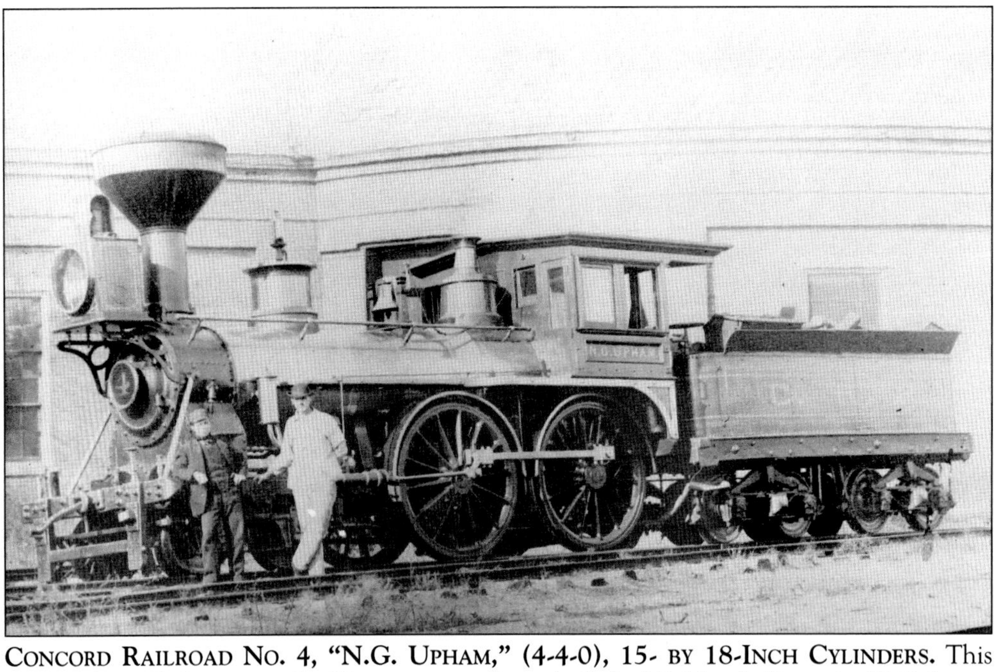

CONCORD RAILROAD NO. 4, "N.G. UPHAM," (4-4-0), 15- BY 18-INCH CYLINDERS. This engine, formerly known as the "Passaconaway," was built by Hinkley & Drury in 1848. It was rebuilt in 1855 and scrapped in 1886.

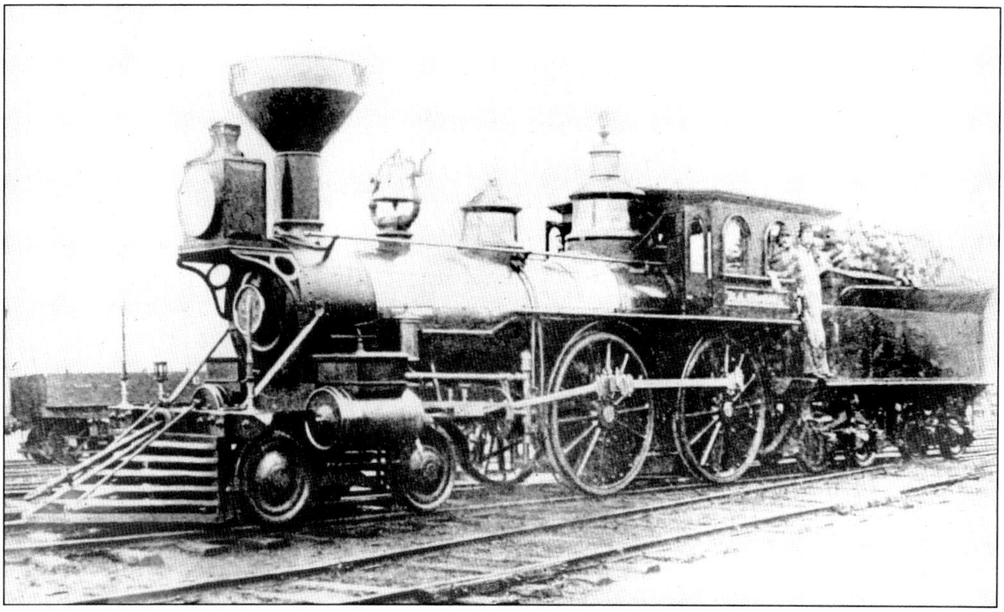

Concord Railroad No. 24, "B.A. Kimball" (4-4-0). Formerly the "John Kimball," this locomotive was built by the Amoskeag Manufacturing Company in 1856 and rebuilt in 1865. Benjamin A. Kimball, after whom this locomotive is named, was the president of the Concord Railroad.

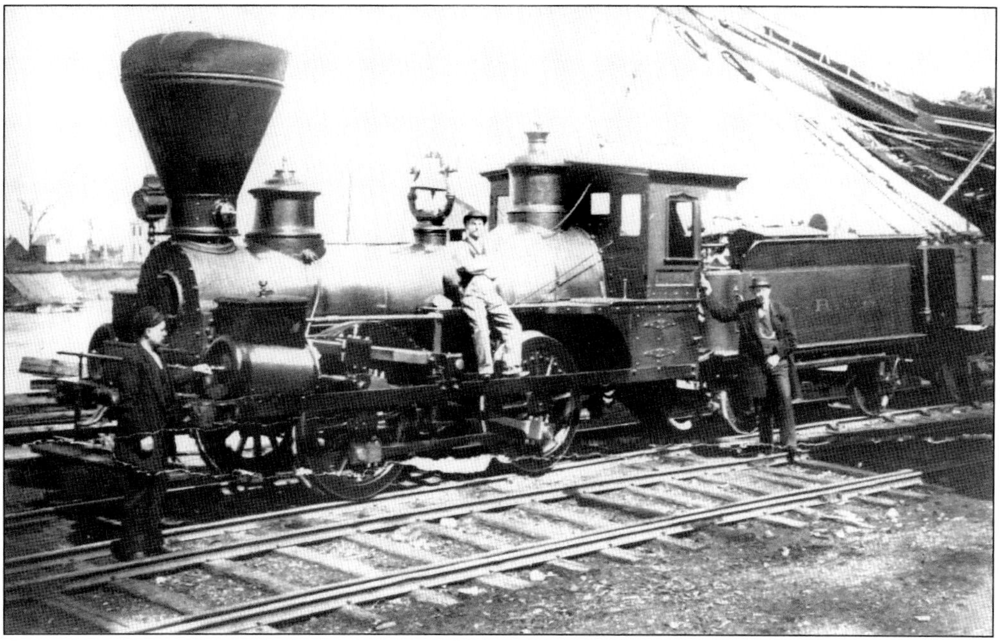

Concord Railroad No. 21, "Liberty" (0-4-0), 15- by 20-Inch Cylinders. The "Liberty" was built in 1863. Additions and improvements to the Concord Railroad paid out of earnings included 32 miles of additional track, new station buildings, and extensive renovation on buildings in Concord, Manchester, and Nashua, New Hampshire. The company also acquired car houses, shops, roundhouses, and 23 acres of land in Manchester while making many improvements to the Concord & Portsmouth and Suncook Valley Railroads.

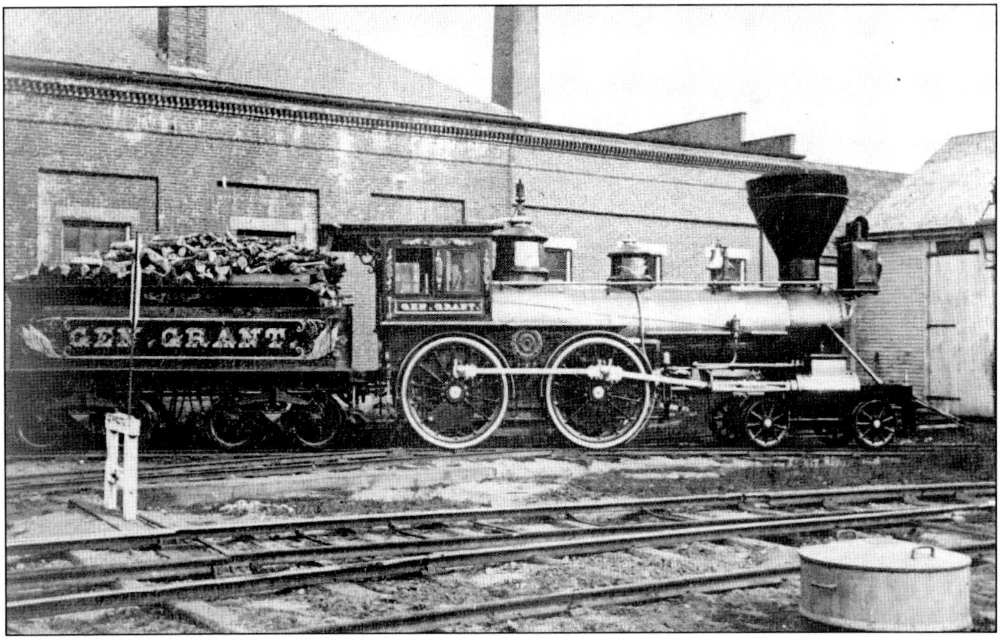

Concord Railroad No. 25, "General Grant" (4-4-0), 16- by 24-Inch Cylinders. Built by the Manchester Locomotive Works in 1865, the "General Grant" was scrapped in 1892.

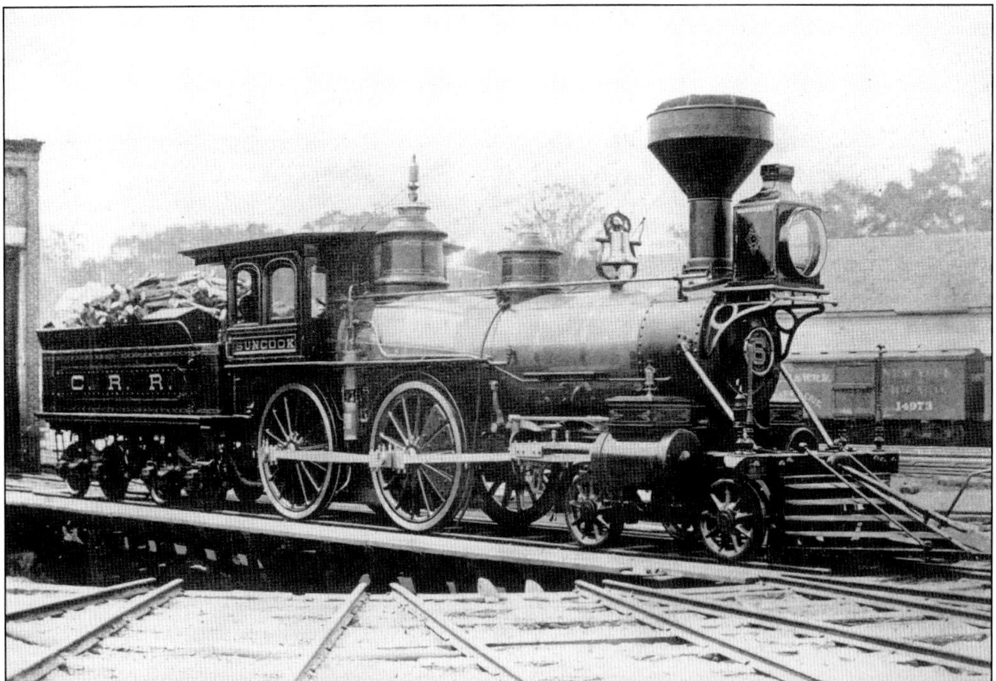

Concord Railroad No. 6, "Suncook," (4-4-0). The "Suncook" was built in 1880 by the Concord Railroad Company in Concord, New Hampshire. In 1889, the New Hampshire legislature permitted the consolidation of the Concord Railroad with the Boston, Concord & Montreal Railroad.

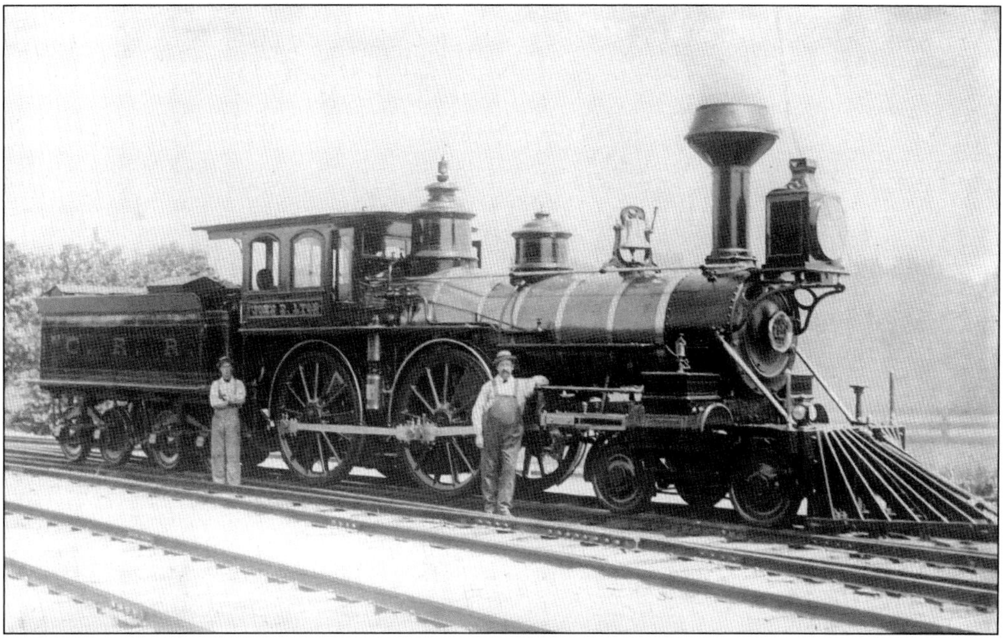

CONCORD RAILROAD NO. 12, "JOHN E. LYON," (4-4-0). Built by the Manchester Locomotive Works in 1878, this engine was scrapped by the Boston & Maine in 1897. In 1895, the Concord & Montreal Railroad leased its lines to the Boston & Maine.

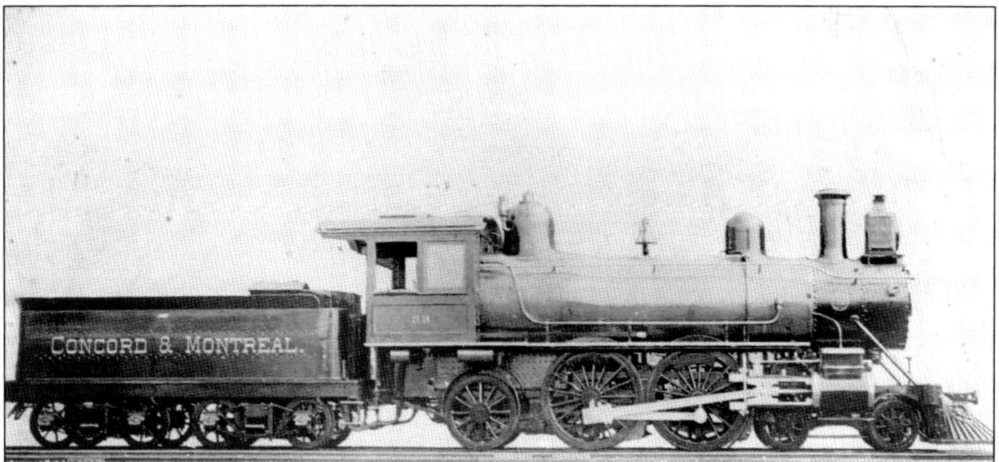

CONCORD & MONTREAL NO. 33, 19- BY 24-INCH CYLINDERS. Built by Baldwin in 1895, this engine is reportedly the oldest Atlantic type in New England. It later became B & M No. 733 and finally No. 3200.

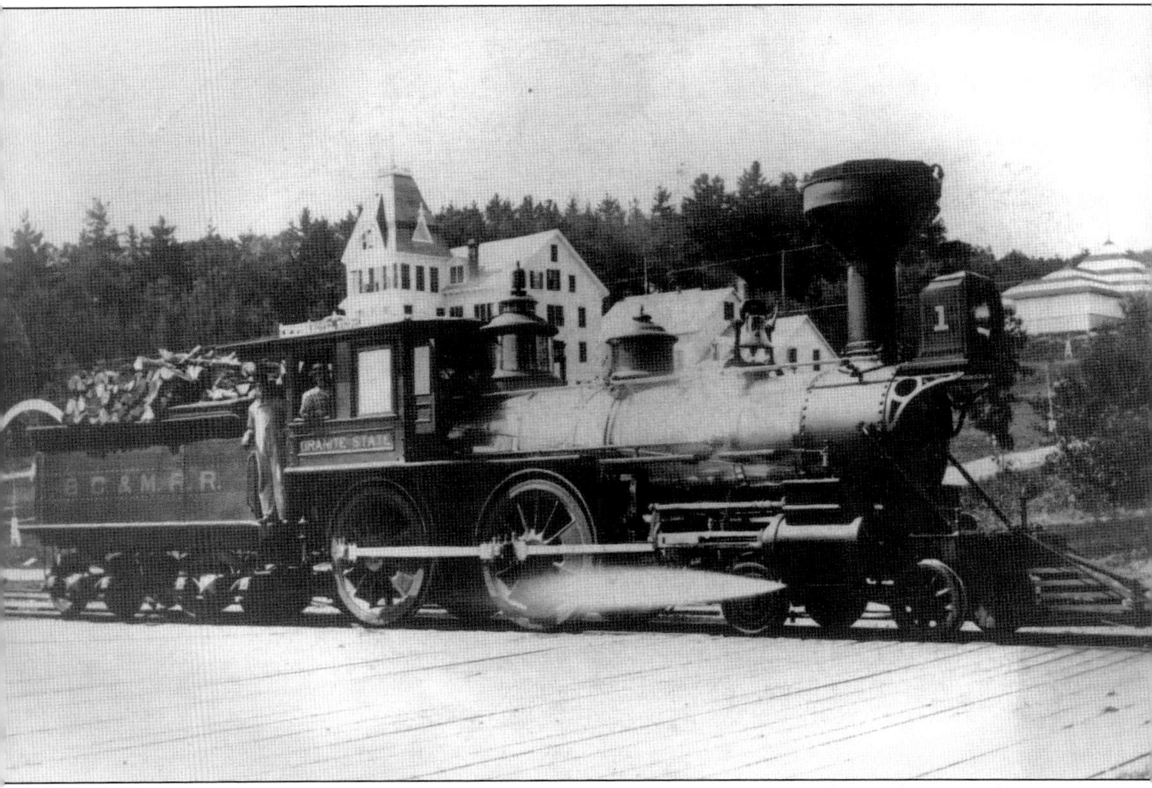

BOSTON, CONCORD & MONTREAL NO. 1, "GRANITE STATE." Shown here at the Weirs, New Hampshire, this locomotive was built by Hinkley & Drury in 1856. Originally, the Boston, Concord & Montreal was established as a single-track line from Concord to Groveton Junction, New Hampshire, a distance of 145.45 miles. This charter for the line from Concord to Wells River, Vermont, was granted on December 27, 1844. The engine was scrapped by the Boston & Maine in 1887.

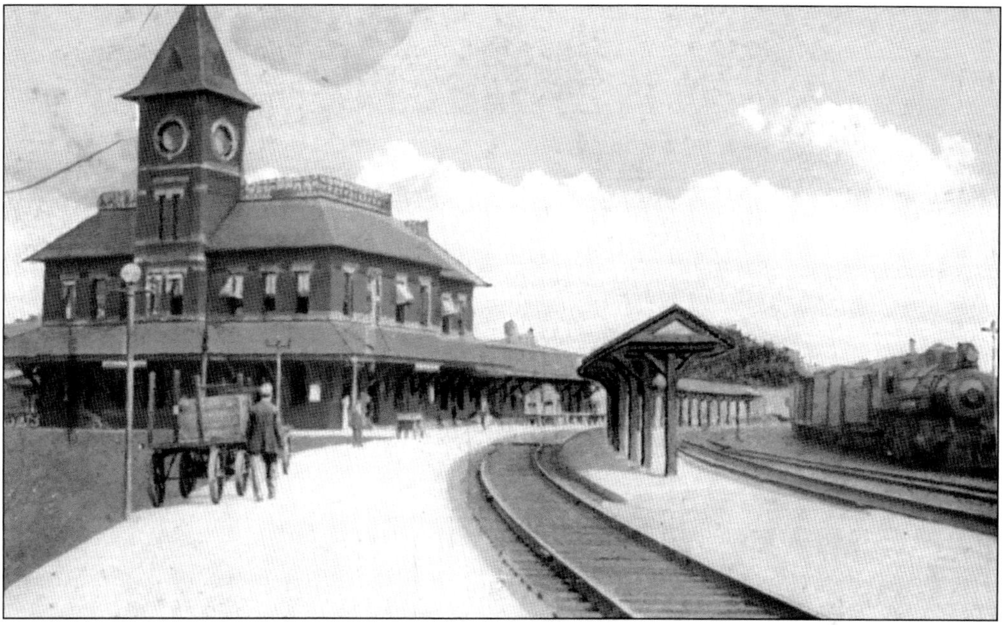

THE NASHUA UNION STATION, NASHUA, NEW HAMPSHIRE. Nashua, the gate city to New Hampshire, was an important junction point on the route between Lowell, Massachusetts, and Manchester, New Hampshire. Nashua was also the terminal of a direct line that ran to Keene from east to west. This depot was used by the Nashua & Lowell Railroad; the Concord Railroad; the Nashua & Keene line; and the Worcester, Nashua & Rochester Railroad.

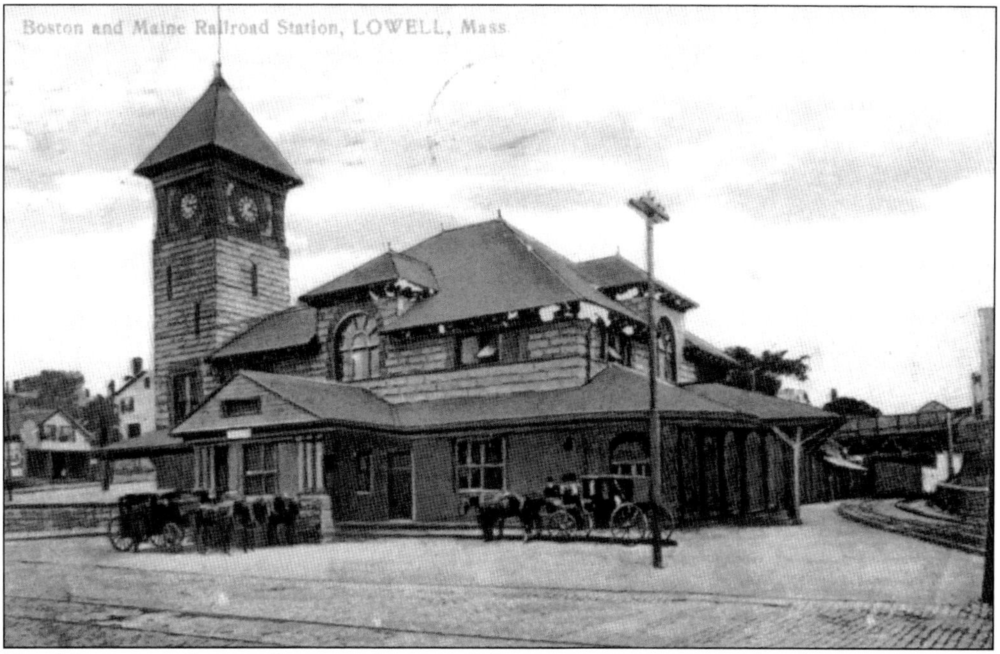

THE MIDDLESEX STREET STATION, LOWELL, MASSACHUSETTS, 1908. This depot was a popular stop and terminus for most rail service to northern New England. The imposing edifice was built of granite with brownstone trimming, the inside being finished in quartered oak. It was erected in 1893–1894 at a cost of about $80,000 and was opened for use on April 28, 1894.

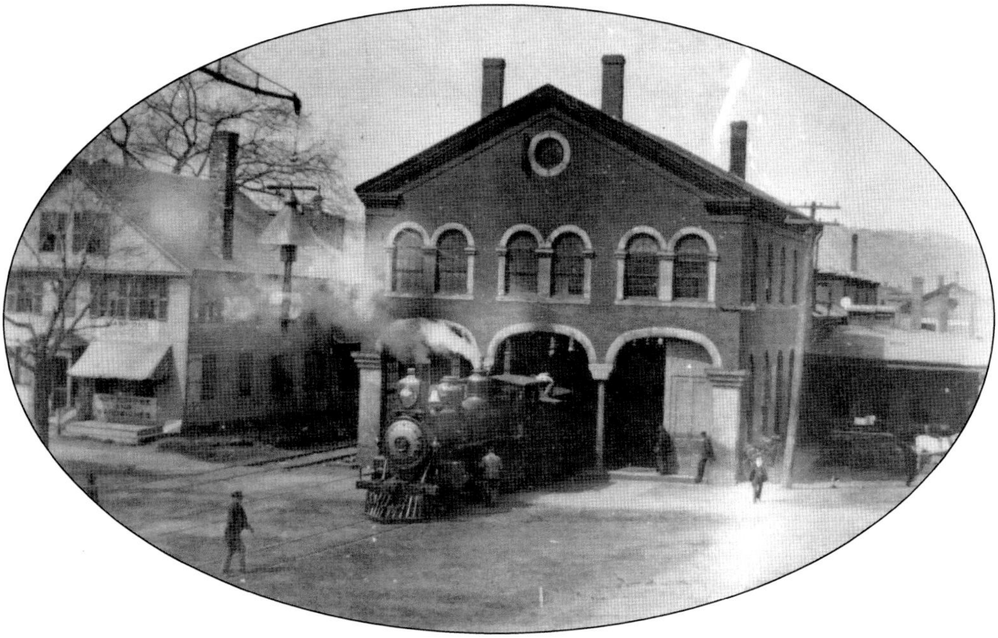

The First Railroad Station in Keene, New Hampshire. Keene was a major junction point in the southwest corner of New Hampshire. There was an east-west main line between Keene and Nashua. From the south came a pair of former Fitchburg Railroad lines, one from Fitchburg and the other from Greenfield, Massachusetts. To the north is the railroad town of Bellows Falls.

During the early years, Keene featured a covered station (as pictured here) where the tracks ran directly into the building so that the passengers could board and disembark comfortably regardless of the weather. The building covered three tracks and was graced with Romanesque arched windows.

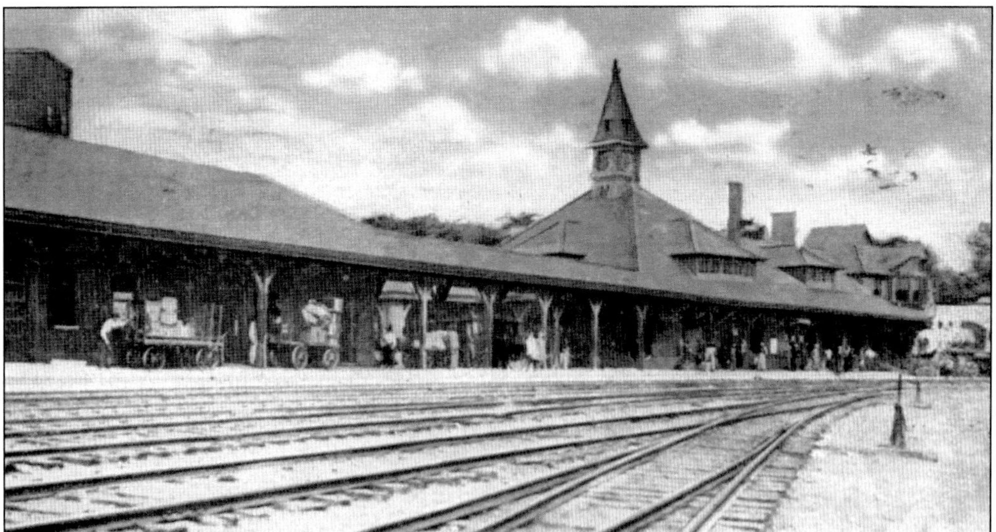

The Railroad Station in Greenfield, Massachusetts, Early 1920s. This was a major rail link for Central and Northern New England from the mid-1800s to the first half of the 20th century.

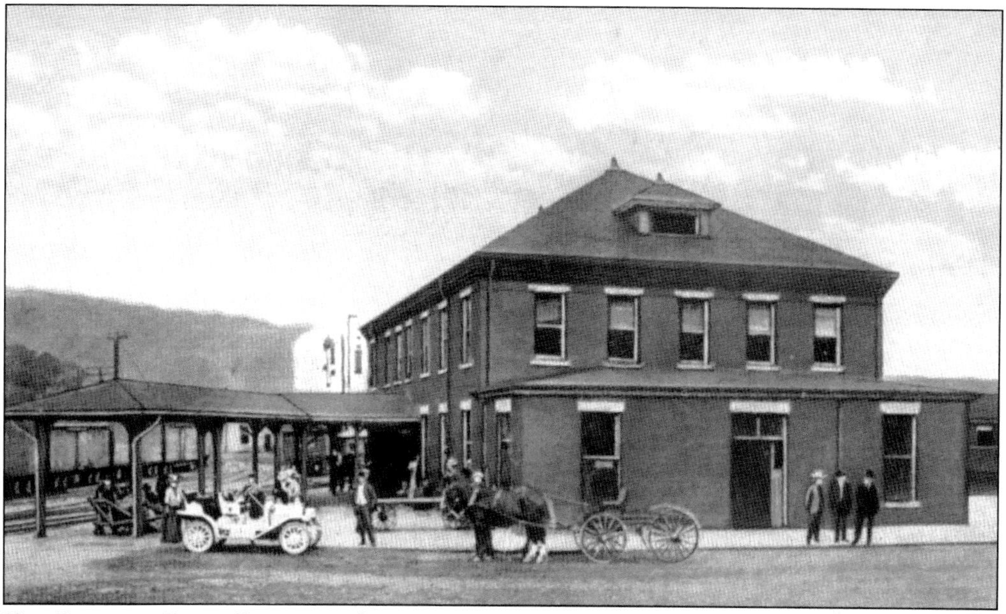

THE BELLOWS FALLS RAILROAD STATION, BELLOWS FALLS, VERMONT, EARLY 1920S. To the north, many railroads of the Connecticut Valley, New York, Massachusetts, and New Hampshire used this depot for both passenger and freight convenience.

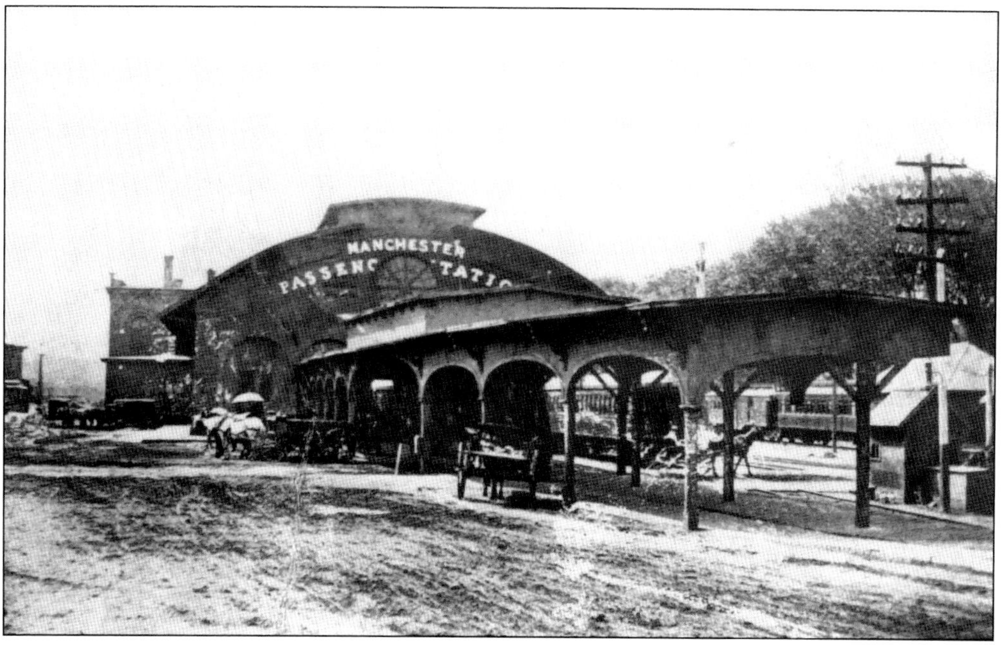

THE FIRST PASSENGER RAILROAD STATION, MANCHESTER, NEW HAMPSHIRE, 1857. In the heyday of passenger service in northern New England, the Union Station became the hub of five routes: those from Lowell and Lawrence, Massachusetts; Concord and Portsmouth, New Hampshire; and the Atlantic coast of New Hampshire and Maine.

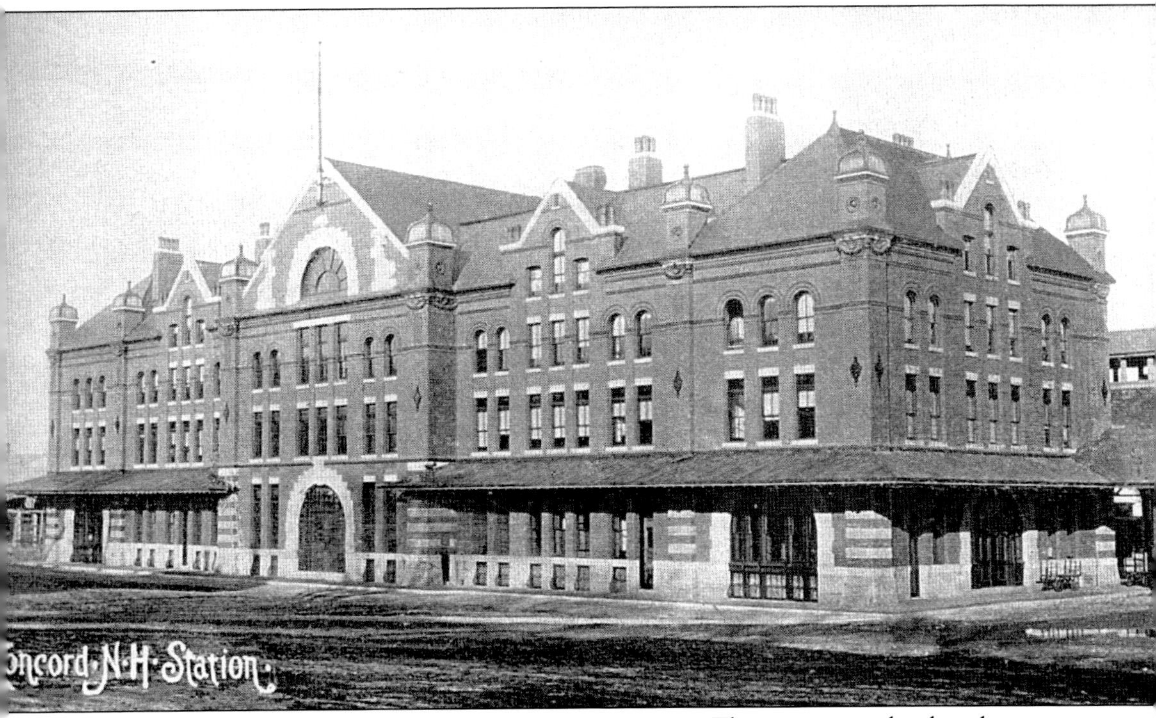

The Concord Depot, Concord, New Hampshire. This impressive brick rail center was built in the 1880s at a cost of $250,000 and was one of the finest buildings of its kind. The entire establishment occupied upward of 2 acres of land. The style was that of the English Renaissance. The main building, 280 feet long and 65 feet wide, contained three completely furnished stories, a basement, and an attic. It was constructed of dark-red brick with base walls and window sills of Concord granite. The rotunda in the center measured 60 by 65 feet and divided the building into two wings. The structure was designed by Bradford Gilbert, who became famous for work on New York City's Grand Central Station. From this terminal, trains ran north to Wells River, Vermont, and south to White River Junction to connect with the Central Vermont. In the early 1960s, this passenger station was torn down to make way for a parking lot and shopping mall.

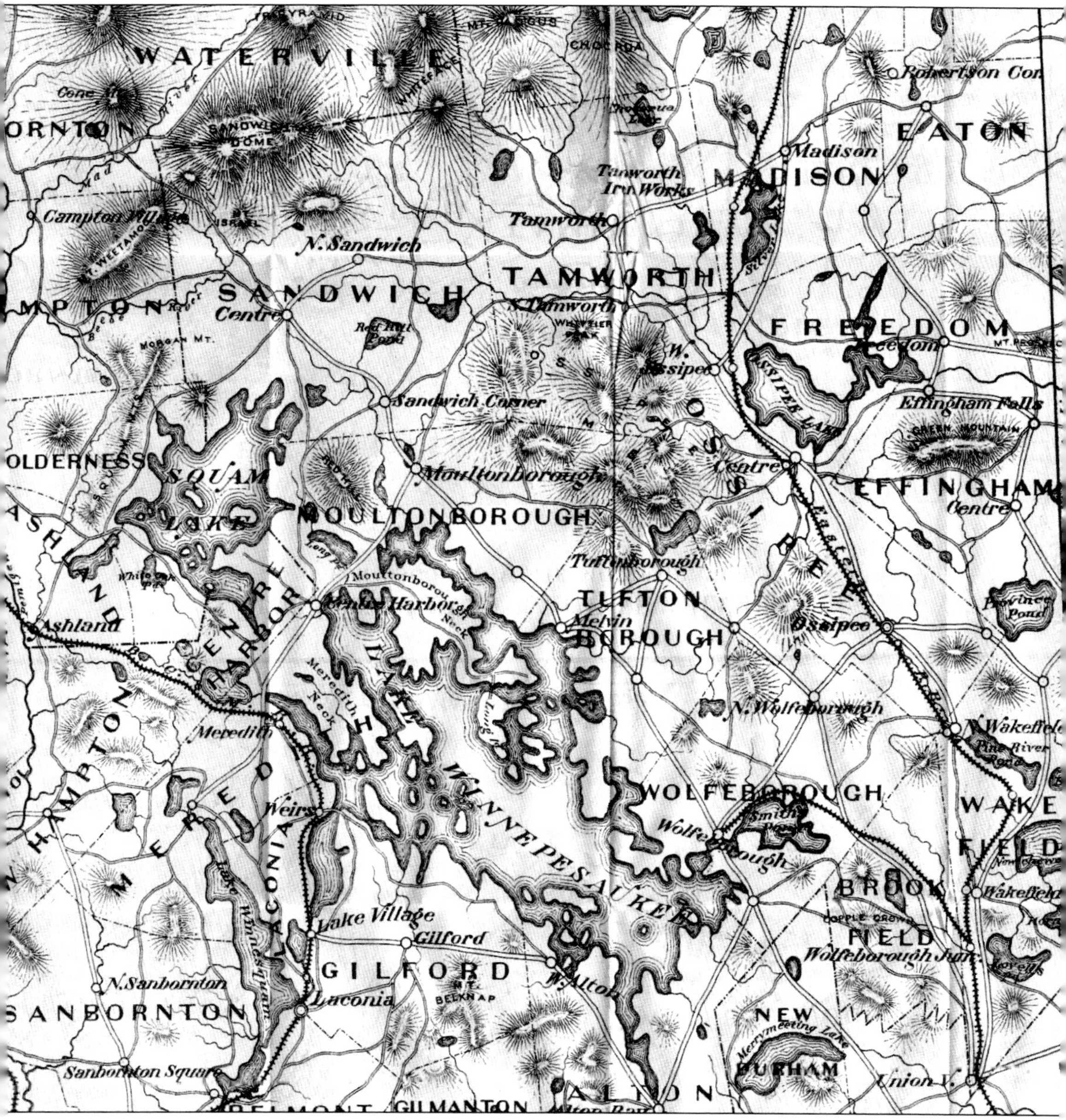

A MAP OF THE LAKES COUNTRY OF NEW HAMPSHIRE, 1876. Note that the railroad line on the east side of Lake Winnipesaukee is that of the Eastern Railroad (right), and the line on the west shore is the Boston, Concord & Montreal Railroad.

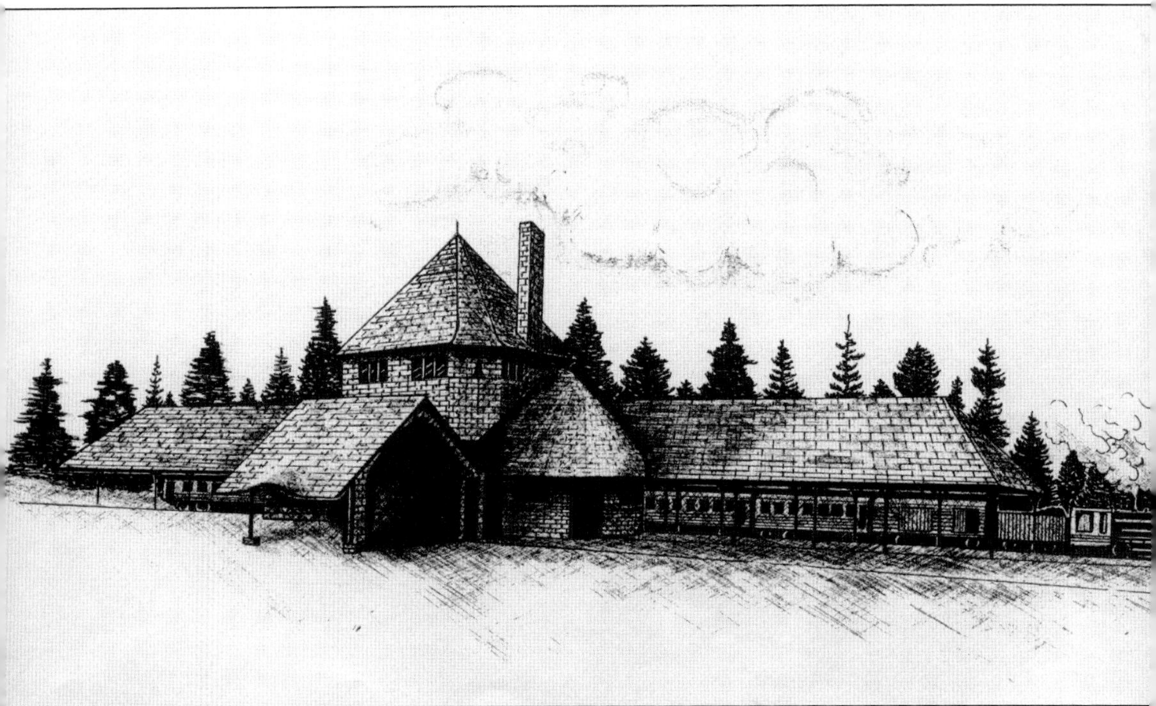

THE RAILROAD DEPOT, VETERANS SQUARE IN LACONIA, NEW HAMPSHIRE, 1917. When the Boston, Concord & Montreal Railroad was extended to Meredith Bridge in Laconia, passengers were provided with a small wooden station, which soon became inadequate as the community grew. After the merge of the Boston, Concord & Montreal Railroad with the Concord Railroad in 1889, the new railroad company (the Concord & Montreal Railroad) immediately modernized its many railroad stations. Charles A. Busiel—a prominent Laconia businessman and one of the railroad's managing directors—made sure that a new station was built in his city. The city responded to this effort by widening Depot Street in order to create the present Veterans Square. On August 22, 1892, the station was dedicated and opened to the public.

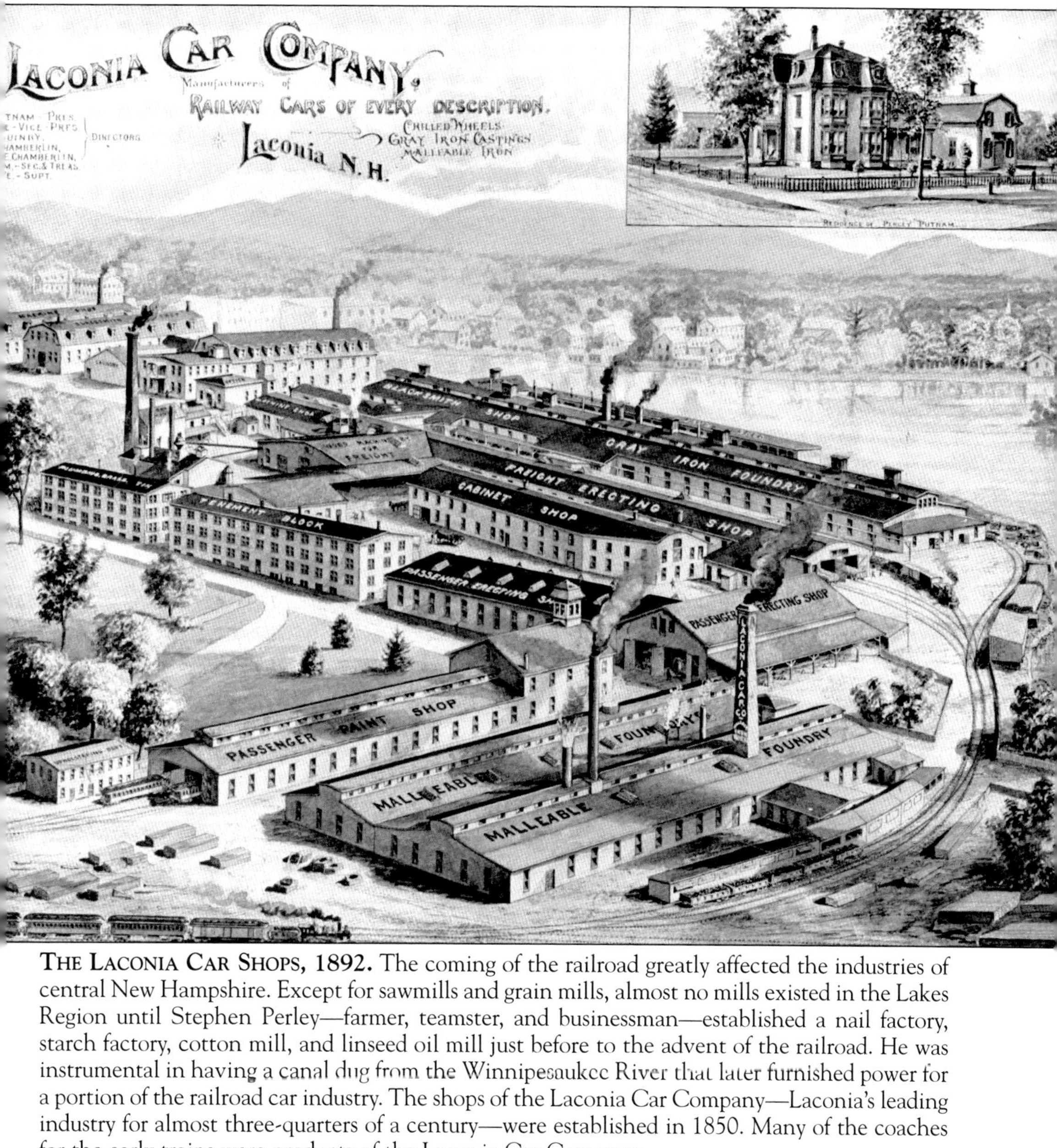

The Laconia Car Shops, 1892. The coming of the railroad greatly affected the industries of central New Hampshire. Except for sawmills and grain mills, almost no mills existed in the Lakes Region until Stephen Perley—farmer, teamster, and businessman—established a nail factory, starch factory, cotton mill, and linseed oil mill just before to the advent of the railroad. He was instrumental in having a canal dug from the Winnipesaukee River that later furnished power for a portion of the railroad car industry. The shops of the Laconia Car Company—Laconia's leading industry for almost three-quarters of a century—were established in 1850. Many of the coaches for the early trains were products of the Laconia Car Company.

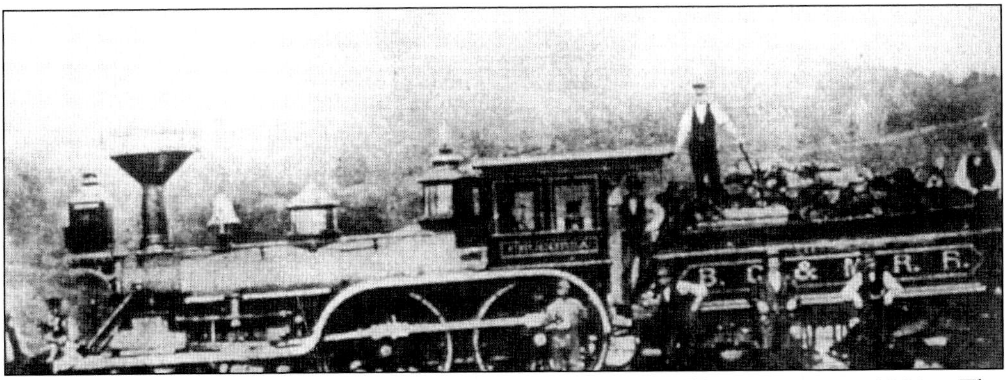

THE LOCOMOTIVE "CHOCORUA" IN LAKE VILLAGE, NEW HAMPSHIRE, C. 1880S. The "Chocorua," a favorite Boston, Concord & Montreal locomotive built in the Lake Village shops, sported high drivewheels for passenger assignments. In 1847, a charter was granted to build the Lake Shore Railroad between Laconia and Alton Bay. This 18-mile road was to be established to connect the Cocheco Road on the eastern side of New Hampshire with the Boston, Concord & Montreal Railroad at Meredith. Due to the lack of finances, the project was postponed for 40 years. Finally, in 1883, the charter was granted to Charles A. Busiel and his associate. This line was finally constructed by the Concord Railroad Corporation and officially opened in Laconia on June 17, 1890.

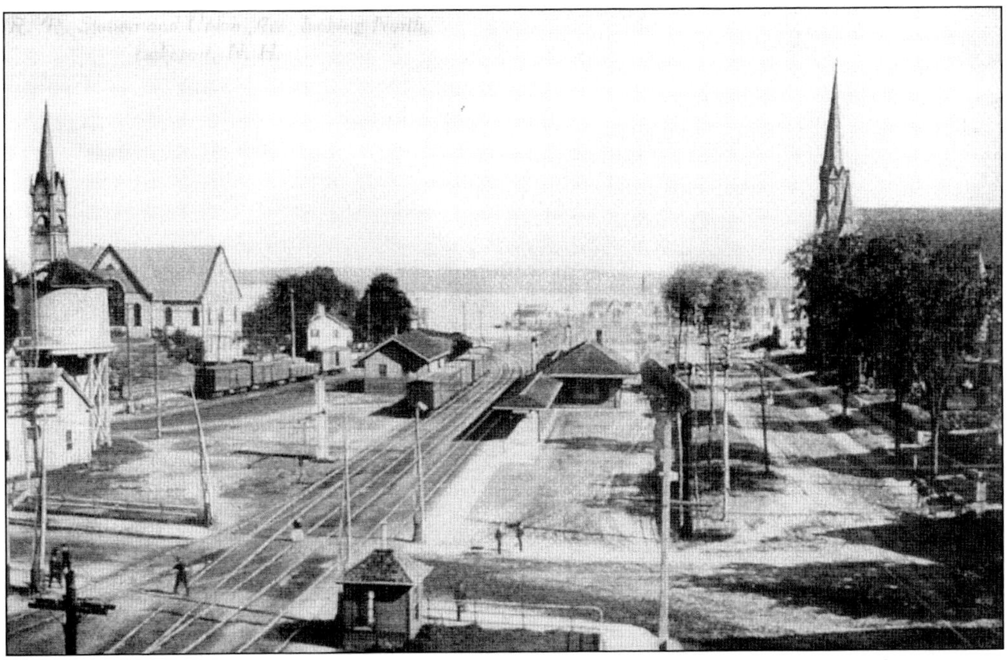

THE LAKE VILLAGE PASSENGER STATION AND UNION AVENUE, LACONIA, NEW HAMPSHIRE. This *c.* 1900 view looks north toward Paugus Bay in Laconia. On August 8, 1848, the opening of the Boston, Concord & Montreal Railroad between Concord and Meredith Bridge was established, marking an important development in the growth of what is now Laconia. The following year, the road was extended to Lake Village, known today as Lakeport. This event caused one of the largest celebrations these towns had ever seen.

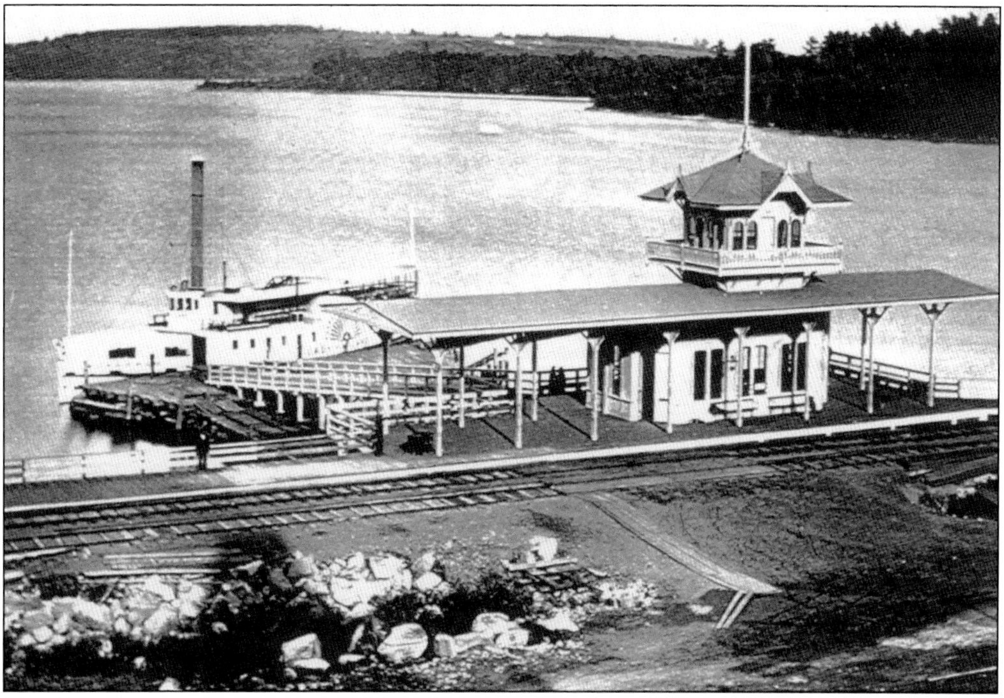

THE *LADY OF THE LAKE* AT THE WEIRS DOCK, 1880S. From 1848 until 1893, this very popular side-wheeler operated as a passenger vessel connecting with Center Harbor, Wolfeboro, and the Weirs. It was built and operated by the Boston, Concord & Montreal Railroad Company to provide passenger service across the lake for those wishing to go to the Mountain Region.

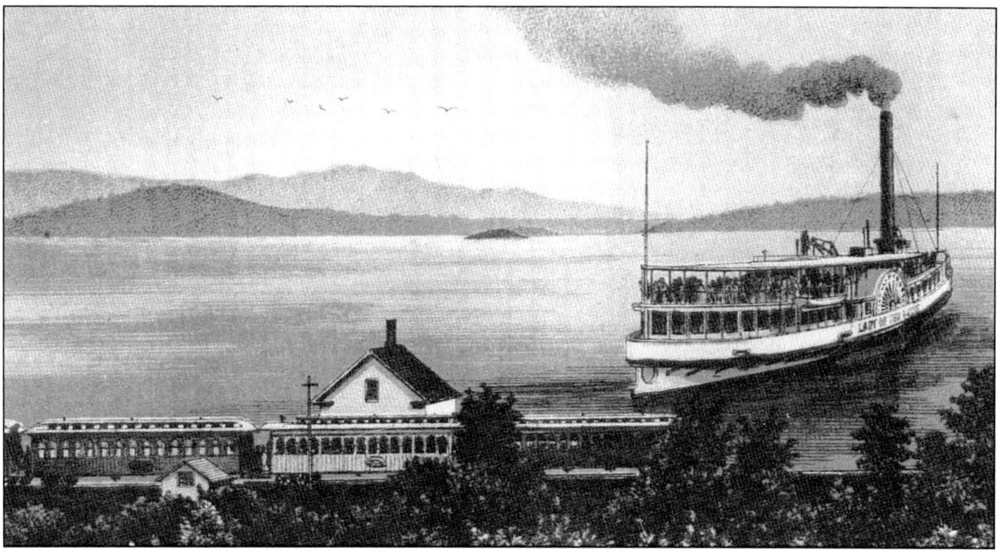

THE *LADY OF THE LAKE* LEAVING THE WEIRS STATION. The *Lady of the Lake* at this time had no rival, and business boomed for the rail company. This was difficult for the competitor, the Cocheco Railroad Company, to withstand. The Cocheco Railroad served the southern half of the lake and could easily see its business going under as the result of competition from the Boston, Concord & Montreal side-wheeler. The company therefore ordered the construction of a new vessel, the *Chocorua*, at Alton Bay.

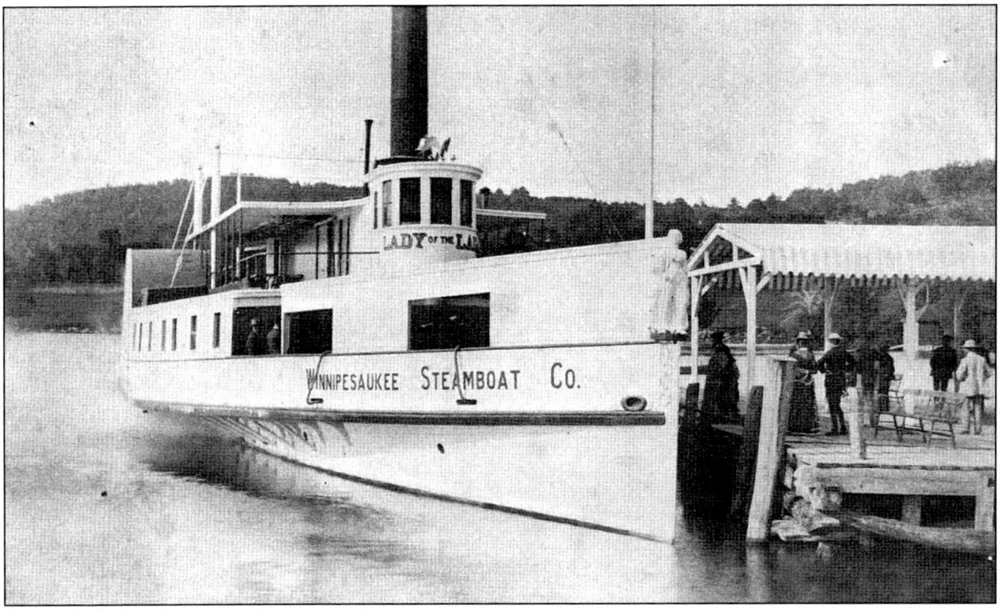

THE *LADY OF THE LAKE* AT CENTER HARBOR, NEW HAMPSHIRE. Population was growing and railroading was coming in fast. The mid-1800s saw the construction of the famous *Lady of the Lake* and the development of marine transportation in Lake Winnipesaukee. The side-wheeler *Lady of the Lake* was built in Lake Village in 1849 by the Winnipesaukee Steamboat Company. It was a large craft of 125 feet and completely designed for commercial lake travel.

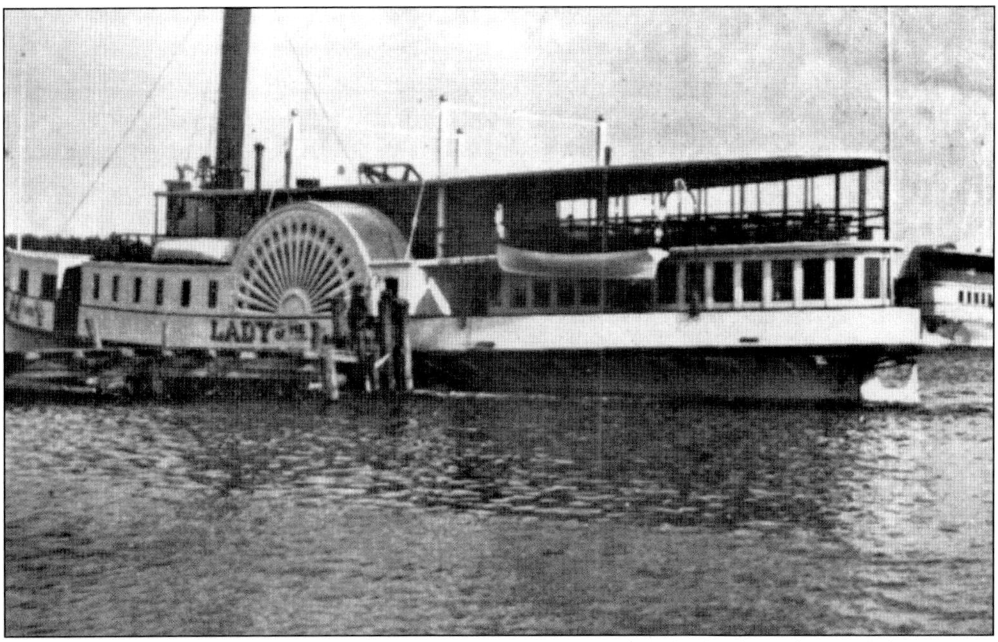

THE *LADY OF THE LAKE* AND THE *MOUNT WASHINGTON*. With the launching of the Boston & Maine's new side-wheeler *Mount Washington* in 1872, the *Lady of the Lake* was outclassed. Regardless of the rivalry, the two railroad companies continued unabated for 18 more years. The *Lady of the Lake* finally ceased operation on Lake Winnipesaukee on September 14, 1893.

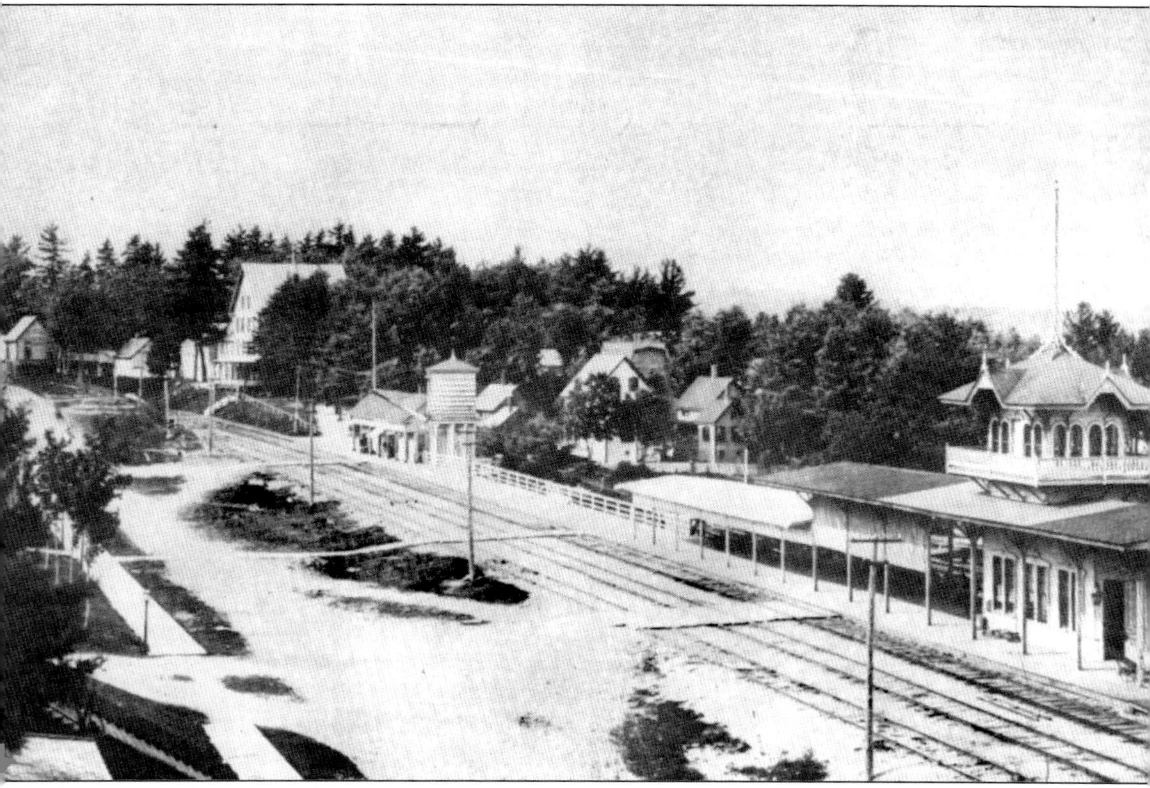

THE WEIRS RAILROAD STATION IN THE LATE 1800S. At the Weirs, the Boston, Concord & Montreal skirted the western shoreline of Lake Winnipesaukee. From the 1850s until its retirement in 1893, the most popular tourist side-wheeler *Lady of the Lake* met the train and transferred passengers to the vessel to cross the lake en route to the White Mountain and the grand resort hotels. When the Boston & Maine leased the Boston, Concord & Montreal Railroad, the *Lady of the Lake* was retired in favor of its own steamer, the *Mount Washington*. In this view looking north, notice that there are three lines passing the old station with the Veterans Association campground on the left.

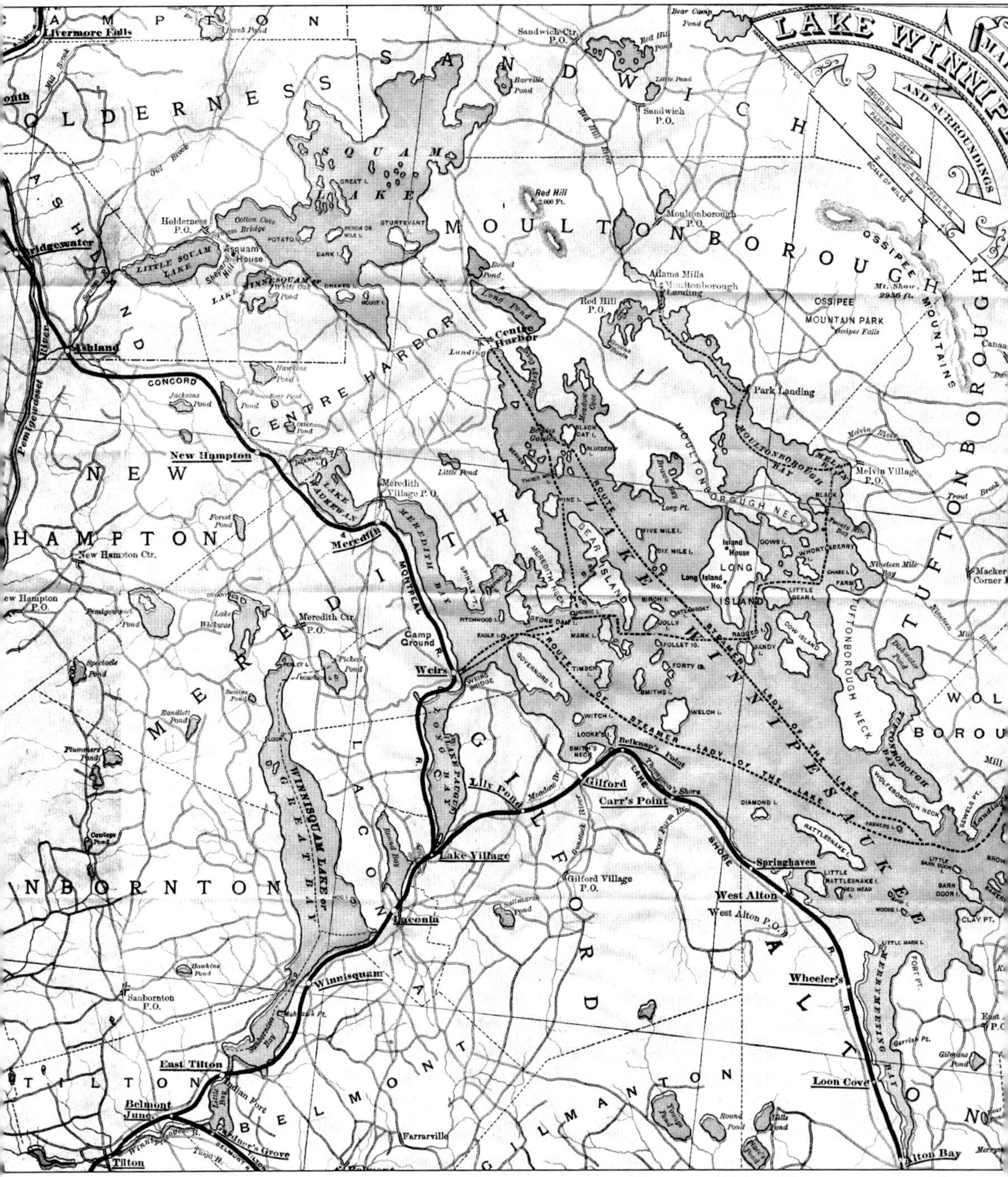

A Map of Lake Winnipesaukee and Surroundings, Early 1890s. This map, issued by the Concord & Montreal Railroad, indicates two major routes of the railroad: the rails from Concord through the towns in the Lakes Region en route to Montreal and the lake route of the steamer *Lady of the Lake* and its ports of call around the lake.

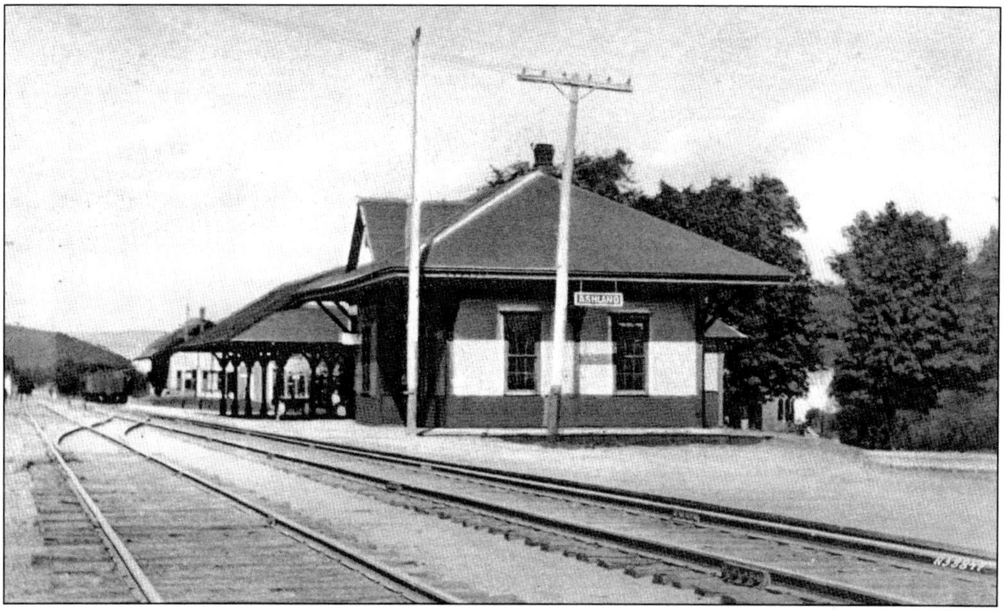

The Ashland Railroad Station. The Boston, Concord & Montreal Railroad ran the first train from Concord to Plymouth on Friday, January 18, 1850. The regular passenger service started on Monday, January 22, with one train daily from Concord. This was due at Ashland at 11:45 A.M. and left Ashland on the return journey to Concord at 12:30 P.M.

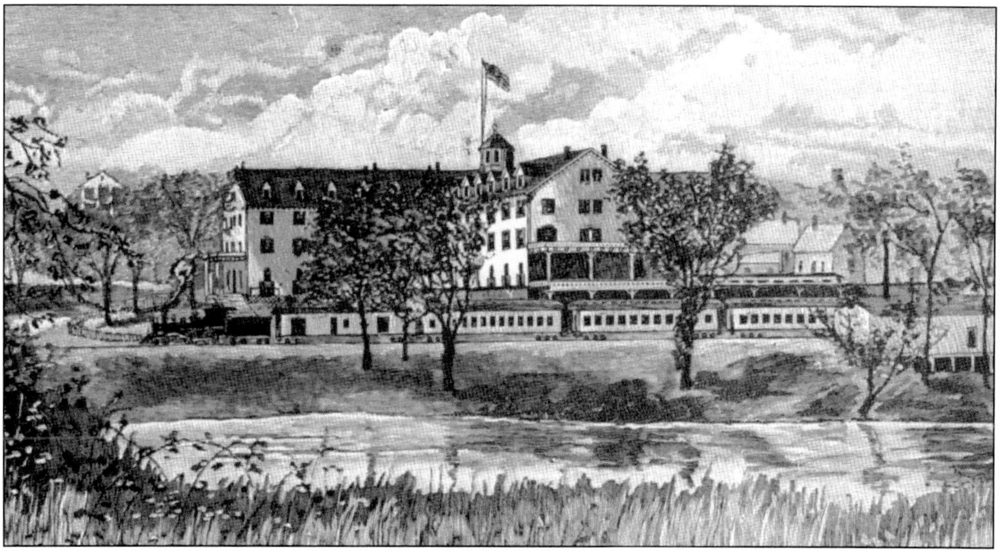

The Pemigewasset House and the Boston, Concord & Montreal Station, Plymouth, New Hampshire, 1877. In 1850, the Boston, Concord & Montreal Railroad completed the road to Plymouth from Concord. In 1858, the company leased the White Mountain Railroad, which continued the road from Plymouth to Littleton. The railroad began building an extension of the White Mountain Railroad beyond Littleton in 1869, and the track from Wing Road toward the base of Mount Washington was begun in 1872. In 1877, the original White Mountain Railroad between Woodsville and Littleton was taken over by the Boston, Concord & Montreal. The company exchanged $300,000 in six-percent bonds for the capital stock of the reorganized road.

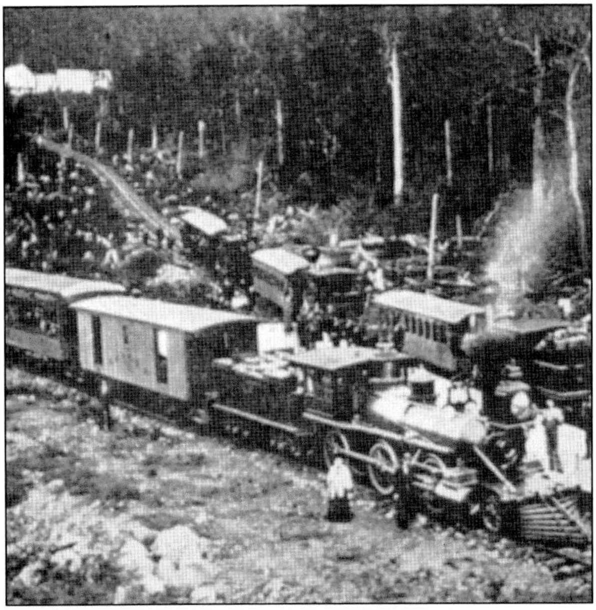

Boston, Concord & Montreal No. 29, "Mount Washington." Built in the 1870s, this locomotive is shown at the base of Mount Washington. On June 1, 1883, this road was leased to the Boston & Lowell. On May 1, 1889, however, the lease to the Boston & Lowell was declared void, and the road was consolidated with the Concord Railroad under the name of the Concord & Montreal Railroad.

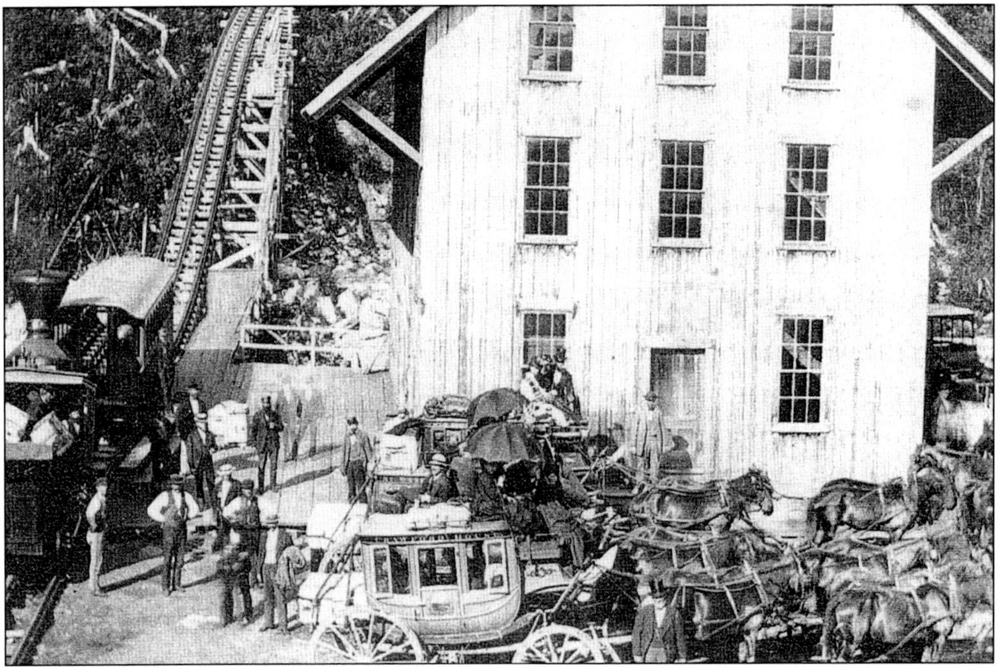

The Mount Washington Base Station with Concord Stagecoach and Passengers from the Grand Hotels in the White Mountains, c. 1875. Whether by train or by stagecoach, thousands of visitors came to ride the railway. It is interesting to note that the first U.S. president to visit Mount Washington during his term of office was Ulysses S. Grant. On August 27, 1869, he and the First Lady with their son, Jesse, drove from the Crawford House to Marshfield. He was welcomed by Sylvester Marsh, whom he complimented on his enterprise. At the summit, he was greeted by Col. J.R. Hitchcock, landlord of the Tip Top House, where the party dined and was entertained. On August 20, 1877, Pres. Rutherford B. Hayes and family made the ascent via the Cog Railway.

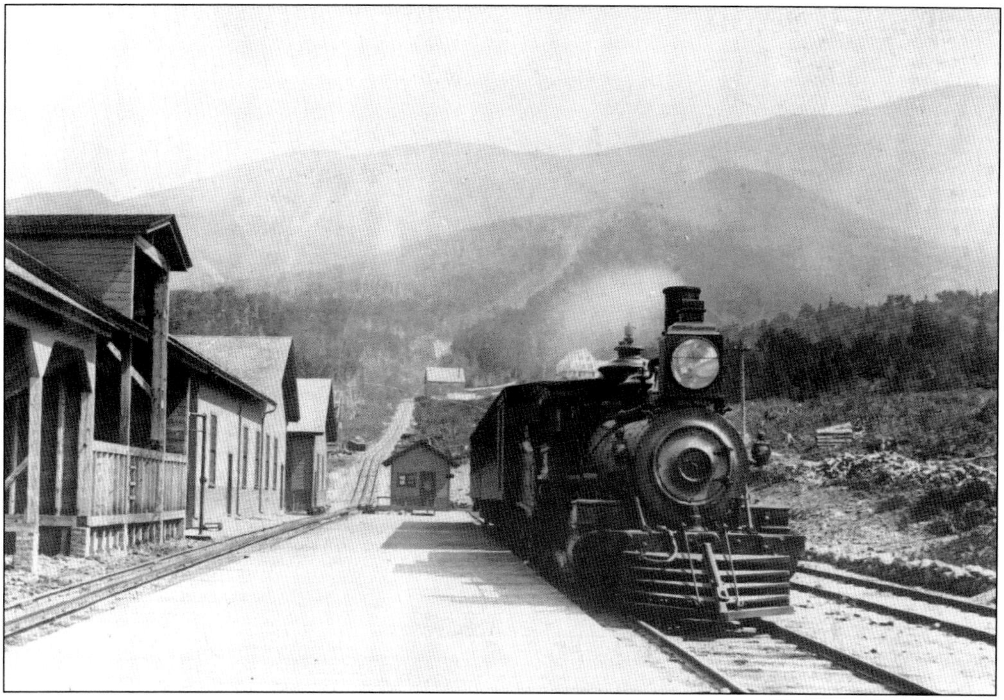

B & M No. 782 at the Base Station. In 1895, the Boston & Maine leased this line connecting the Base Station to the Cog Railway with Fabyan's Station.

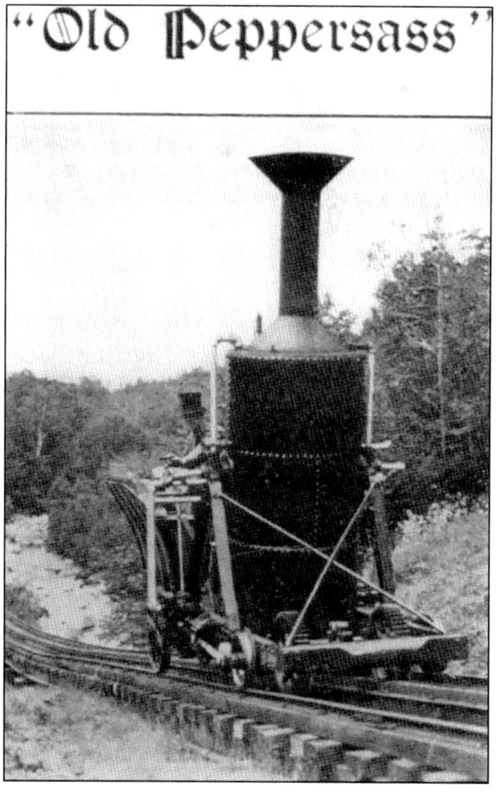

"Old Peppersass," the First Cog Railway Engine, 1866. At first, this engine was christened the "Hero." However, one old-timer thought it looked like a bottle of peppersass and the name stuck. After 12 years of faithful service, the engine was retired but not scrapped. It was put on display at the World's Columbian Exposition in Chicago, later at the Field Museum of Natural History in Chicago and, in 1904, at the Louisiana Purchase Exposition in St. Louis.

"Old Peppersass" did return to the Cog Railway in 1929 for a rechristening ceremony, but upon its last trip on the mountain on July 20, 1929, the front axle broke and the engine let loose down the side of Mount Washington to smash on the rocks below Jacob's Ladder. The broken parts were taken to a Boston & Maine repair shop, where they were reassembled for display at the base station.

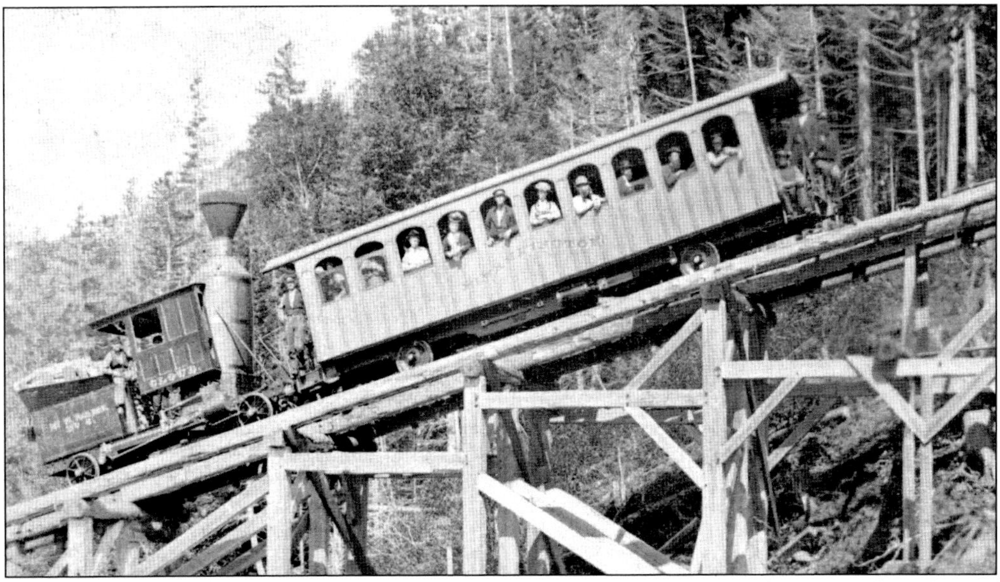

THE COG RAILWAY UP MOUNT WASHINGTON, C. 1870S. Credit is due Herrick Aiken of Franklin, New Hampshire, for cooperating with Sylvester Marsh in making a success of the Cog Railway and for producing the present type of cog engine. Aiken also helped finance the Cog Railway and served as its manager for several years. On August 29, 1866, the first practical demonstration of the Cog Railway was held. Pictured is a load of passengers ascending the mountain up a grade of 15 degrees.

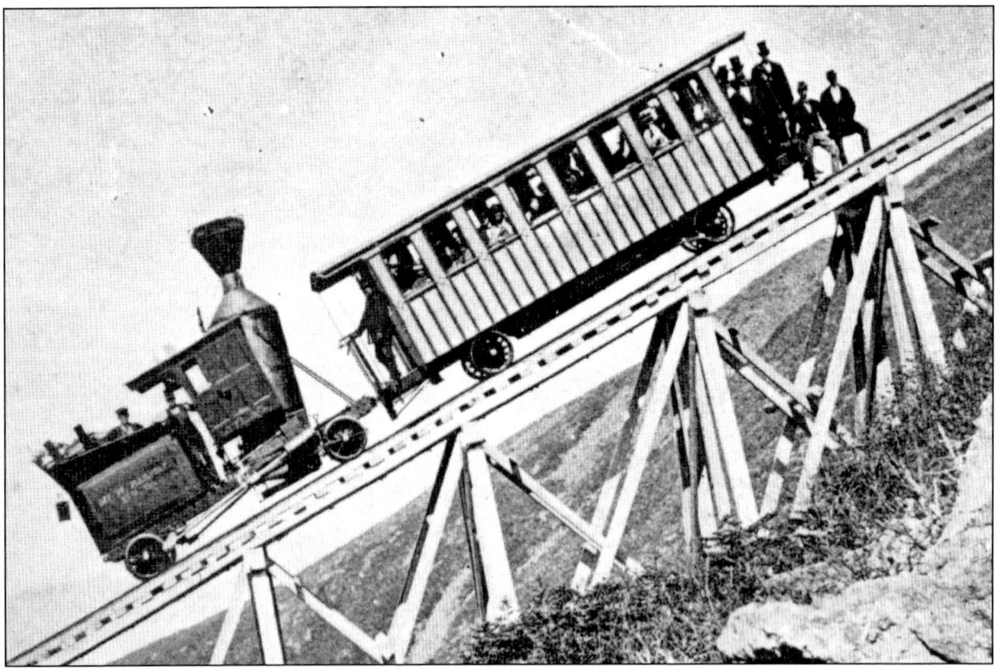

THE RAILROAD UP MOUNT WASHINGTON, C. 1870S. In the summer of 1866, a quarter-mile section of the Cog Railway track was built, including a trestle bridge crossing the Ammonoosuc River. The steepest pitch in this railway is found here at Jacob's Ladder. The trestle has an average grade of 1,300 feet to the mile and a maximum grade of 1,980 feet to the mile.

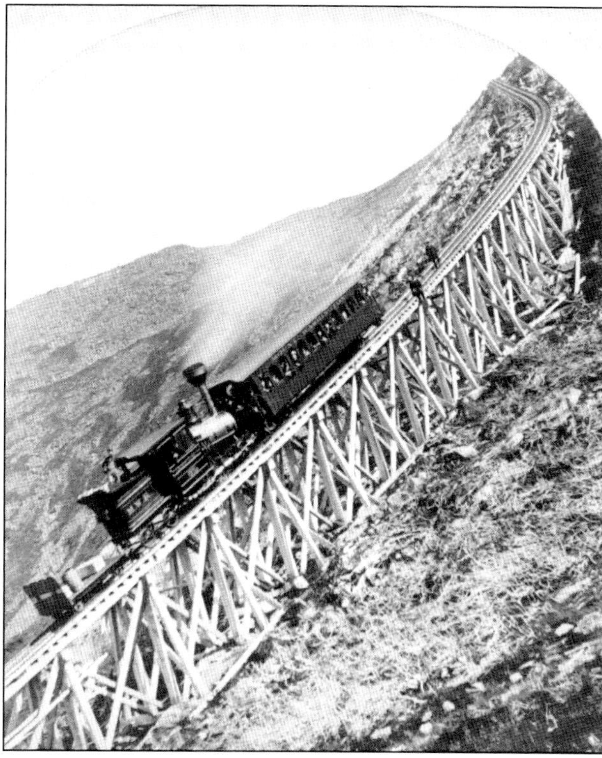

Jacob's Ladder, Mount Washington Railway, c. 1870s. This photograph shows an awe-inspiring view into Burt's Ravine. This ravine was named in honor of the late Henry M. Burt, founder and publisher of *Among the Clouds*, a newspaper published and printed in the old Tip Top House on the summit of Mount Washington.

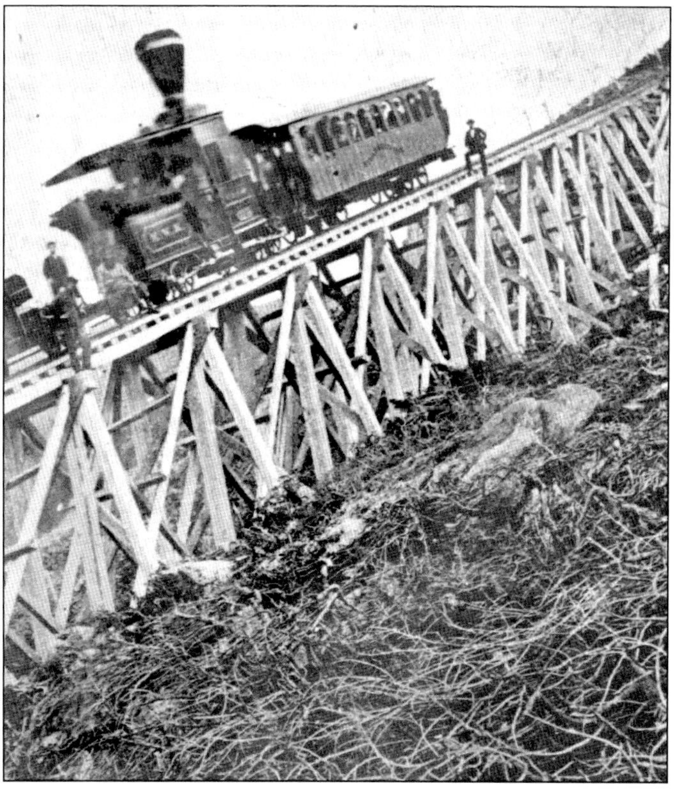

The Cog Railway Trains Crossing Jacob's Ladder, c. 1870s. The ascent of Mount Washington over this unique road can be taken with complete assurance of safety. The Cog Railway advertises that "it is much safer than any other railroad, as no passenger has ever been killed or injured during the entire life of the road."

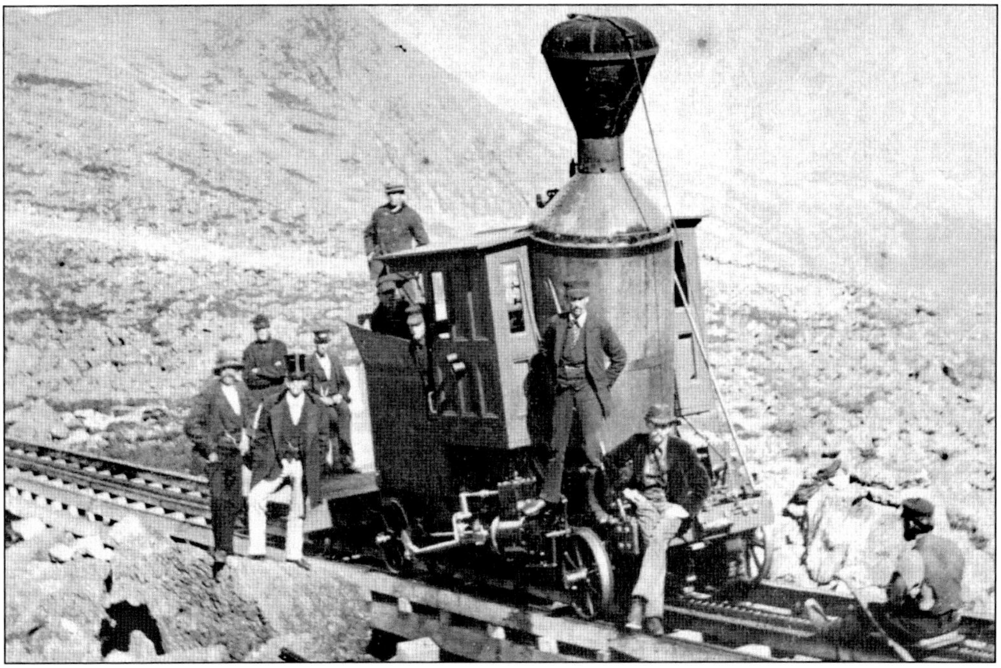

A VIEW FROM THE SUMMIT OF MOUNT WASHINGTON WITH THE COG RAILWAY IN THE FOREGROUND. As the engine leaves Jacob's Ladder, it soon passes the tree line and enters the region of subalpine vegetation.

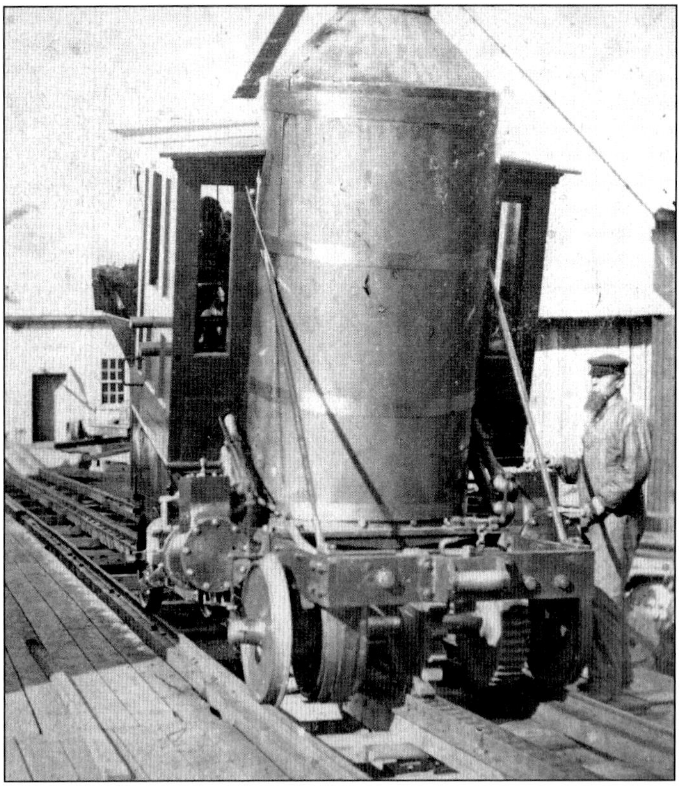

THE RAILWAY UP MOUNT WASHINGTON, C. 1870S. The essential feature of the Cog Railway is the driving mechanism. Looking closely at this picture, one can see the the central cog as well as the outside rails. The cog consists of two pieces of wrought-angle iron placed parallel and connected by iron pins 4 inches apart. Teeth on the driving wheel mesh with the cog rails and draw the whole train up the mountainside.

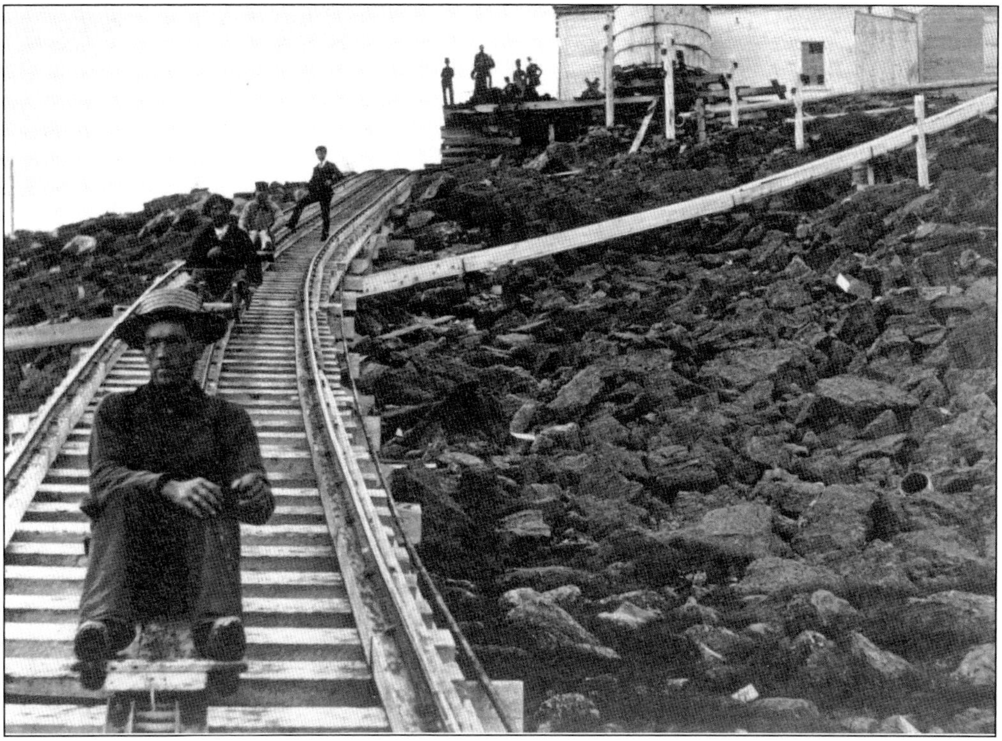

SLIDING DOWN THE RAILWAY, C. 1890S. Until recent years, the Cog Railway provided not only the slowest and safest railway journey, but also the fastest and most dangerous. A type of slide board called "the Devil's Shingle" gave railway workers a way to get down the mountain after a day's work on the summit. The boards were banned c. 1930 after a few fatal accidents occurred.

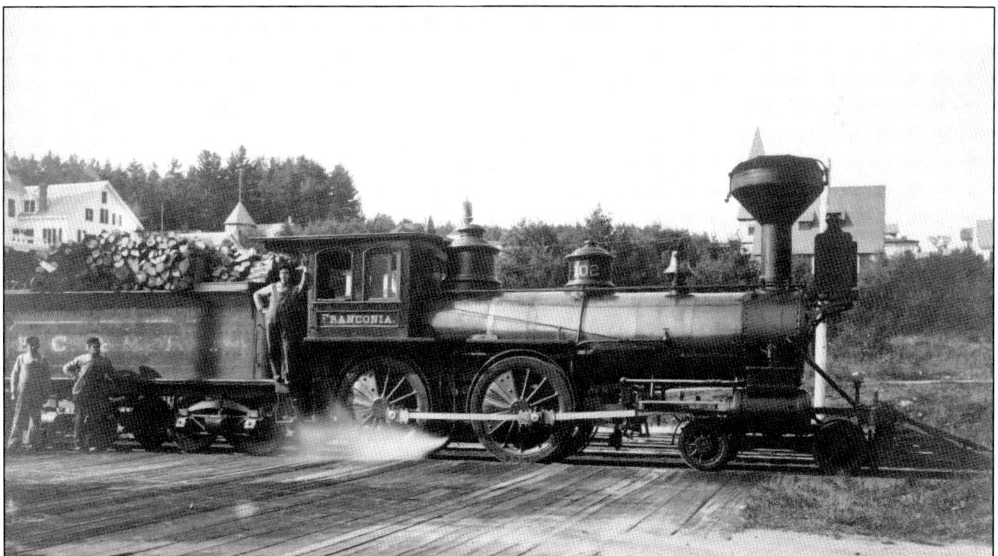

BOSTON, CONCORD & MONTREAL NO. 16, "FRANCONIA." This locomotive was built in 1870 by McKay and Aldus for the Boston, Concord & Montreal line. It was later used by the Concord & Montreal line as No. 74.

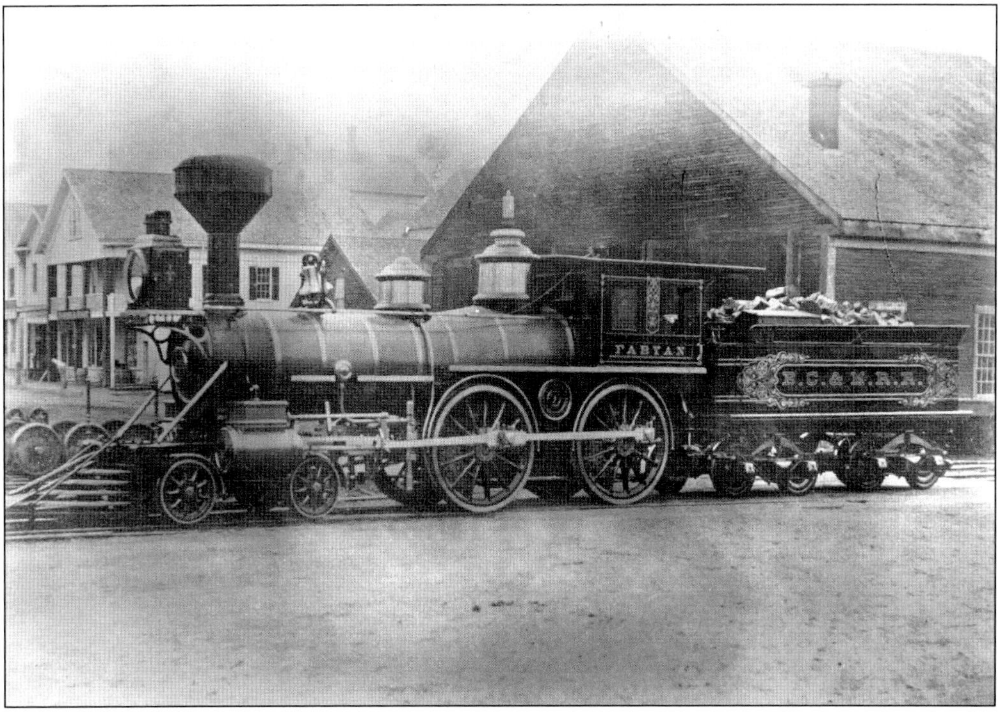

BOSTON, CONCORD & MONTREAL NO. 25, "FABYAN." The Manchester Locomotive Works built this locomotive in 1874.

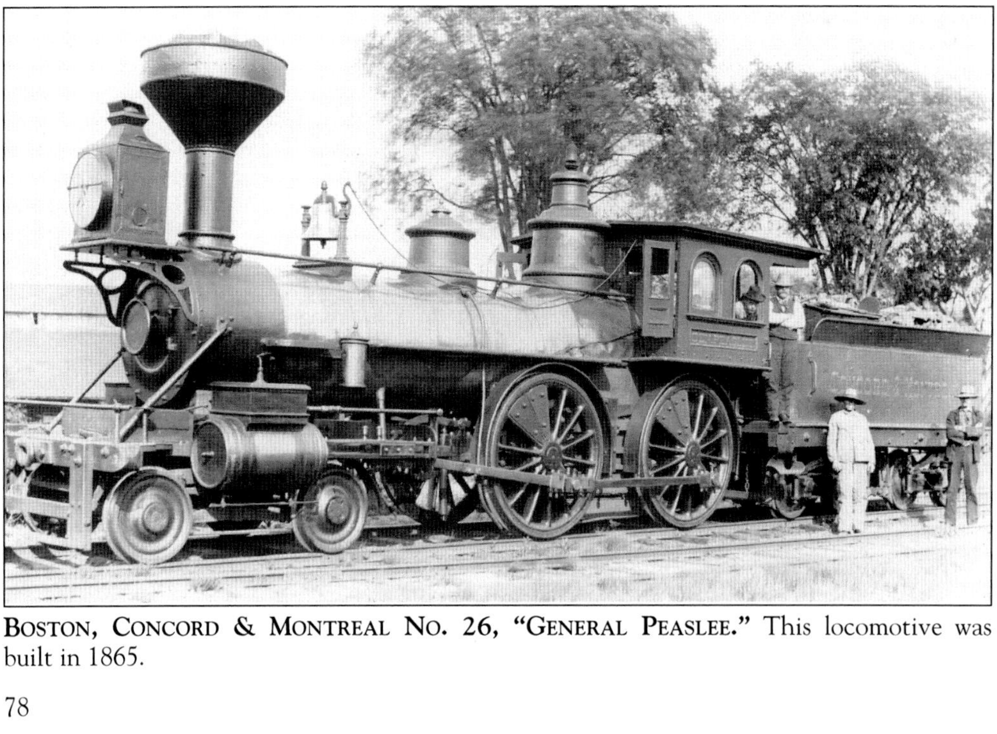

BOSTON, CONCORD & MONTREAL NO. 26, "GENERAL PEASLEE." This locomotive was built in 1865.

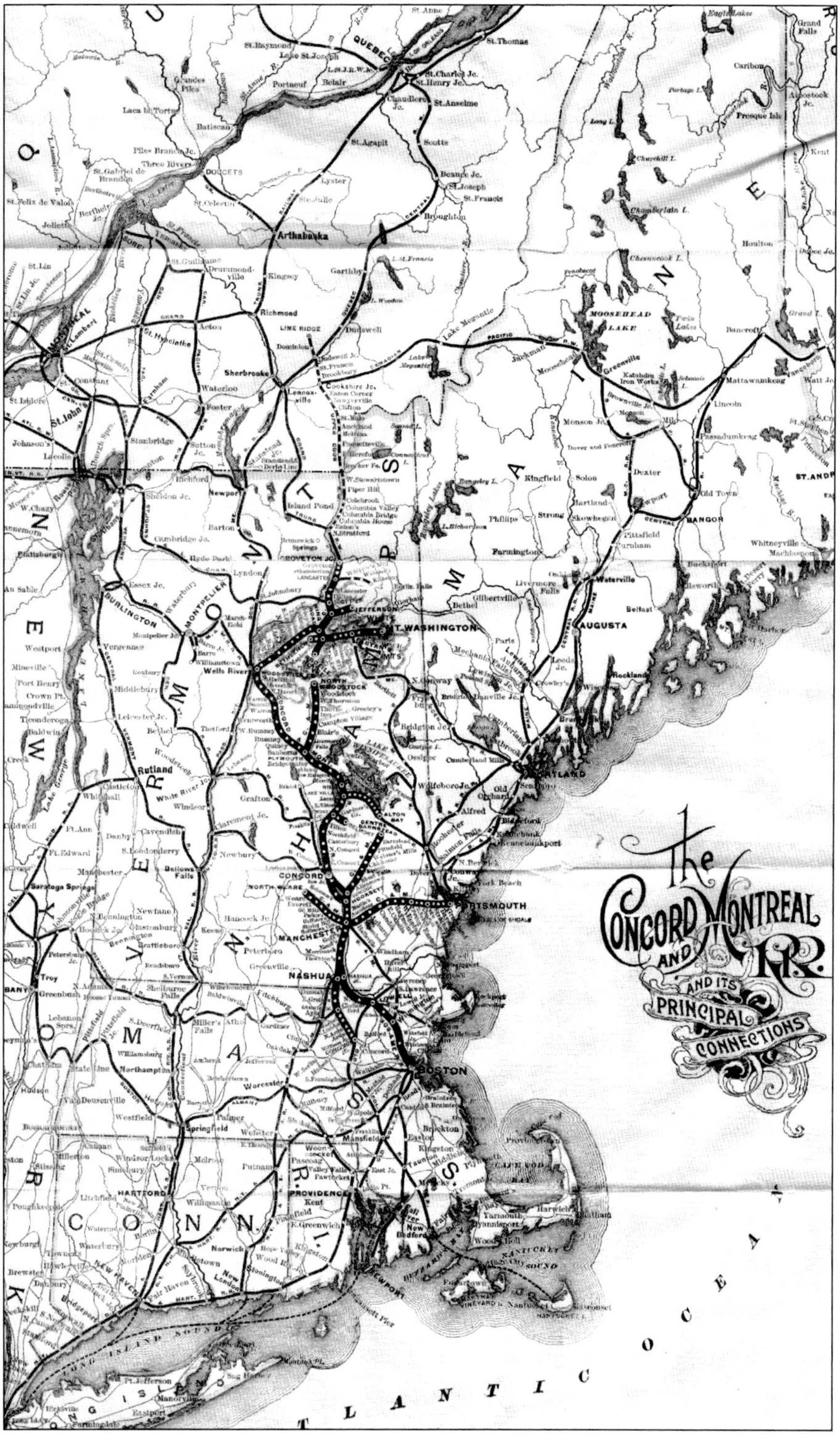

A Map of the Concord & Montreal Railroad System. This map shows the major routes and principal connections of the Concord and Montreal Railroad throughout New England.

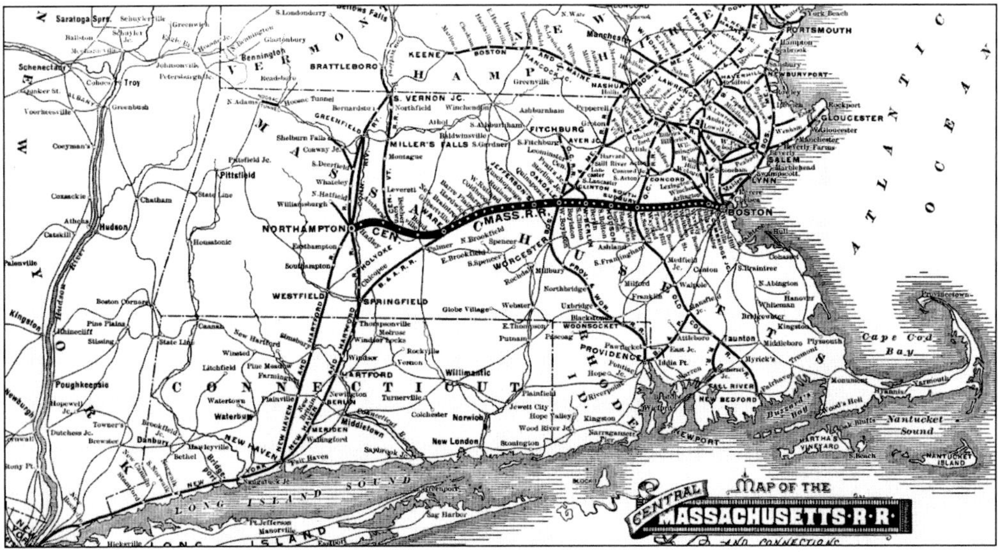

A MAP OF THE CENTRAL MASSACHUSETTS RAILROAD AND CONNECTIONS, JULY 23, 1888. On October 16, 1868, a group of citizens met in Barre, Massachusetts, to draft a petition to the Massachusetts legislature for "a charter of a railroad from Northampton to Boston, through Ware, and crossing the Worcester & Nashua Railroad, to pass over the present chartered road called the Wayland & Sudbury Branch, and to be united with the Williamsburgh and North Adams road at Williamsburgh or some other point, and to be called and known as the Massachusetts Central Ry."

On May 10, 1869, an act by the Massachusetts legislature created the Massachusetts Central Railroad and authorized a union with the Wayland & Sudbury Branch Railroad and the right to construct a line of road from Stony Brook on the main line of the Fitchburg Railroad to Northampton, a distance of some 98 miles. It should be noted that the Massachusetts Central went bankrupt and was reorganized as the Central Massachusetts Railroad.

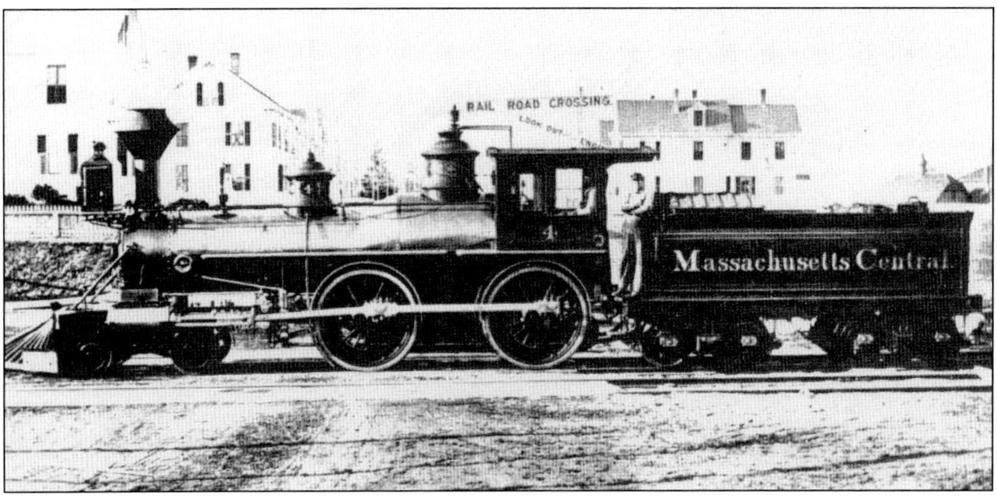

MASSACHUSETTS CENTRAL NO. 4. This locomotive stands on the Pope Street crossing in Hudson, Massachusetts, probably in the fall of 1881. This is the only known photograph of a locomotive lettered and numbered for that road. Near the turn of the century, under the Boston & Lowell control, the Central Massachusetts line entered a period of relative fiscal and managerial tranquility.

MASSACHUSETTS CENTRAL RAILROAD.

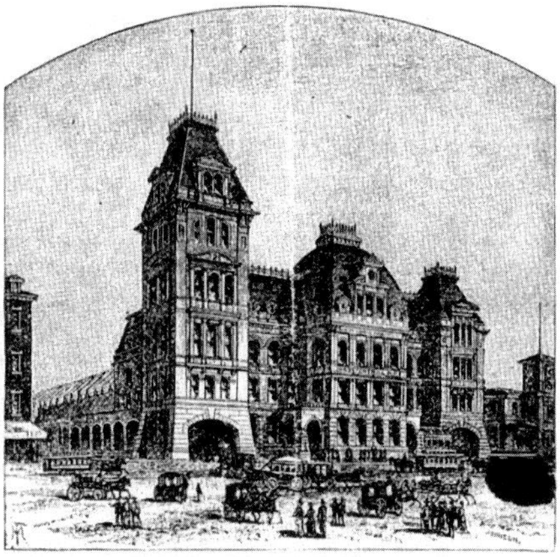

—TIME-TABLE,—

LOCAL, COMMUTATION, SEASON AND MILEAGE,

TICKET TARIFF.

In effect December 29, 1881.

N. C. MUNSON, Gen. Manager. E. G. ALLEN, Supt.

TRAINS STOP ONLY WHERE TIME IS GIVEN BELOW.

WEST-BOUND.

STATIONS. LEAVE	A. M.	P. M.	P. M.	P. M.	P. M.	Sund'y P. M.
Boston	7 15	12 05	3 45	5 00	5 30	4 45
East Cambridge	†7 20	†12 10	†3 50	†5 05	†5 34	†4 50
North Cambridge	†7 28	†12 18	†3 58	†5 13	†5 42	†4 58
Belmont	7 32	12 22	4 02	5 18	5 46	5 02
Waverly	7 35	12 25	4 05	5 21	5 49	5 05
Waltham	7 40	12 30	4 10	5 28	5 54	5 10
W. Waltham	†7 42	†12 32	†4 12	†5 30		†5 12
Weston	7 46	12 36	4 16	5 35	6 00	5 17
Tower Hill	†7 52	†12 42	†4 22	†5 42	†6 06	†5 25
Wayland	7 55	12 45	4 25	5 50	6 09	5 28
South Sudbury	8 01	12 51	4 31	6 23	6 18	5 39
Wayside Inn		†12 55		†6 27		†5 43
Rockbottom	†8 13	†1 03	†4 43	†6 35		†5 51
Hudson	8 18	1 08	4 48	6 40	6 30	6 00
Berlin	8 26	1 16			6 38	6 08
S. Clinton	8 33	1 23			6 45	6 15
Boylston	†8 36	†1 26			†6 48	†6 18
W. Boylston	8 42	1 32			6 54	6 24
Oakdale	8 45	1 35			6 57	6 27
Holden	†8 56	†1 46			†7 08	†6 38
Holden Junction		†1 51			7 13	
Jefferson's	9 02	1 52			7 14	6 45
WORCESTER via W. & N. RR Lincoln Sq	9 20	2 10			7 25	
WORCESTER via W. & N. RR Union St'n	9 25	2 15			7 30	
WORCESTER via B., B.&G. RR Lincoln Sq	9 24					
WORCESTER via B., B.&G. RR Union St'n	9 29					
Princeton, via B., B.&G. RR		2 58			7 25	
Hubbardston " "		*3 10			7 34	
Gardner, " "		3 30			7 55	
WINCHENDON, " "		4 00			8 25	
Arrive	A. M.	P. M.	P. M.	P. M.	P. M.	P. M.

EAST-BOUND.

STATIONS. LEAVE	A. M.	A. M.	A. M.	A. M.	P. M.	Sund'y A. M.
WINCHENDON via B., B.&G. RR			7 56		4 16	
Gardner, " "			8 20		4 40	
Hubbardston " "			*8 38		4 58	
Princeton, " "			8 42		5 07	
WORCESTER via B., B.&G. RR Union St'n			8 00			
WORCESTER via B., B.&G. RR Lincoln Sq			8 05			
WORCESTER via W. & N. RR Union St'n			7 30	11 15	5 00	
WORCESTER via W. & N. RR Lincoln Sq			7 35	11 20	5 05	
Jefferson's			8 55	11 40	5 15	7 15
Holden Junction			9 01		5 21	
Holden			†9 05	†11 45	†5 25	†7 20
Oakdale			9 15	11 55	5 35	7 30
W. Boylston			9 18	11 58	5 38	7 33
Boylston			†9 24	†12 04	†5 44	†7 39
S. Clinton			9 26	12 06	5 46	7 41
Berlin			9 32	12 12	5 52	7 47
Hudson	6 45	7 30	9 40	12 20	6 00	8 00
Rockbottom	†6 50	†7 34	†9 44	†12 24	†6 04	†8 05
Wayside Inn	†6 58			†12 32		†8 13
South Sudbury	7 07	7 46	9 56	12 36	6 16	8 21
Wayland	7 20	7 53	10 03	12 43	6 23	8 32
Tower Hill	†7 23	†7 56	†10 06	†12 46	†6 26	†8 35
Weston	7 30	8 01	10 13	12 53	6 33	8 43
W. Waltham	†7 35		†10 17	†12 57	†6 37	†8 47
Waltham	7 39	8 07	10 20	1 00	6 40	8 50
Waverly	7 44	8 11	10 25	1 05	6 45	8 55
Belmont	7 47	8 14	10 28	1 08	6 48	8 58
North Cambridge	†7 52	†8 20	†10 32	†1 12	†6 52	†9 02
East Cambridge	†8 00	†8 29	†10 40	†1 20	†7 00	†9 10
BOSTON	8 05	8 34	10 45	1 25	7 05	9 15
Arrive	A. M.	A. M.	A. M.	P. M.	P. M.	P. M.

† Flag Stations.
* Connect with Barre Coach.

Coaches run between Cochituate and Wayland, connecting with all trains to and from Boston.

Coaches run between Clinton and S. Clinton, connecting with all trains to and from Boston.

A MASSACHUSETTS CENTRAL TIMETABLE. By 1882, the road was complete to Oakdale and Jefferson's. This timetable shows three trips each way to Jefferson's, one each way to Hudson, and one round-trip to Jefferson's on Sunday. Grading and related work were in progress to the west, and it appeared on the surface that the goal of Northampton would soon be reached, but not until a great deal of financial trouble.

CENTRAL MASSACHUSETTS R. R.

TRAINS WEST.

Mls.	Train No. / Stations.	23	27		117	123		205	219	245	261	273		SUN. 729
		A. M.	A. M.		A. M.	P. M.		P. M.	P. M.	P. M.	P. M.	P. M.		P.M.
	B. & L. R. R.													
	BOSTON ..lv.	7 05	7 25		11 40	12 05		3 40	4 20	5 25	6 00	6 25		1 15
1.1	East Cambridge								G		G	G		1 20
1.8	Prospect Hill..													
2.5	Winter Hill....	G									6 09			
2.8	Somerville.....										6 11			
3.3	Som'le H'lands													
3.7	Willow Avenue													
4.	W. Somerville.				11 51						6 14			
	C. M. R. R.													
4.4	No.Camb'ge Jc.	7 17			11 53			B	F		6 16			F
5.9	Hill's Crossing				D						D			D
6.7	Belmont......	7 22			11 59				4 36		6 22	6 43		1 35
7.7	Waverley......	7 26			12 02				4 39		6 25			1 38
8.6	Clematis Brook	D			D						D			D
10.	Waltham......	7 32			12 08	12 26		4 01	4 44	5 46	6 31	6 50		1 45
10.5	Hammond St..	D			D				D		D			D
13.2	Weston........	7 40			12 18	12 33		4 09	4 52	5 54	6 40	6 57		1 54
14.	Cherry Brook..	D			D				D		D			D
15.6	Tower Hill	D			D				D		D			D
16.8	Wayland.......	7 50	7 57		12 30	12 40		4 15	5 02	6 01	6 50	7 04		2 04
18.8	East Sudbury..								D					D
20.	S. SUDBURY		8 03			12 46		4 21	5 09	6 07		7 10		2 11
	O. C. R. R.													
	So.Framingham ar.		8 36			1 46			5 29					
	Lowell.........ar.		9 02							6 59				
	C. M. R. R.													
21.9	Wayside Inn..								D					D
23.6	Mirror Lake...													
25.6	Rockbottom....		F					D	D					D
28.	Hudson........		8 18			1 01		4 36	5 30	6 22		7 24		2 30
29.7	South Bolton..		D			D		D						
31.7	Berlin		8 26			1 10		D						
35.6	South Clinton..		D			D		D						
36.9	Boylston.......		D			1 21		D						
40.	West Bolyston.		8 44			1 27		5 03		6 50				
41.3	OAKDALE...		8 50			1 31		5 18		6 54				
	B. & M. R. R.													
	Worcester ......ar.		9 25			2 15		5 32		7 27				
	Worcester ......lv.		7 50					4 50		6 25				
	C. M. R. R.													
45.8	Quinapoxet....		D			D		D						
48.1	Jefferson		D			1 48		D		D				
51.	Muschopauge..							D						
53.5	Rutland........		9 21			2 01		5 52		D				
55.6	West Rutland.		D			D		D						
59.2	Coldbrook		D			2 16		6 07		D				
61.	Barre..........		9 40			2 20		6 11		7 44				
62.6	Barre Plains...		9 44			2 24		6 15		D				
64.2	Hardwick		D			D		D						
66.	New Braintree.		D			D		D						
69.8	Gilbertville....		9 59			2 39		6 31		8 02				
75.	WARE.....ar.		10 10			2 49		6 40		8 11				
	B. & A. R. R.													
	Ware........lv.		10 20											
	Thorndike ..ar.		10 40											
	Palmer......ar.		10 49											
	Palmer ......lv.		11 04											
	Springfield.....		11 35											
	Westfield		11 53											
	Pittsfield		1 23 P											
	Albany .....ar.		2 50 M											
	N.Y., N.H.& H.R.R.		A.M.											
	Springfield......lv.		11 45											
	Hartford ....ar.		12 24 P											
	New Haven		1 24 M											
	Bridgeport		1 57											
	New York.........		3 30											
		LOCAL. A.M.	A.M.						LOCAL, P.M.					
	C. M. R. R.													
75.	WARE .....lv.	7 25	10 10			2 49			4 55	8 11				
81.	Bondville	D	D			D			5 10	D				
87.	Belchertown ...	7 56	10 39			3 16			5 25	8 40				
93.9	South Amherst	D	10 54			D			D	D				
96.4	Amherst.......	8 20	11 00			3 37			5 50	9 00				
100.9	Hadley	8 30	11 10			3 47			6 00	9 10				
105.	Northampton ar	8 35	11 15			3 52			6 05	9 15				
	Conn. R. R. R.													
	Northampton lv	8 46				3 57								
	Hatfield........	8 54				4 06								
	North Hatfield.	9 02				4 12								
	Whately.......	9 06				4 18								
	South Deerfield	9 14				4 25								
	Deerfield	9 24				4 35								
	Greenfield	9 35				4 47								
	Conn. R. R. R.													
	Northampton lv	9 23	11 20			4 00			6 1[illegible]					
	Mt. Tom ...ar.	9 28	11 26			4 06								
	Smith's Ferry..					4 12								
	Holyoke.......	9 45	11 42			4 30			6 35					
	Chicopee.......	9 58	11 54			4 44								
	Chicopee Falls.	10 20	12 05 P			5 25								
	Springfield..ar.	10 07	12 05 M			4 55			6 50					
	N.Y., N.H.& H.R.R.													
	Springfield......lv.	11 45	1 58						7 03					
	Hartford...........	12 24	2 40						7 40					
	New Haven	1 24	3 42						8 33					
	Bridgeport.........	1 57	4 20						9 06					
	New York.........	3 30	6 00						10 30					
	N. Y., N.H.& H.R.R.	A.M.												
	Northampton....lv.	8 51				4 15			6 17					
	Easthampton	9 01				4 50			6 27					
	Southampton	9 07				5 05			6 35					
	Westfield	9 20				5 30			6 44					
	N.Y., N.H. & H.R.R.													
	Northampton ...lv.	10 26							6 17					
	South Deerfield....	10 47							6 36					
	Conway...........	10 59												
	Shelburne Falls....	11 14							7 00					
	N. Y., N.H.& H.R.R.													
	Northampton ... lv.	10 30							6 33					
	Florence..........	10 37							6 40					
	Leeds.............	10 45							6 45					
	Haydenville	10 50							6 50					
	Williamsburgh	10 54							6 55					
		A.M.	P.M.		P.M.	P.M.		P.M.	P.M.	P.M.	P.M.	P.M.		P.M.

B stops only to take passengers for points west of Hudson. D stops only on signal, or to leave passengers on notice to Conductors. E stops only to leave passengers on notice to Conductors.

Brenton Dickson Collection

A CENTRAL MASSACHUSETTS RAILROAD TIMETABLE FROM DECEMBER 19, 1887. Noted on this east-to-west schedule are station names, railroad connections, and departure times.

Three

A Dynasty Is Born: The Boston & Maine

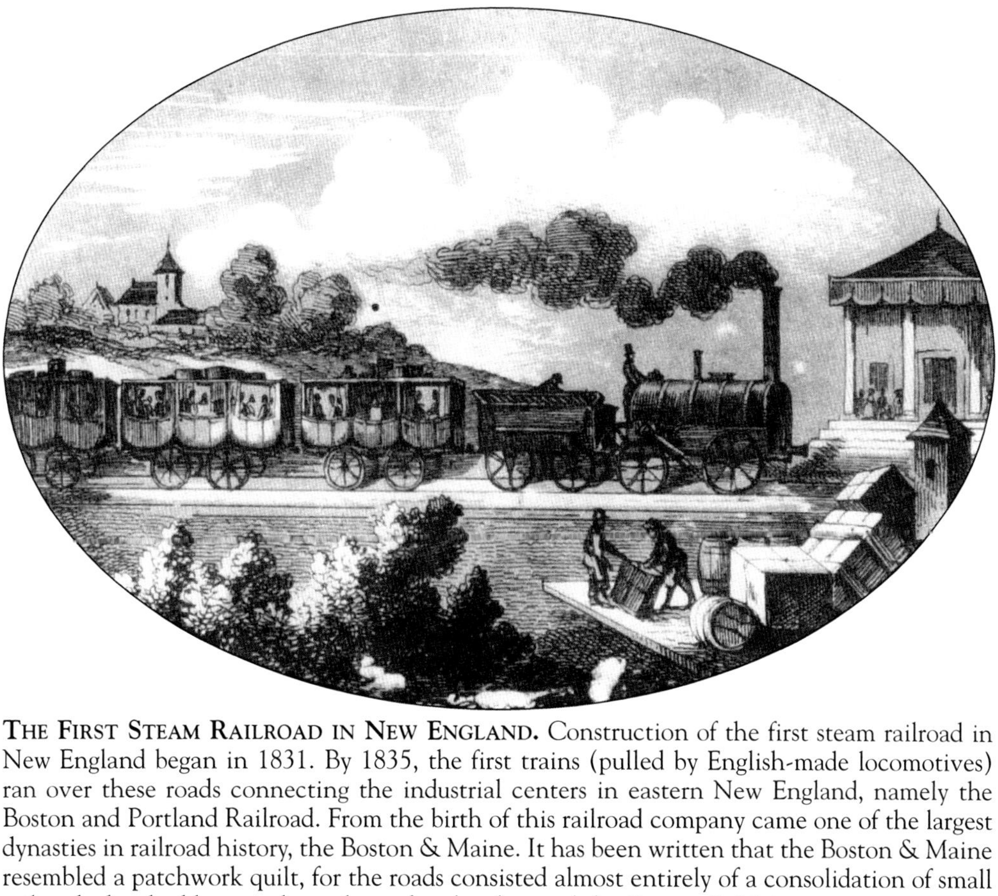

The First Steam Railroad in New England. Construction of the first steam railroad in New England began in 1831. By 1835, the first trains (pulled by English-made locomotives) ran over these roads connecting the industrial centers in eastern New England, namely the Boston and Portland Railroad. From the birth of this railroad company came one of the largest dynasties in railroad history, the Boston & Maine. It has been written that the Boston & Maine resembled a patchwork quilt, for the roads consisted almost entirely of a consolidation of small railroads that had been independent of each other and the Boston & Maine.

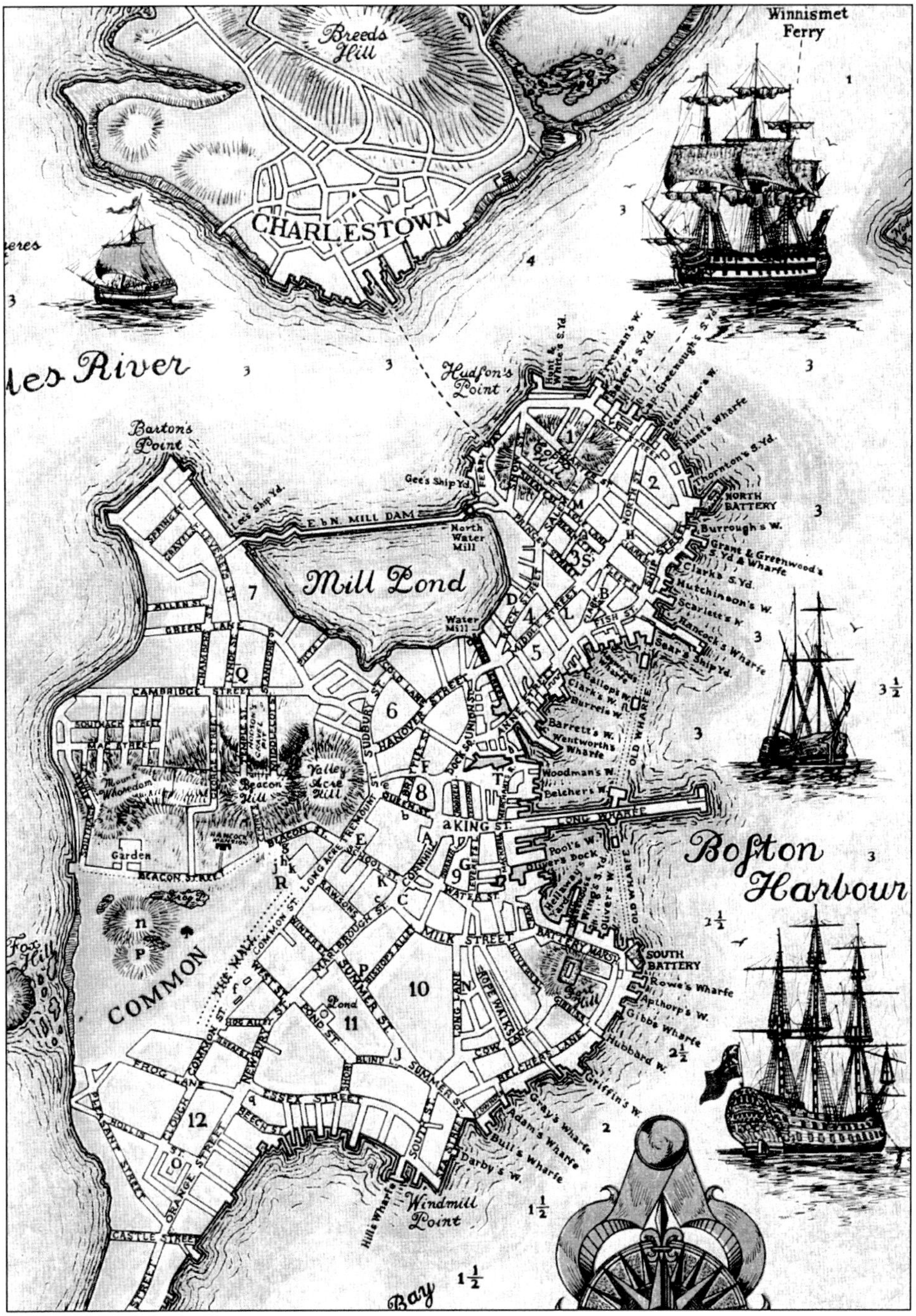

A Map of Boston's Original Shoreline. The Boston & Maine's original Haymarket Square depot was located near what was once a millpond. Due to the growing population, this pond was filled in completely from land taken from Copp's and Beacon Hill. The Boston & Lowell Railroad played an important part in the total filling-in process so that new land would be available by Causeway Street. As this area developed into Boston's northern railroad terminal, the number of railroads using the area continued to increase. By 1871, a total of four railroad companies were located there.

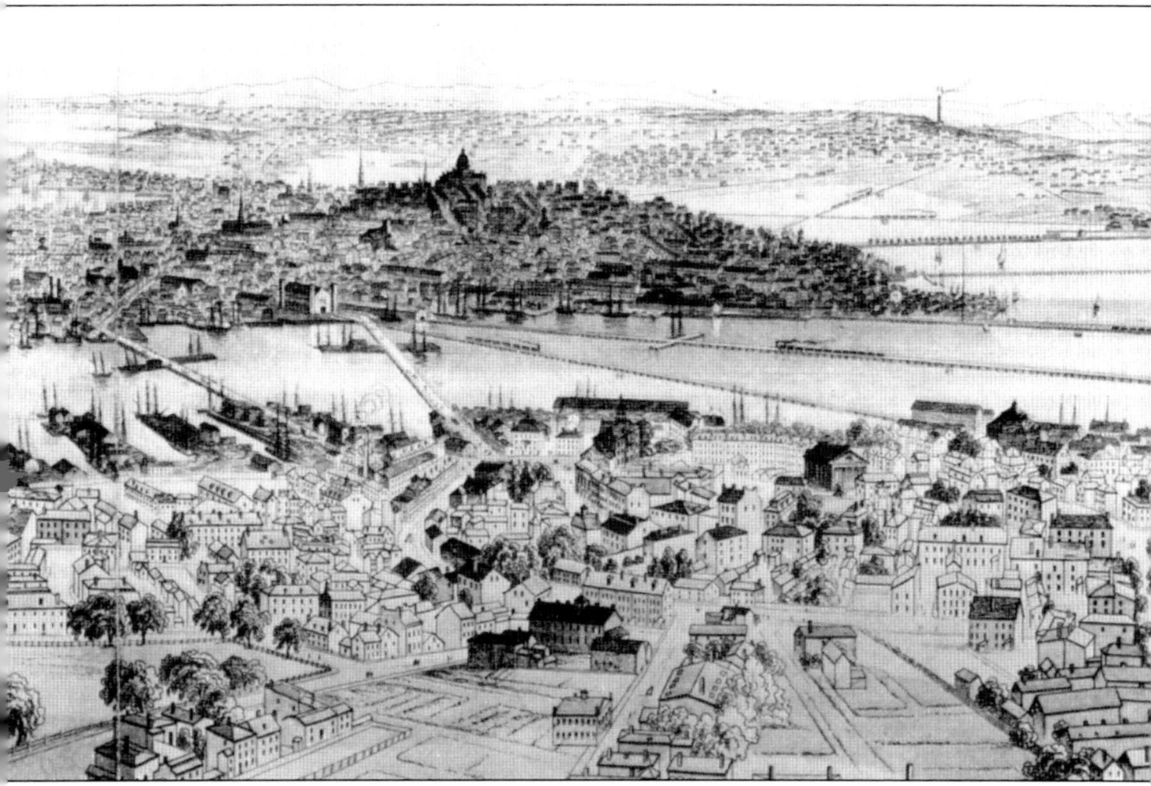

BOSTON'S CAUSEWAY STREET DEPOTS, 1856. This image shows the city of Boston during the early days of railroading. The three railroad bridges in the center are, from left to right, those of the Fitchburg, the Boston & Maine, and the Boston & Lowell. The Fitchburg's depot, with its tall, castlelike towers, stands out in the center on the west bank of the Charles River. The dome of the State House can be seen on Beacon Hill in the distance.

ACTS OF MASSACHUSETTS.

An Act, incorporating the Andover and Wilmington Railroad Corporation, passed March 15, 1833.

An Act, authorizing the extension of the above to Haverhill, passed April 7, 1835.

An Act, authorizing a further extension, from Haverhill to the State line of New Hampshire, and changing the name to the Andover and Haverhill Railroad Corporation, passed April 7, 1837.

An Act, changing the name of the Andover and Haverhill Railroad Corporation to that of the Boston and Portland Railroad Corporation, passed April 3, 1839.

An Act, to incorporate the Boston and Maine Extension Railroad Corporation, bringing the road directly into Boston to the terminus in Haymarket square, passed March 16, 1844.

ACTS OF NEW HAMPSHIRE.

An Act to incorporate the Boston and Maine Railroad Corporation, from the State line of Massachusetts to the State line of Maine, passed June 27, 1835.

An Act, to incorporate the Dover and Winipisiogee Railroad, passed July 2, 1839.

ACTS OF MAINE.

An Act, incorporating the Maine, New Hampshire and Massachusetts Railroad Corporation, passed March 30, 1836.

An Act, in addition to the above, passed April 2, 1841, uniting the above-named corporation into one company, by the name of the Boston and Maine Railroad.

ACTS OF LEGISLATURE: MASSACHUSETTS, NEW HAMPSHIRE, AND MAINE. To understand the development of Boston & Maine's early history, it is best to examine the acts of legislature that incorporated the various small railroads into what became known as the "old" Boston & Maine roads. In these acts, this company was just the beginning of a long line of travel. They were chartered in New Hampshire simply to build across the state to its eastern edge, thus attaining their objective: to accommodate the general travel from eastern New Hampshire to the state of Maine. In this fashion, a New Hampshire corporation has been introduced into New England in the form of the Boston & Maine. Thus the Boston & Maine of New Hampshire and Massachusetts are united as one corporation.

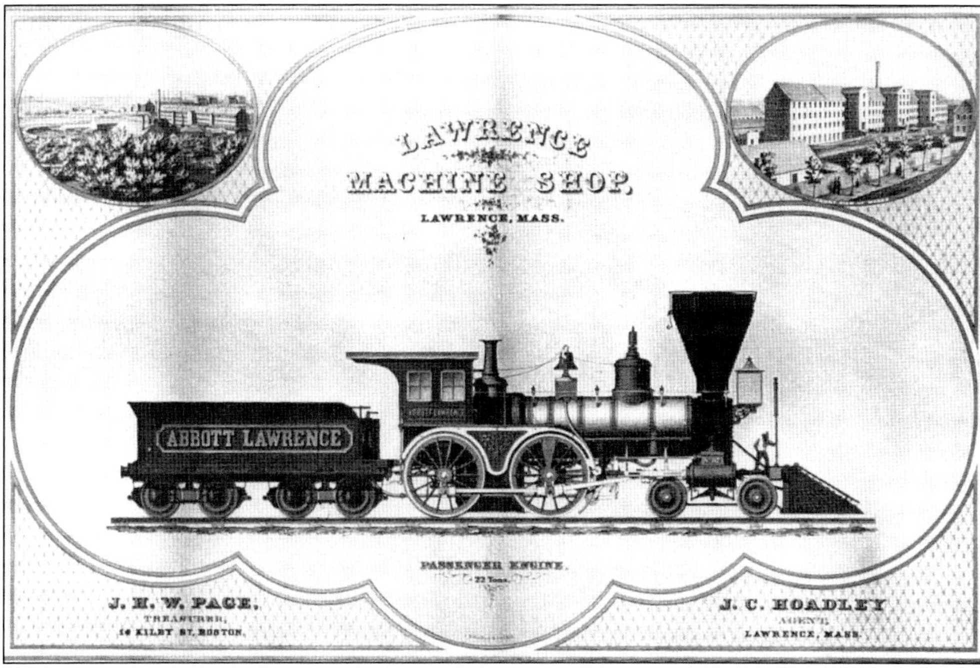

THE LAWRENCE MACHINE SHOP, LAWRENCE, MASSACHUSETTS. Soon, these locomotives were being manufactured in Massachusetts at Lawrence.

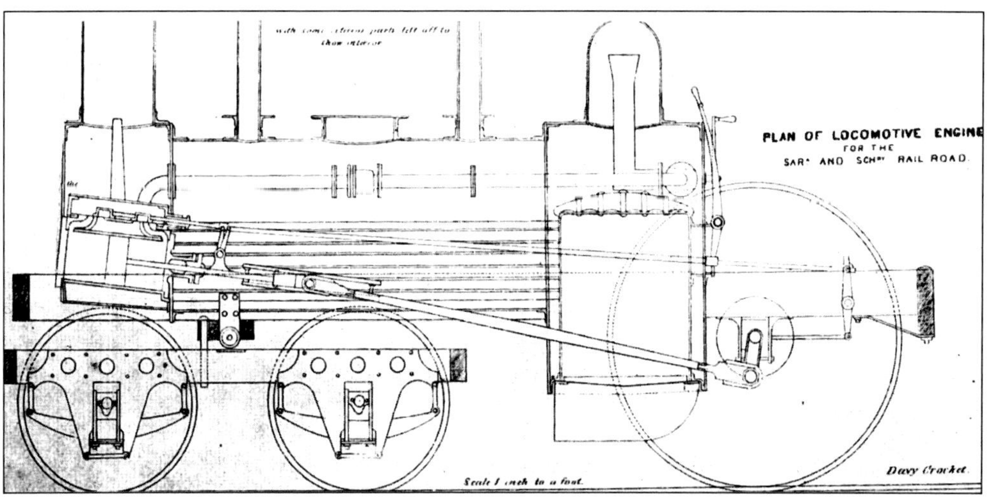

PLAN OF THE "DAVY CROCKETT." A lithography firm in Boston published this print of the American locomotive "Davy Crockett" to show people how the remarkable new engine worked.

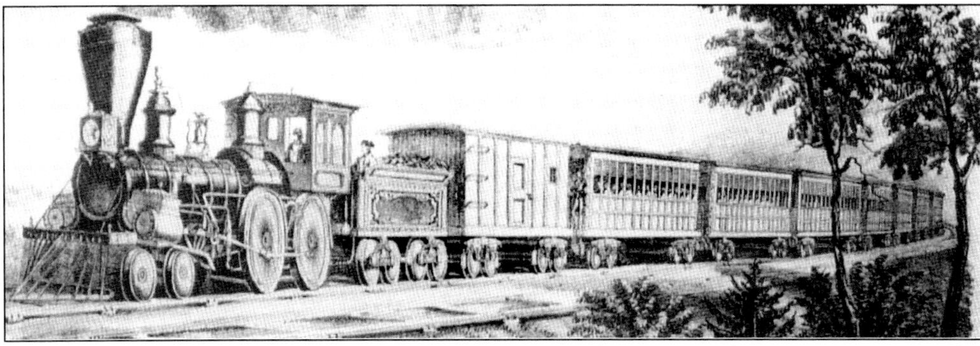

A Steam Locomotive with Passenger Trains. On July 24, 1843, the Boston & Maine's first branch was opened. It extended from Rollinsford, Massachusetts, to Great Falls, New Hampshire, a distance of 3 miles. From 1839 to 1841, the road was known as the Boston and Portland Railroad, but in the latter year the more familiar name of Boston & Maine was adopted.

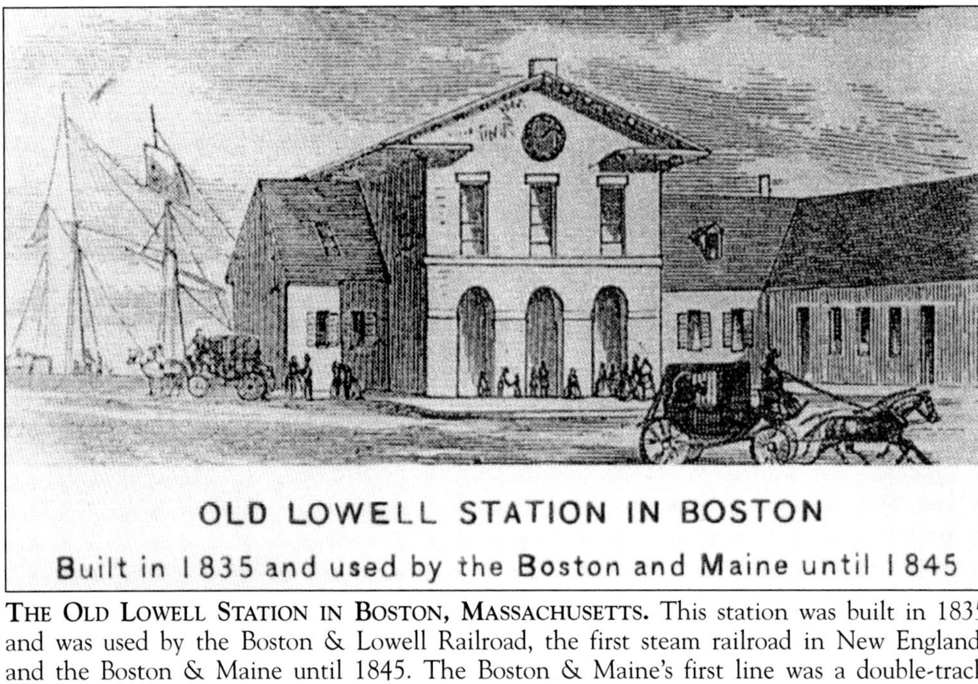

The Old Lowell Station in Boston, Massachusetts. This station was built in 1835 and was used by the Boston & Lowell Railroad, the first steam railroad in New England, and the Boston & Maine until 1845. The Boston & Maine's first line was a double-track line from Boston to Portland, Maine—115.5 miles, with 34.75 miles in New Hampshire. The road was chartered in New Hampshire in 1835 and was opened from the Massachusetts state line to Exeter, New Hampshire, in 1840, and to Dover, New Hampshire, in 1841. From a November 1, 1841 timetable entitled "Boston and Portland Railroad—road opened to Dover—48 miles from Portland," we learn that trains left Boston at "7 1-2 and 11 1-2 A.M., and 5 P.M. for Andover, Haverhill, Exeter, New-Market, Durham and Dover [leaving] Dover for Boston . . . at 5 1-2 and 9 A.M. and 3 1-2 P.M." The timetable continues, "The depot in Boston is on Lowell Street, and passengers taking the cars of this road are subjected to no detention by change of conveyance. Travellers from the northern and eastern parts of New Hampshire, or any part of the State of Maine, will find that this route has superior advantages in passing to and from the city of Boston."

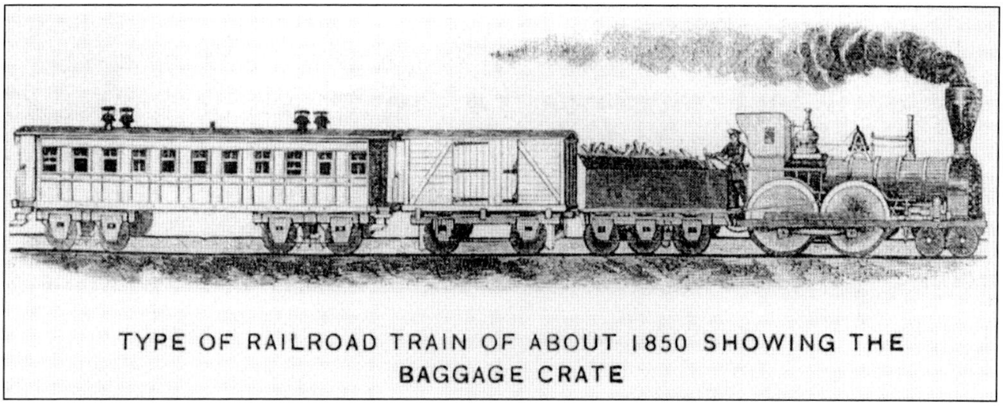

TYPE OF RAILROAD TRAIN OF ABOUT 1850 SHOWING THE BAGGAGE CRATE. Merchandise trains left Boston and Dover every morning at six. It is interesting to note that a little Nile's express had been established on the Boston & Maine and advertised itself "leaving Boston for Dover every afternoon at 5 o'clock, and any packages left at No. 11 Elm Street by 4 o'clock will meet with attention. All packages for Great Falls, South Berwick, Kennebunk, Saco and Portland, as well as for any of the towns in the the N.E. part of New Hampshire."

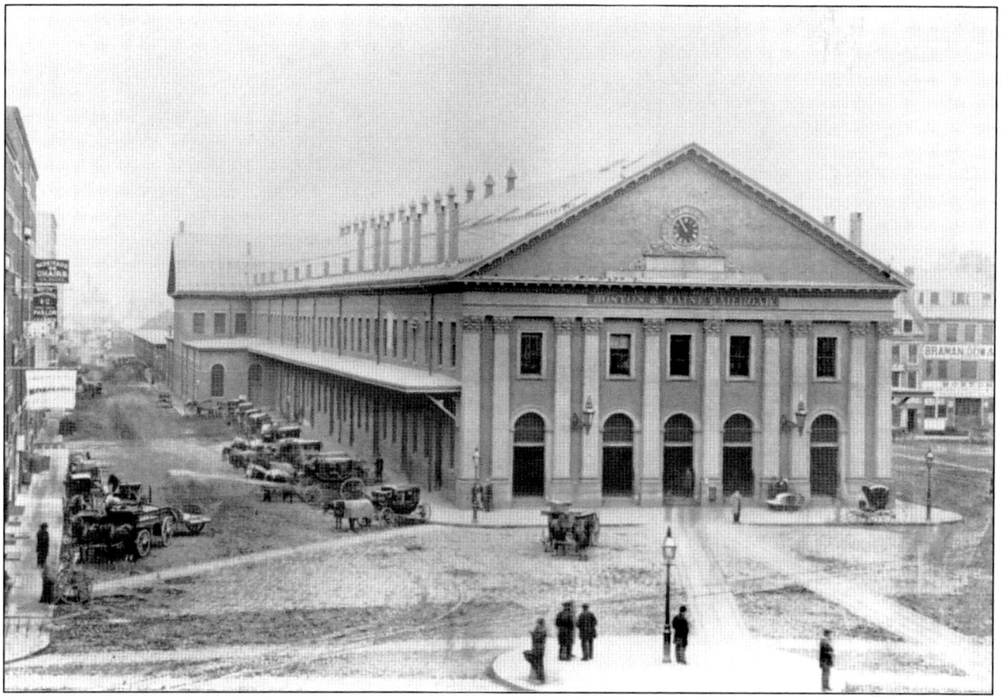

THE OLD BOSTON & MAINE STATION IN HAYMARKET SQUARE, BOSTON, MASSACHUSETTS, 1845. In 1841, the Boston & Portland consolidated with the Boston & Maine. It was chartered to Haymarket Square in Boston in 1844 and opened in 1845. In 1843, the Boston & Maine, in connection with the Eastern Railroad Company, leased the Portland, Saco & Portsmouth Railroad for a term of 99 years. Boston became New England's major transportation center. From the Boston & Maine depot, vacationers left for Maine and the White Mountains of New Hampshire. This station was used until the completion of the North Station in 1894; it was finally torn down in 1897 to make way for the Boston City Hospital. This photograph was taken c. 1865.

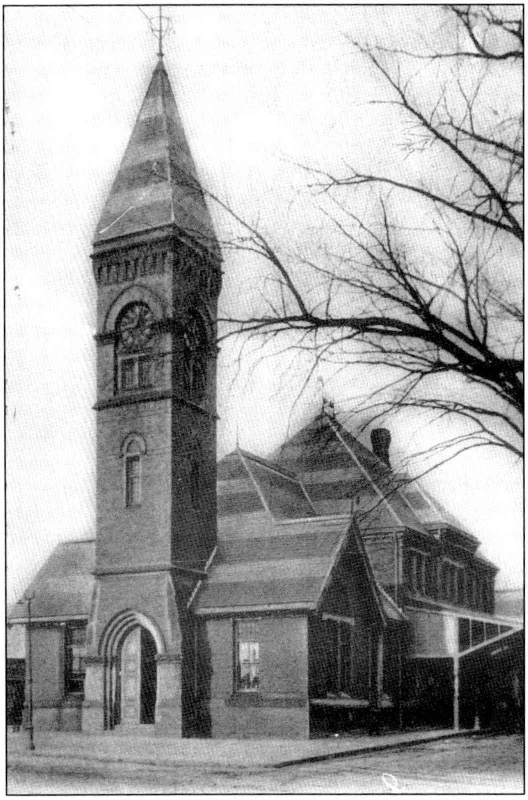

The Boston & Maine Depot, Lawrence, Massachusetts. In the mid-1800s, Lawrence had begun to show signs of becoming a prosperous manufacturing town; the Essex Company had settled there and commenced an extensive outlay of capital. The directors of the Boston & Maine realized that Lawrence would soon require greater railroad facilities. On March 3, 1846, they therefore obtained the approval of an act changing the location of the road between Andover and North Andover: it would run down the valley of the Shawsheen River to a point near Andover bridge and from there along the south bank of the Merrimack River to the old line of the road at North Andover. A new bridge was built across the Merrimack to deliver passengers in Lawrence directly upon its north bank. The new line was completed and opened to the public on July 3, 1848. It was built with one track only; the double track at that time extended only as far as Reading, 10 miles from Boston.

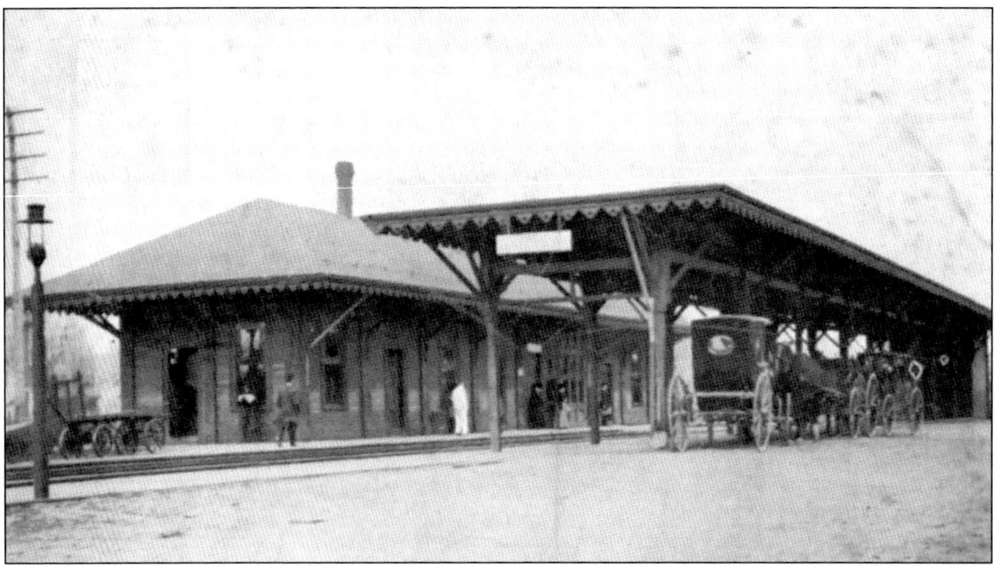

The Boston & Maine Station, Reading, Massachusetts. The line completed in 1848 was furnished with 60-pound T rails, but culverts and bridges were constructed for the future reception of a double track. These two extensions of the Boston & Maine meant the construction of 26 miles of new road and necessitated the removal of the company's repair and car shops from Andover to Lawrence.

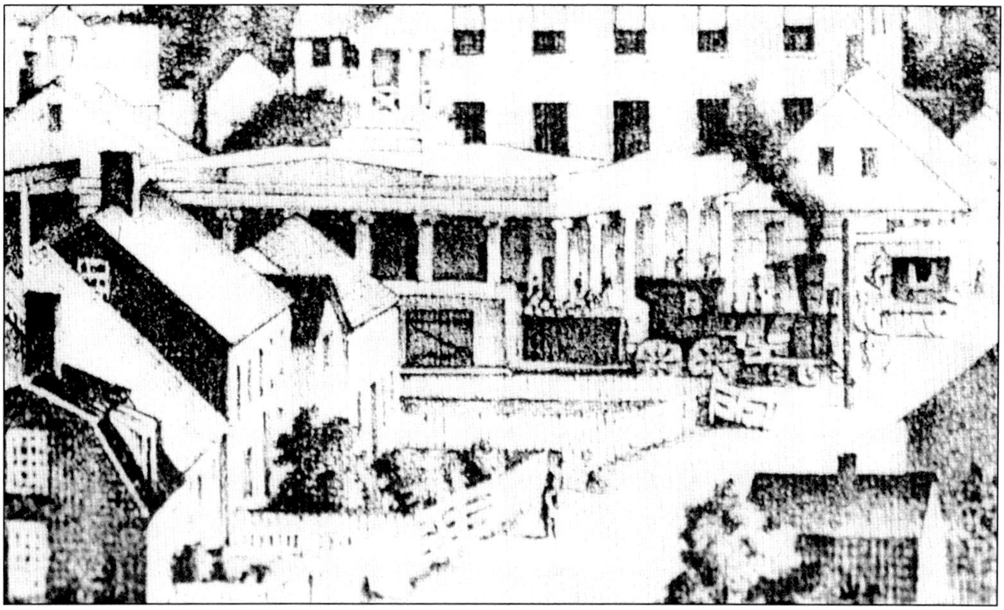

THE BOSTON & MAINE STATION, HAVERHILL, MASSACHUSETTS, 1850 LITHOGRAPH. At the time of these extensions, the road began to show signs of becoming prosperous due to the manufacturing towns on the Merrimack River. Thus, additional stations were constructed all along the road. The extensions and additions to the road encountered bitter opposition from minority stockholders, who could not foresee the future wants of the company. However, the Boston & Maine became a financial success from the time it entered Boston on its own tracks.

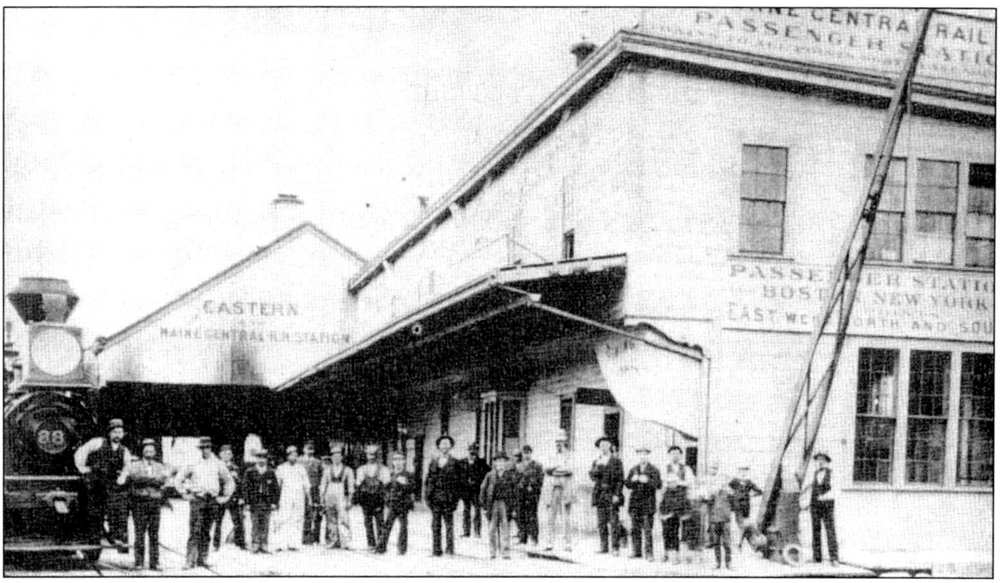

THE RAILROAD STATION IN PORTLAND, MAINE. Built in 1842 for the Portland, Saco & Portsmouth Railroad, this station was used by the Boston & Maine until 1873. The first station in Portland was of the "dead end" variety and was situated on Commercial Street near the steamboat docks. This location, not far from the waterfront, was of great importance to the railroad, accommodating the steamboat traffic from Boston.

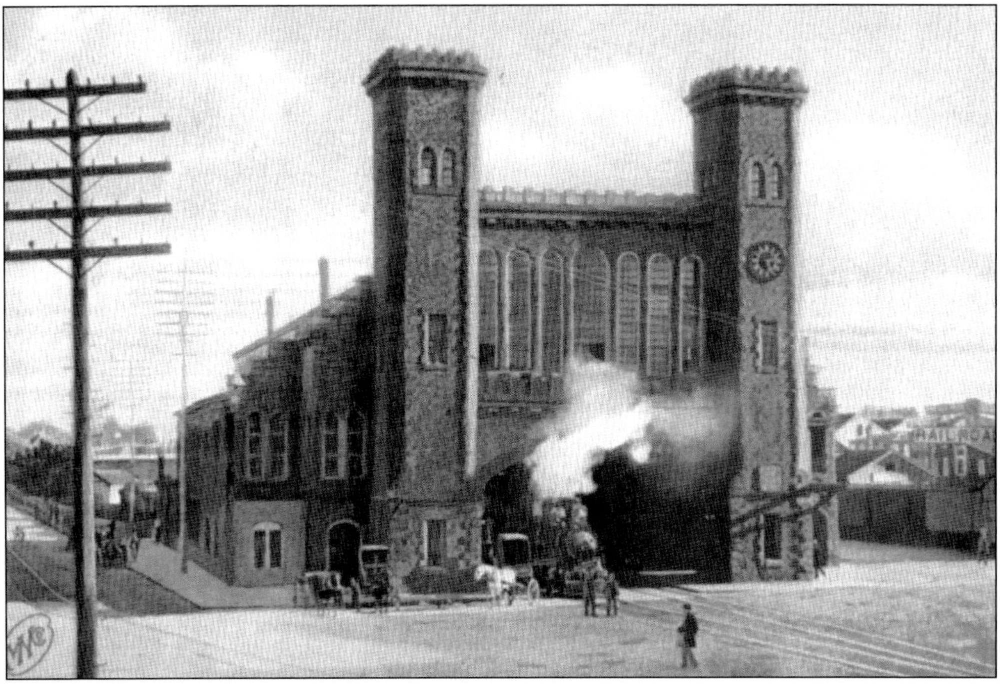

THE BOSTON & MAINE RAILROAD STATION, SALEM, MASSACHUSETTS. In 1848, the Massachusetts legislature chartered a railroad that was to be built from South Danvers (now Peabody) to South Reading, a distance of 8 miles. There it would connect with the Boston & Maine. By using the Salem and Lowell Railroad track between Peabody and Salem, the new road afforded another means of communication between Boston and Salem, Massachusetts. The road was opened to the public on August 31, 1850, using the Salem and Lowell station in Salem.

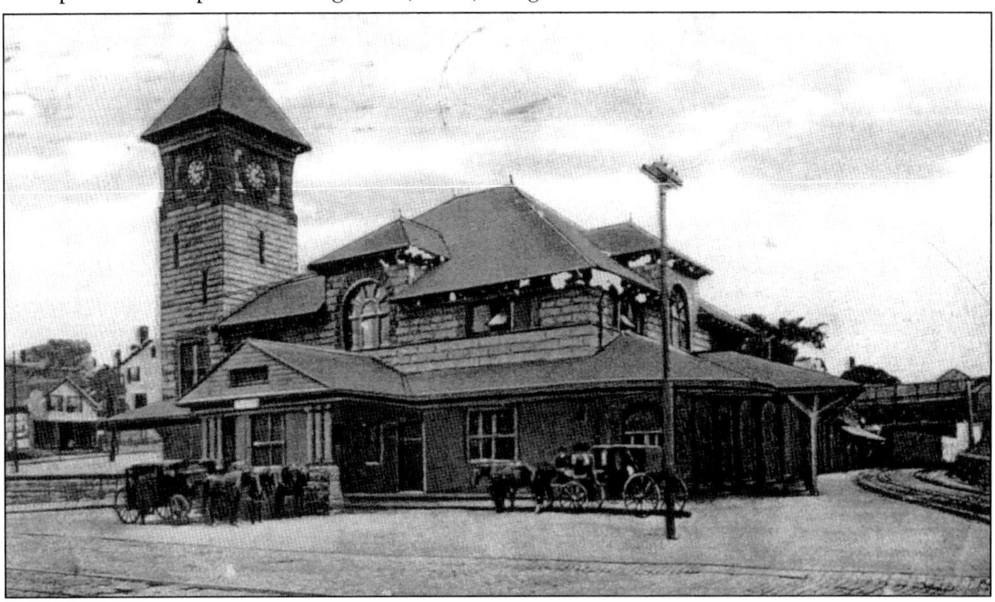

THE BOSTON & MAINE RAILROAD STATION, LOWELL, MASSACHUSETTS. This imposing granite depot, built in 1893–1894, was a major passenger and freight stop for all Boston & Maine trains.

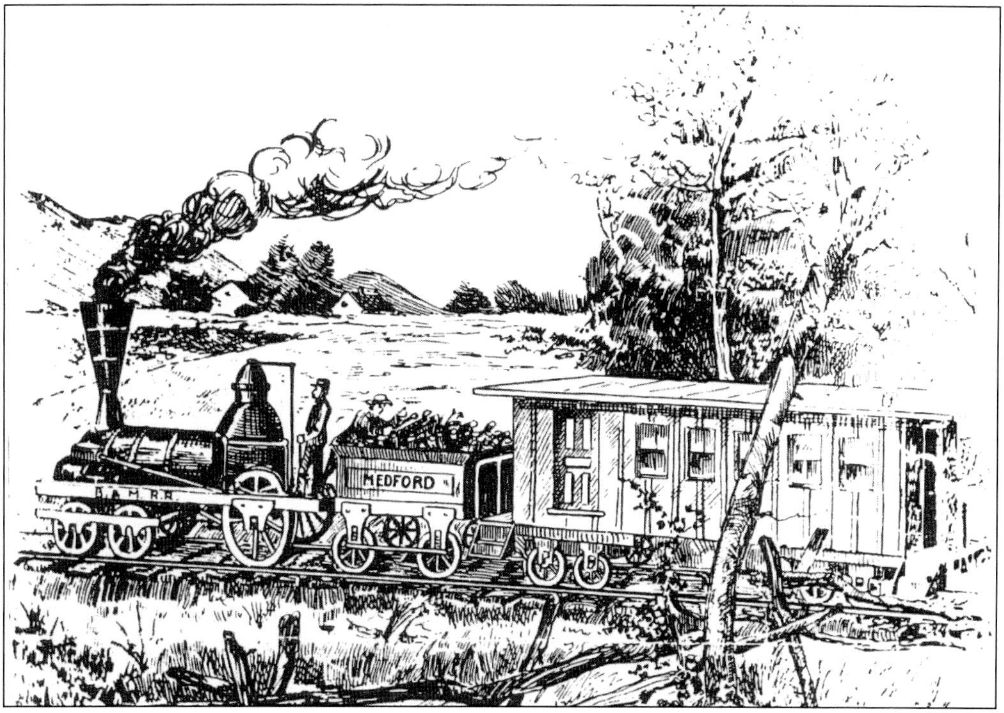

THE LOCOMOTIVE "MEDFORD" AND THE FIRST TRAIN ON THE MEDFORD BRANCH, 1847. All the early locomotives were named and ornamented. The tenders and cabs were ornamented with fancy scroll designs, and the oil cups and other parts of the running machinery were kept polished and cleaned by the firemen.

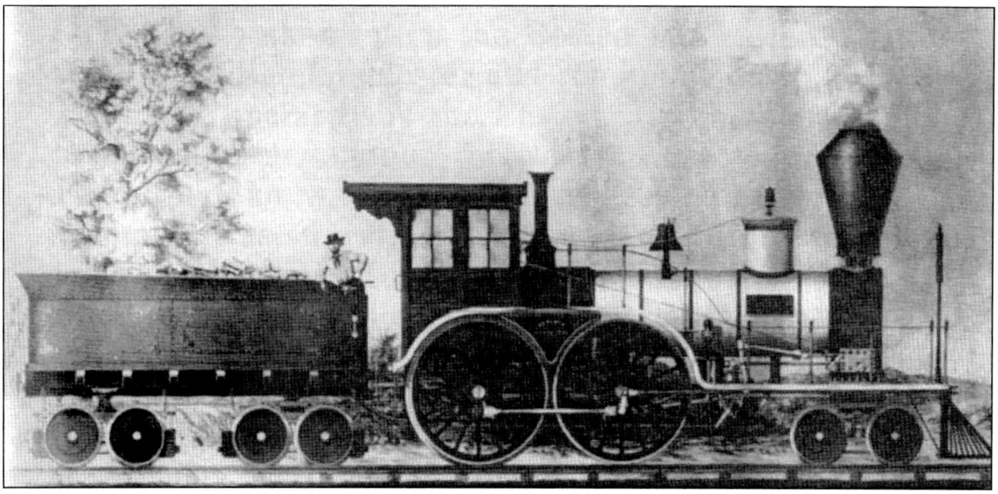

THE LOCOMOTIVE "LAWRENCE" (4-4-0). This locomotive, built by the Lawrence Machine Shop in 1853, weighed 25 tons. By 1850, the engines were all provided with cabs to shelter their occupants from the weather. Many of the early locomotives were of a type now obsolete, called "insiders," shown in the picture of the "Lawrence." The term "insider" meant that the cylinders were close together under the forward end of the boiler. These required a cracked axle for the forward pair of driving wheels.

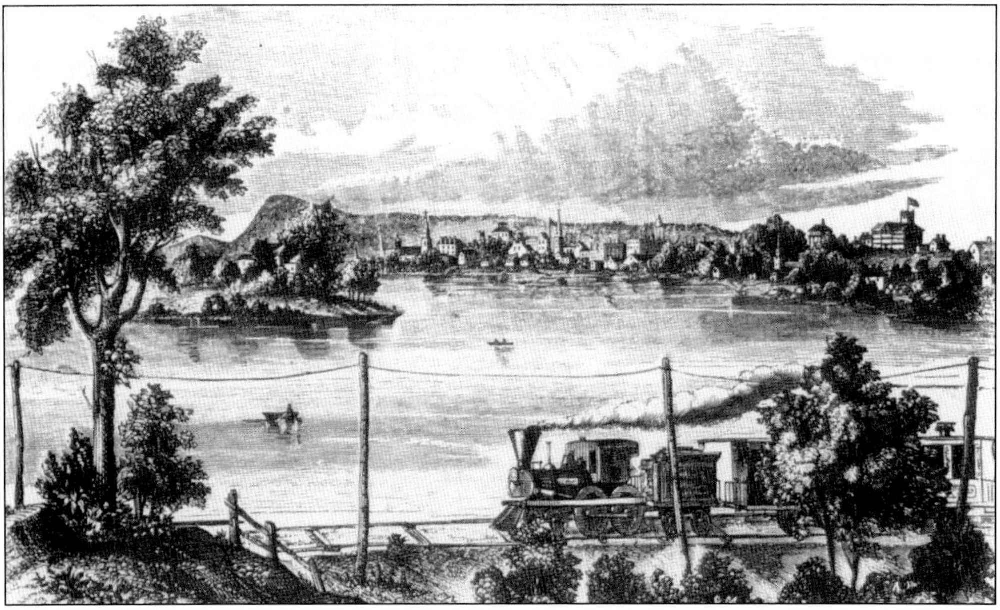

RAIL SERVICE ALONG THE CONNECTICUT RIVER, 1846. While eastern Massachusetts grew, the western region remained sparsely settled. Industry was almost nonexistent except along the Connecticut River, as seen in this illustration of the oxbow of the river near Northampton, Massachusetts. South of the oxbow were several industrial towns connected by both river and rail.

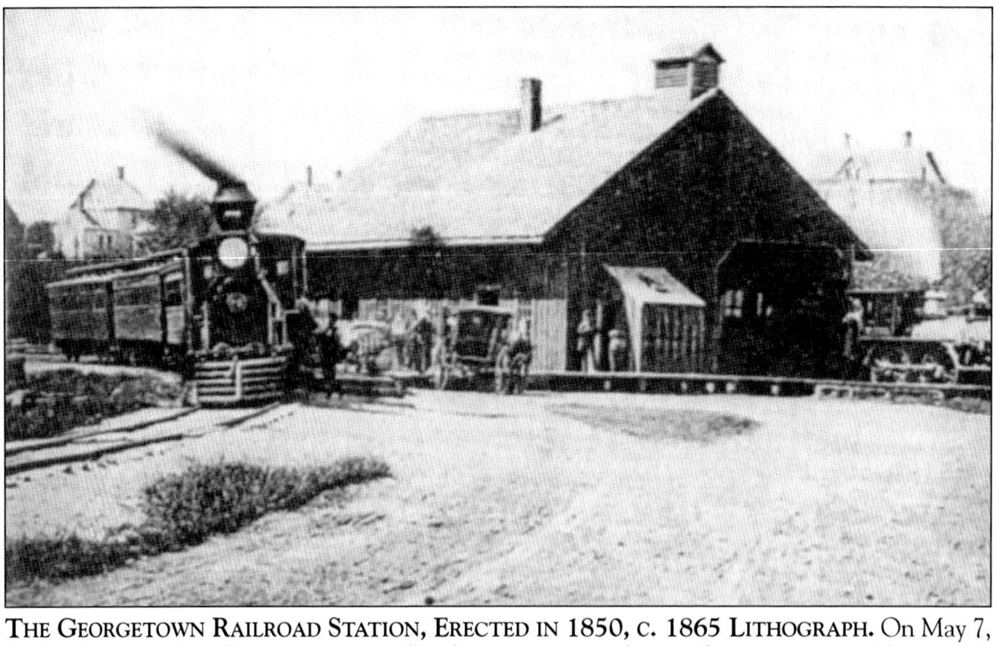

THE GEORGETOWN RAILROAD STATION, ERECTED IN 1850, C. 1865 LITHOGRAPH. On May 7, 1851, the Danvers and Georgetown Railroad Company was chartered "to construct and maintain a railroad, commencing at some convenient point in Georgetown, thence running through Rowley, Ipswich, Boxford, Topsfield, Wenham, or any of the said towns, to the village of North Danvers, there to enter upon and unite with the Essex Railroad at some convenient point."

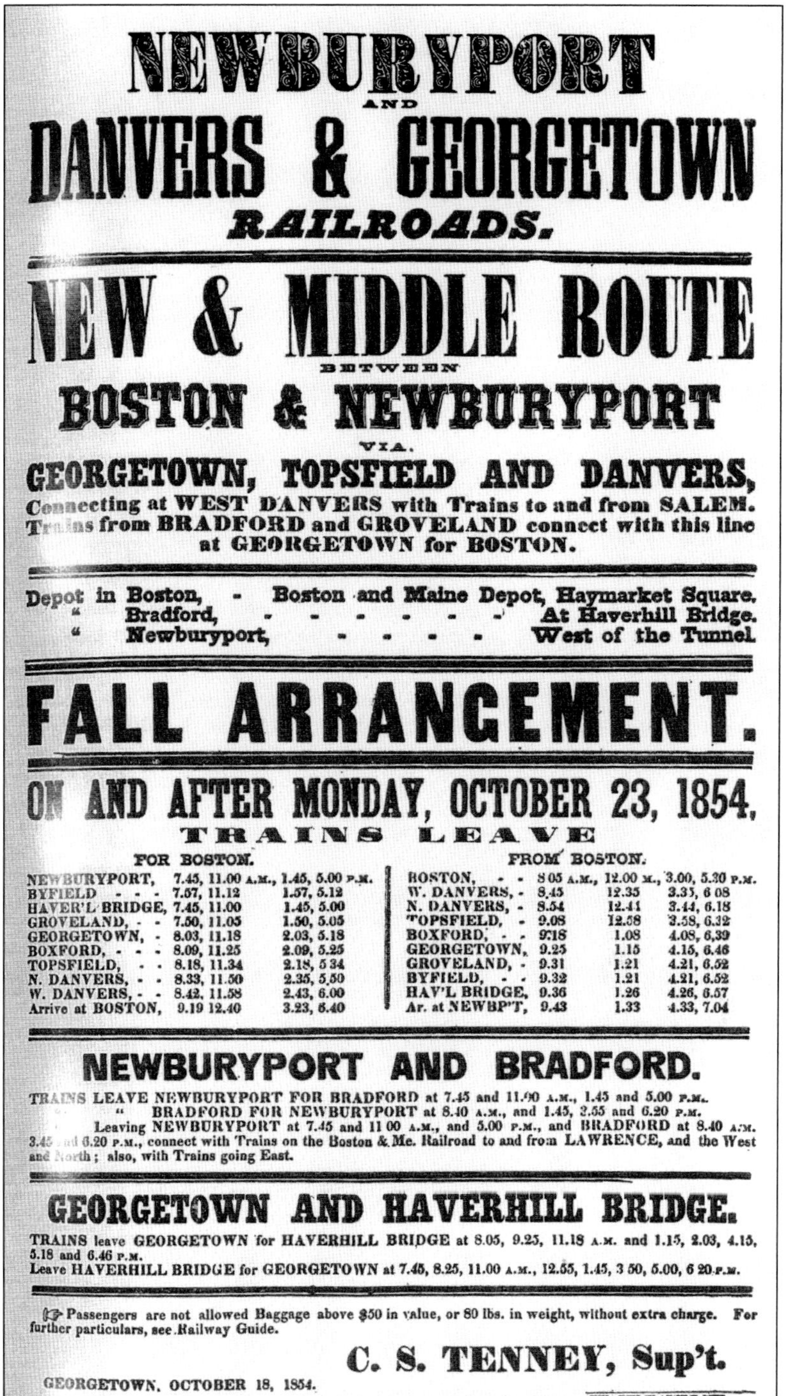

NEWBURYPORT
AND
DANVERS & GEORGETOWN
RAILROADS.

NEW & MIDDLE ROUTE
BETWEEN
BOSTON & NEWBURYPORT
VIA.
GEORGETOWN, TOPSFIELD AND DANVERS,

Connecting at WEST DANVERS with Trains to and from SALEM.
Trains from BRADFORD and GROVELAND connect with this line at GEORGETOWN for BOSTON.

Depot in Boston, - Boston and Maine Depot, Haymarket Square.
" Bradford, - - - - - - - At Haverhill Bridge.
" Newburyport, - - - - West of the Tunnel.

FALL ARRANGEMENT.

ON AND AFTER MONDAY, OCTOBER 23, 1854,
TRAINS LEAVE

FOR BOSTON.

NEWBURYPORT,	7.45, 11.00 A.M.,	1.45, 5.00 P.M.
BYFIELD - - -	7.57, 11.12	1.57, 5.12
HAVER'L BRIDGE,	7.45, 11.00	1.45, 5.00
GROVELAND, - -	7.50, 11.05	1.50, 5.05
GEORGETOWN, -	8.03, 11.18	2.03, 5.18
BOXFORD, - - -	8.09, 11.25	2.09, 5.25
TOPSFIELD, - -	8.18, 11.34	2.18, 5 34
N. DANVERS, - -	8.33, 11.50	2.35, 5.50
W. DANVERS, - -	8.42, 11.58	2.43, 6.00
Arrive at BOSTON,	9.19 12.40	3.23, 6.40

FROM BOSTON.

BOSTON, - -	8 05 A.M.,	12.00 M.,	3.00, 5.30 P.M.
W. DANVERS, -	8.45	12.35	3.35, 6 08
N. DANVERS, -	8.54	12.41	3.44, 6.18
TOPSFIELD, -	9.08	12.58	3.58, 6.32
BOXFORD, - -	9.18	1.08	4.08, 6,39
GEORGETOWN,	9.25	1.15	4.15, 6.46
GROVELAND, -	9.31	1.21	4.21, 6.52
BYFIELD, - -	9.32	1.21	4.21, 6.52
HAV'L BRIDGE,	9.36	1.26	4.26, 6.57
Ar. at NEWBP'T,	9.43	1.33	4.33, 7.04

NEWBURYPORT AND BRADFORD.

TRAINS LEAVE NEWBURYPORT FOR BRADFORD at 7.45 and 11.00 A.M., 1.45 and 5.00 P.M.
" BRADFORD FOR NEWBURYPORT at 8.40 A.M., and 1.45, 2.55 and 6.20 P.M.
Leaving NEWBURYPORT at 7.45 and 11 00 A.M., and 5.00 P.M., and BRADFORD at 8.40 A.M. 3.45 and 6.20 P.M., connect with Trains on the Boston & Me. Railroad to and from LAWRENCE, and the West and North; also, with Trains going East.

GEORGETOWN AND HAVERHILL BRIDGE.

TRAINS leave GEORGETOWN for HAVERHILL BRIDGE at 8.05, 9.25, 11.18 A.M. and 1.15, 2.03, 4.15, 5.18 and 6.46 P.M.
Leave HAVERHILL BRIDGE for GEORGETOWN at 7.45, 8.25, 11.00 A.M., 12.55, 1.45, 3 50, 5.00, 6 20 P.M.

☞ Passengers are not allowed Baggage above $50 in value, or 80 lbs. in weight, without extra charge. For further particulars, see Railway Guide.

C. S. TENNEY, Sup't.

GEORGETOWN, OCTOBER 18, 1854.

A NEWBURYPORT ADVERTISEMENT. While the Danvers and the Danvers and Georgetown Railroads were opened for inspection on September 2, 1854, they were not used for public travel until October 23 of that year. This road connected with the Boston & Maine at South Reading (Wakefield) and passed through Lynn and on to Newburyport, Massachusetts.

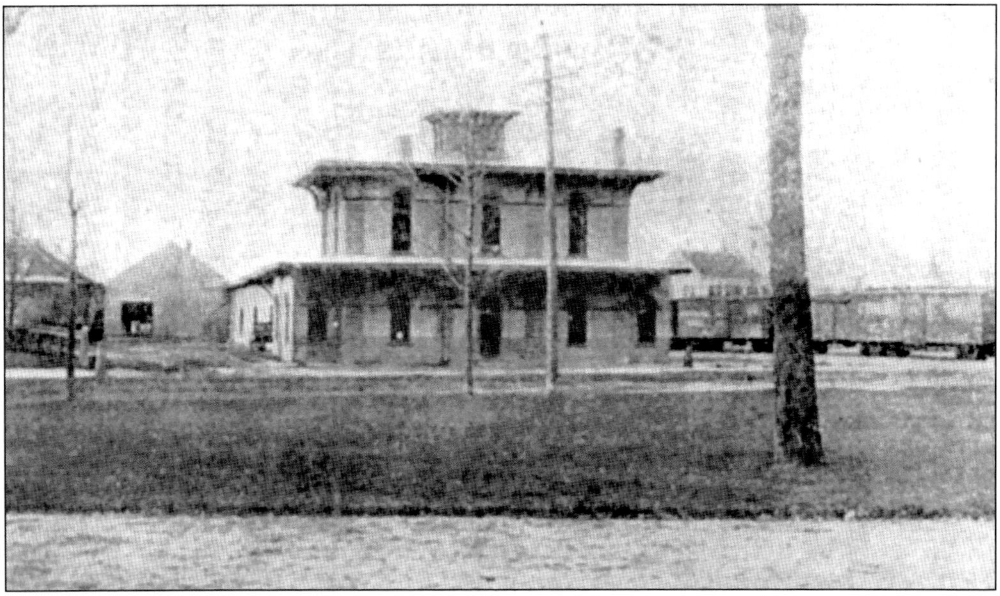

THE NEWBURYPORT RAILROAD COMPANY STATION. This station was built in 1854 on High Street in Newburyport, Massachusetts. The Newburyport Railroad was of the "one horse" variety and a constant source of humor. The slowness of the road was a byword, and it was said that on one occasion the train was so late in arriving to Byfield that many of the citizens gathered at the station to ascertain the cause of its tardiness.

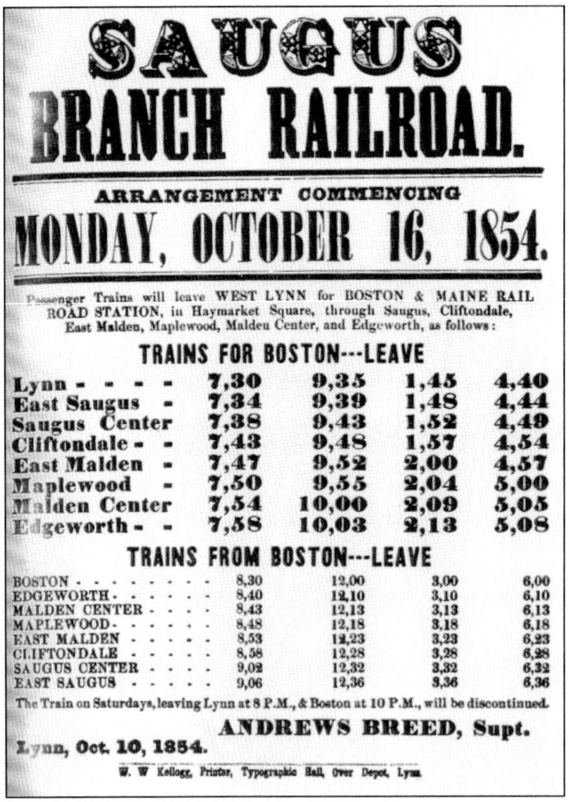

SAUGUS
BRANCH RAILROAD.

ARRANGEMENT COMMENCING
MONDAY, OCTOBER 16, 1854.

Passenger Trains will leave WEST LYNN for BOSTON & MAINE RAIL ROAD STATION, in Haymarket Square, through Saugus, Cliftondale, East Malden, Maplewood, Malden Center, and Edgeworth, as follows:

TRAINS FOR BOSTON---LEAVE

Lynn - - - -	7,30	9,35	1,45	4,40
East Saugus -	7,34	9,39	1,48	4,44
Saugus Center	7,38	9,43	1,52	4,49
Cliftondale - -	7,43	9,48	1,57	4,54
East Malden -	7,47	9,52	2,00	4,57
Maplewood -	7,50	9,55	2,04	5,00
Malden Center	7,54	10,00	2,09	5,05
Edgeworth - -	7,58	10,03	2,13	5,08

TRAINS FROM BOSTON---LEAVE

BOSTON - - - - - - - -	8,30	12,00	3,00	6,00
EDGEWORTH - - - - - -	8,40	12,10	3,10	6,10
MALDEN CENTER - - - -	8,43	12,13	3,13	6,13
MAPLEWOOD - - - - - -	8,48	12,18	3,18	6,18
EAST MALDEN - - - - -	8,53	12,23	3,23	6,23
CLIFTONDALE - - - - -	8,58	12,28	3,28	6,28
SAUGUS CENTER - - - -	9,02	12,32	3,32	6,32
EAST SAUGUS - - - - -	9,06	12,36	3,36	6,36

The Train on Saturdays, leaving Lynn at 8 P.M., & Boston at 10 P.M., will be discontinued.

ANDREWS BREED, Supt.

Lynn, Oct. 10, 1854.

W. W Kellogg, Printer, Typographic Hall, Over Depot, Lynn

SAUGUS BRANCH RAILROAD ADVERTISEMENT. In 1848, the Massachusetts legislature had chartered the Saugus Branch Railroad Company connecting with the main road of the Boston & Maine. The entire project was in reality nothing but an attempt on the part of the Boston & Maine to tap some of the Eastern Railroad's Lynn business. In 1853, the Saugus Branch was opened for travel with four trains each way daily.

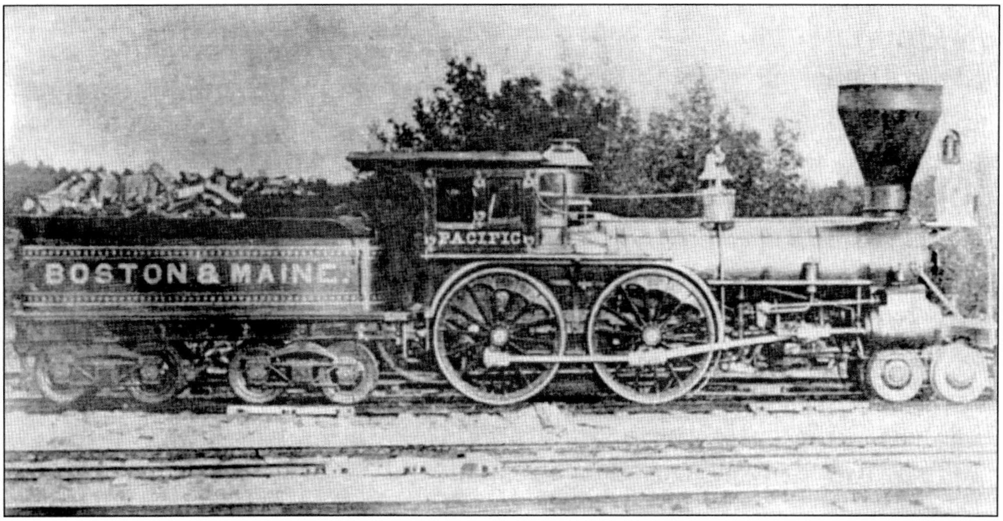

THE WOOD-BURNING LOCOMOTIVE "PACIFIC," 1857. Early locomotives burned coal, or anthracite, but wood soon became widely used. The production of live embers and sparks from wood burners proved to be a constant hazard and increased the number of compensation payments. James F. Baldwin observed, "The locomotives burn pine wood, & the sparks, from the velocity of the cars, fall upon, round, & into the cars so as to endanger the cloths. Great patches are already burned in the lining and curtains of the cars. A bag of biscuits on the top of one car took fire, & the man thru it off to prevent the car from taking fire. I hope you will avoid this in your railroad. You must burn coke or Lehigh coal, and I would provide for it in the outset, for I want your road and travelling to be perfect from the first start."

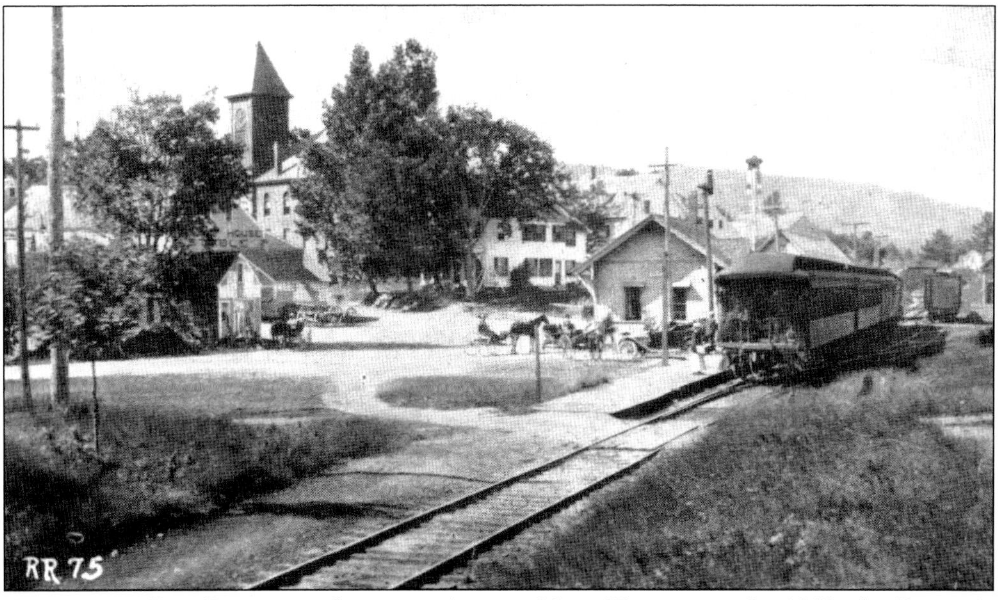

THE ALTON BAY RAILROAD STATION, ALTON, NEW HAMPSHIRE. In 1863, the Dover & Winnipiseogee Railroad was taken under control by a business contract for a term of 50 years. In 1871, the joint lease of the Portland, Saco & Portsmouth was terminated by the Eastern Company, and the Boston & Maine secured a charter and extended its line from South Berwick, Maine, to Portland, completing the extension in 1873.

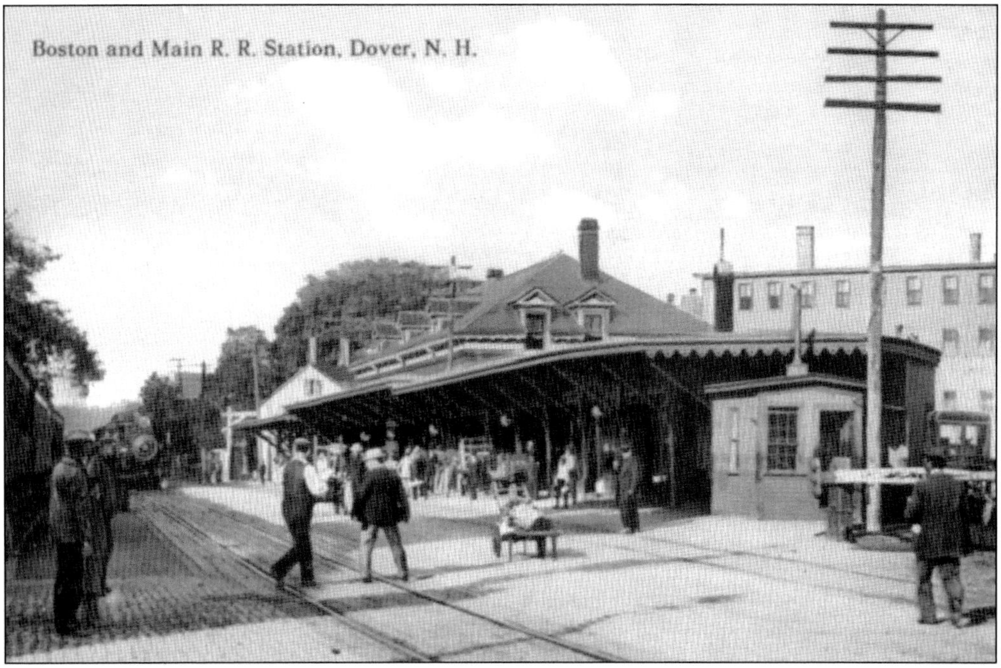

THE BOSTON & MAINE RAILROAD STATION, DOVER, NEW HAMPSHIRE. This popular passenger station was located on the main line between Lawrence, Massachusetts, and Portland, Maine.

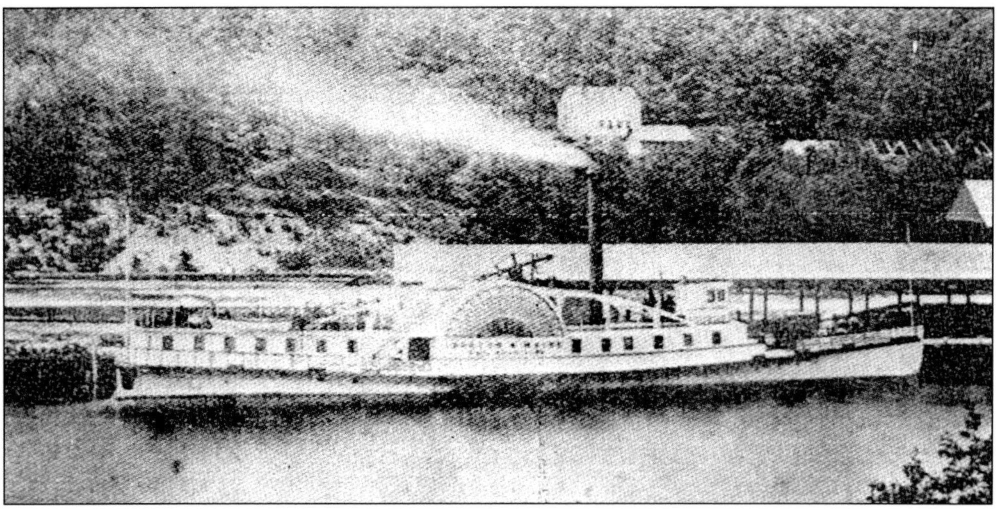

THE SIDE-WHEELER *DOVER*, LAKE WINNIPESAUKEE, LATER THE *CHOCORUA*. Built in 1852, this steamer was owned and operated by the Cocheco Railroad in competition to the *Lady of the Lake* for a number of years until the launching of the side-wheeler *Mount Washington*. Through its connection with the Winnipiseogee Railroad, the Boston & Maine became interested in steamboats running on Lake Winnipiseogee (Winnipesaukee). The *Dover*, a wooden side-wheeler, was later rebuilt and called the *Chocorua*. Weighing some 400 tons, it measured about 170 feet long with a beam of 32 feet.

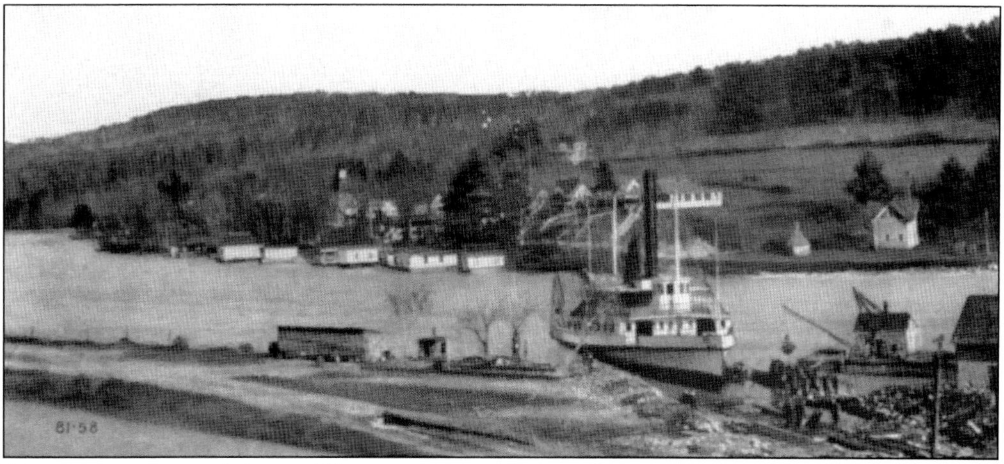

THE SIDE-WHEELER *MOUNT WASHINGTON* AT ALTON BAY, 1872. In 1871, Captain Wiggins of the *Chocorua* persuaded the Boston & Maine to build a vessel that would compete with the Boston, Concord & Montreal's *Lady of the Lake* and take the lake business from them. In 1872, a new steam side-wheeler was launched at Alton Bay and was christened the *Mount Washington*, which was longer and faster than its predecessors. Some consider the *Mount Washington* to be the most beautiful side-wheeler ever built in the United States. A single piston with a diameter of 42 inches and a stroke of 10 feet drove this vessel at more than 20 mph. The piston drove the side wheels by means of a walking beam on top of the superstructure. Picture the tall smokestack belching smoke into the sky, and the walking beam compressing up and down to turn the giant paddle wheels. Its horsepower was 450 at "full ahead" speed, more than enough to leave the *Lady of the Lake* in its wake.

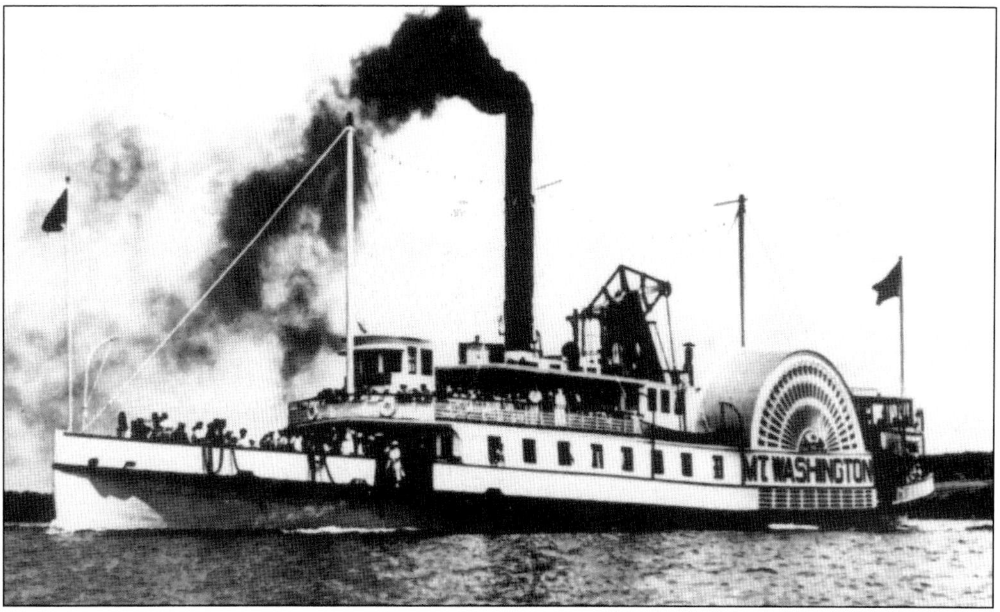

THE *MOUNT WASHINGTON* APPROACHING THE WEIRS DOCK, THE WEIRS, NEW HAMPSHIRE. From 1872 until the early 1920s, the *Mount Washington* ruled the waters of Lake Winnipesaukee. In an effort to capitalize on the expanding and prosperous tourist trade, the Boston & Maine began to compete with—and lease or buy out—many of the smaller independent lines throughout Maine and New Hampshire.

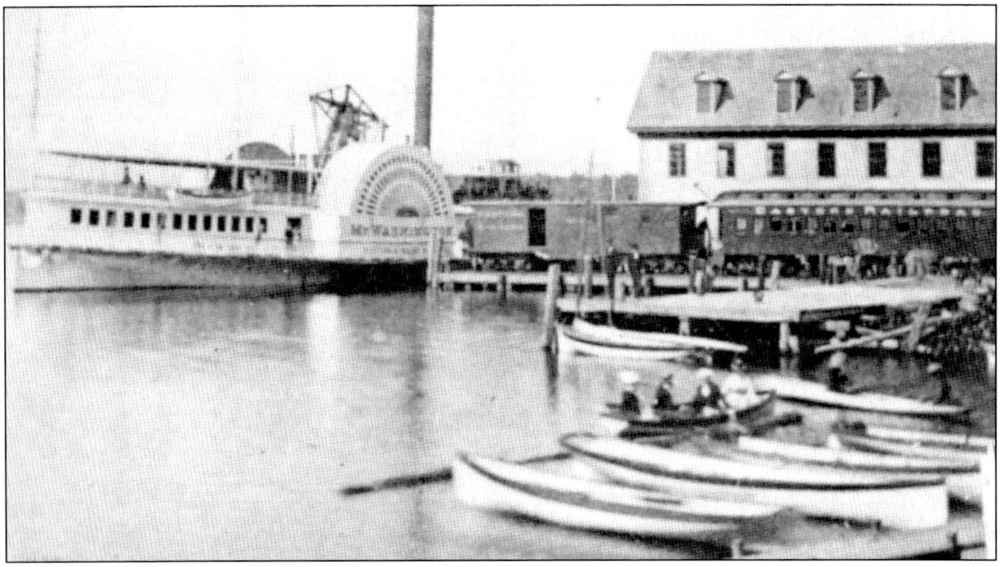

THE MOUNT WASHINGTON AT A WOLFEBORO DOCK, C. 1880. Shown here is the Eastern Railroad train connecting with the Boston & Maine steamer *Mount Washington.* The large Boston & Maine building in the rear burned in 1899. In 1884, in accordance with general legislation obtained for the purpose, the Boston & Maine leased the entire Eastern Railroad system. In 1886, the Boston & Maine system (in addition to the main line) consisted of Great Falls, Dover & Winnipiseogee (Somersworth Branch), West Amsbury Branch, Eastern, Portsmouth, Great Falls and Conway, Wolfeboro, Portsmouth & Dover, Worcester, and Nashua & Portland. The total mileage in New Hampshire was 227.54 miles.

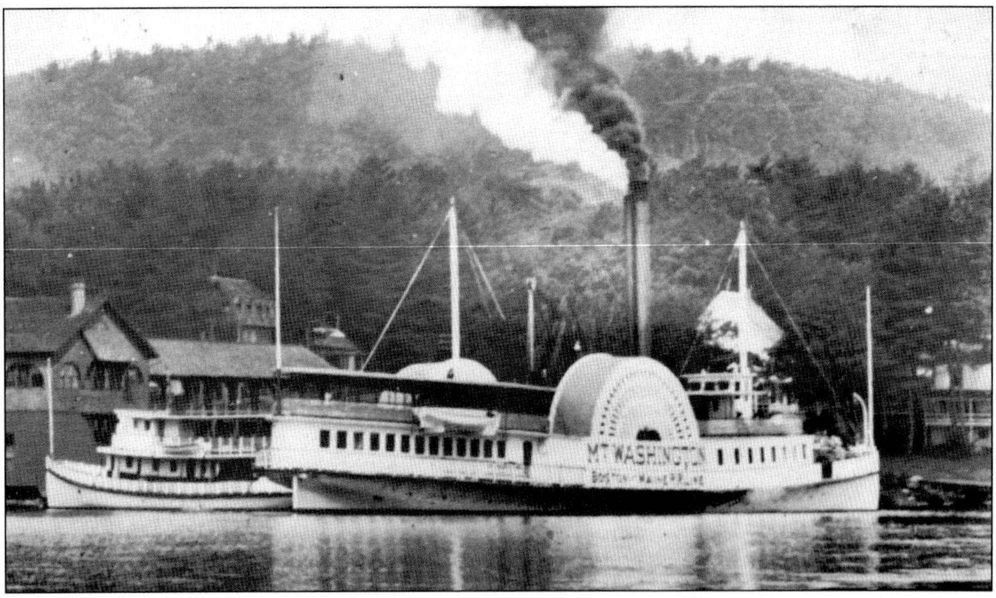

THE MOUNT WASHINGTON AND THE STEAMER CYCLONE AT THE WEIRS DOCK AND RAILROAD STATION, LATE 1800S. The Weirs was a popular resort station in the Lakes Region where Boston & Maine passengers would disembark the train and board the side-wheeler *Mount Washington*. From there, they could sail across Lake Winnipesaukee and make connections via the Concord Coach for the White Mountains.

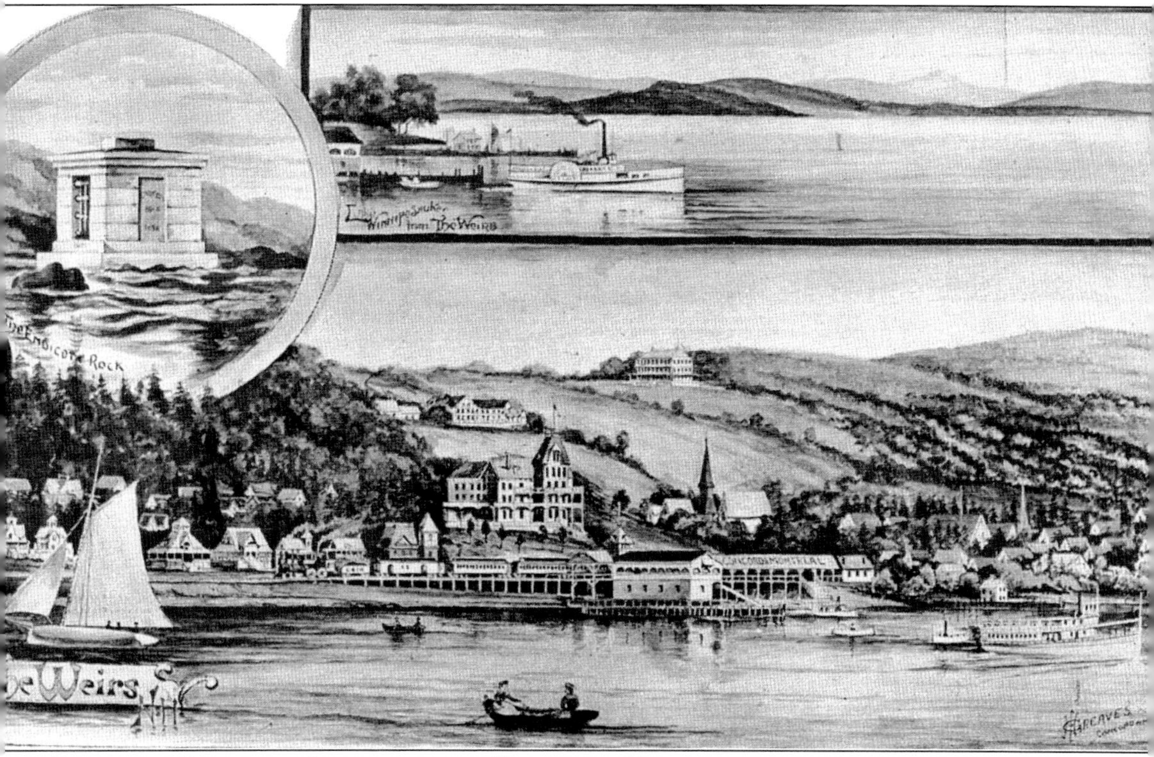

THE WEIRS RAILROAD STATION WITH A PASSENGER TRAIN AT THE STATION, LATE 1800S. On the west shore of Lake Winnipesaukee were the Veterans Association campground, the Methodists' campground, the grand old Hotel Weirs, and many steamboats that plied the waves of the large body of water. In the center of this picture is the steam train making its regular stop from Boston to Montreal. In the corner is Endicott Rock Monument, which indicated the northern boundary of the Massachusetts Bay Colony in 1652.

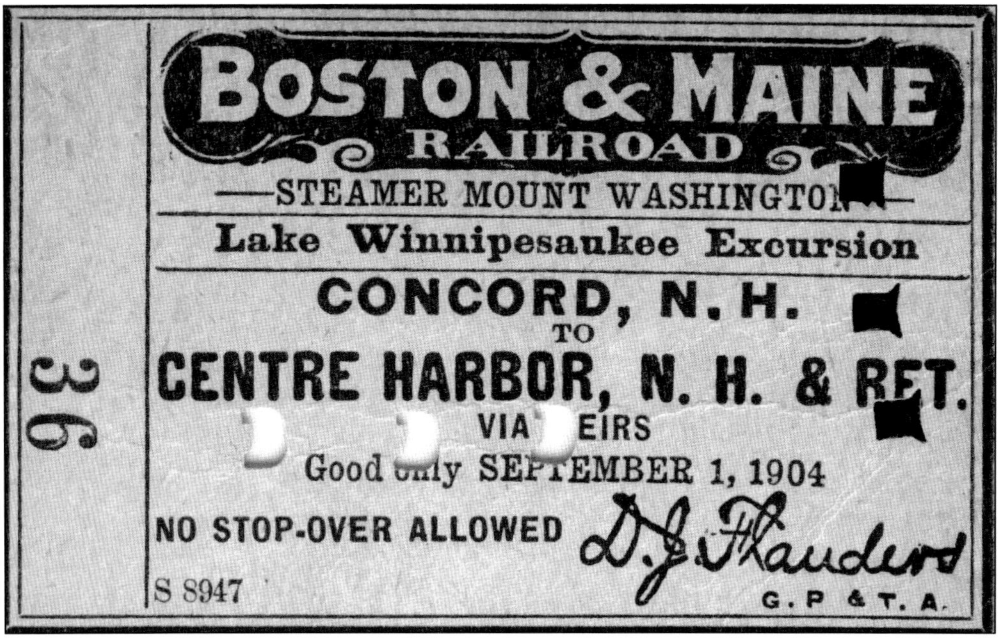

A BOSTON & MAINE RAILROAD TICKET NO. 36. This round-trip railroad ticket was used by a passenger to connect with the steamer *Mount Washington* at the Weirs. It was good for passage between Concord, New Hampshire, and Centre Harbor with "no stop-over allowed."

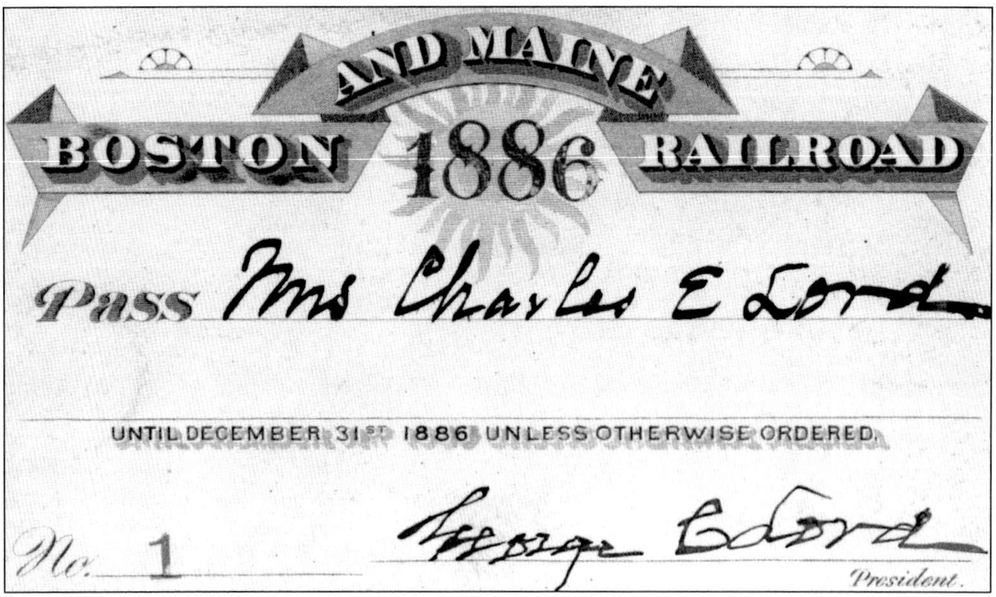

BOSTON & MAINE RAILROAD PASS NO. 1, 1886. This pass was issued to Mrs. Charles E. Lord by Pres. George E. Lord.

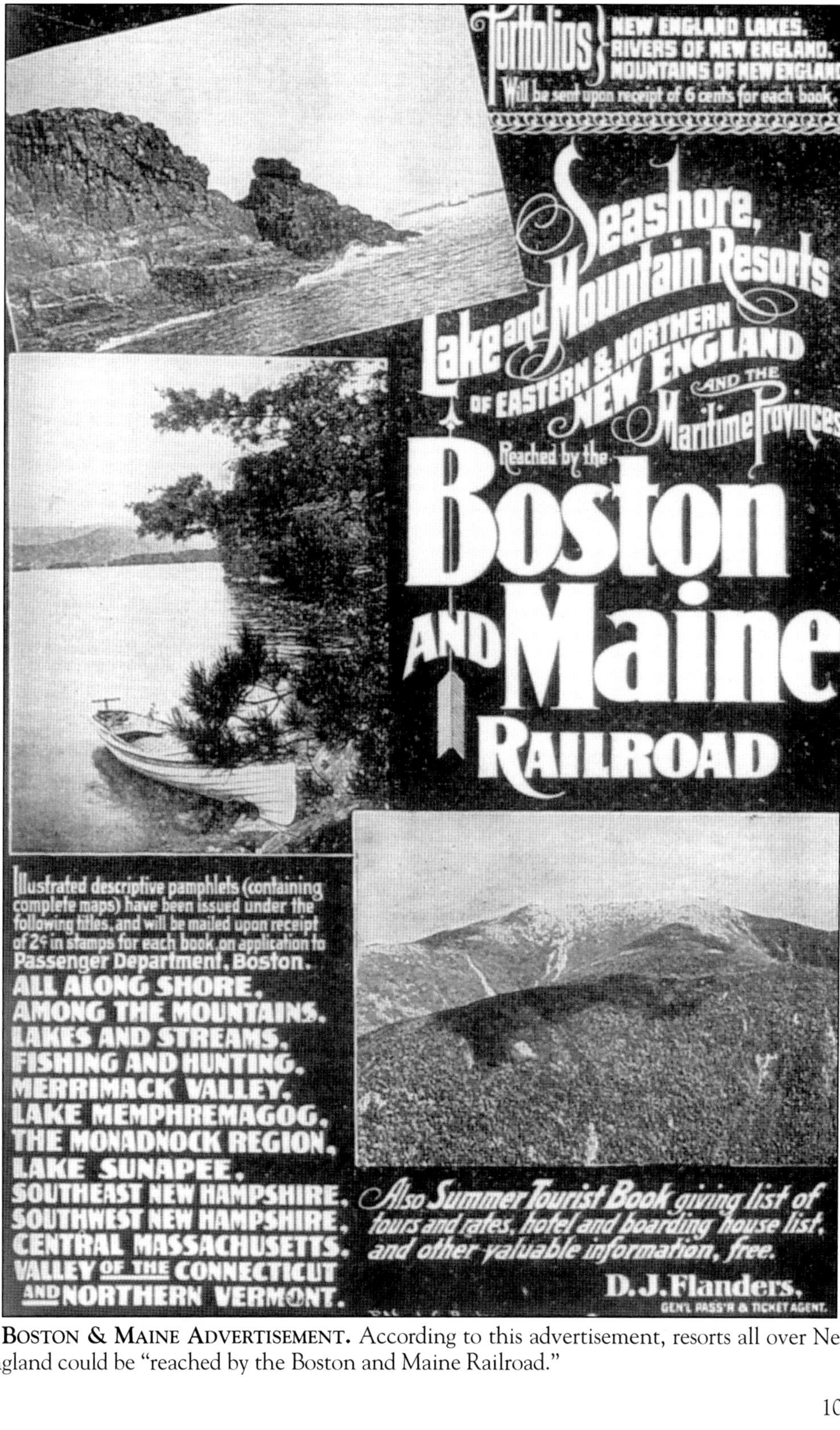

A Boston & Maine Advertisement. According to this advertisement, resorts all over New England could be "reached by the Boston and Maine Railroad."

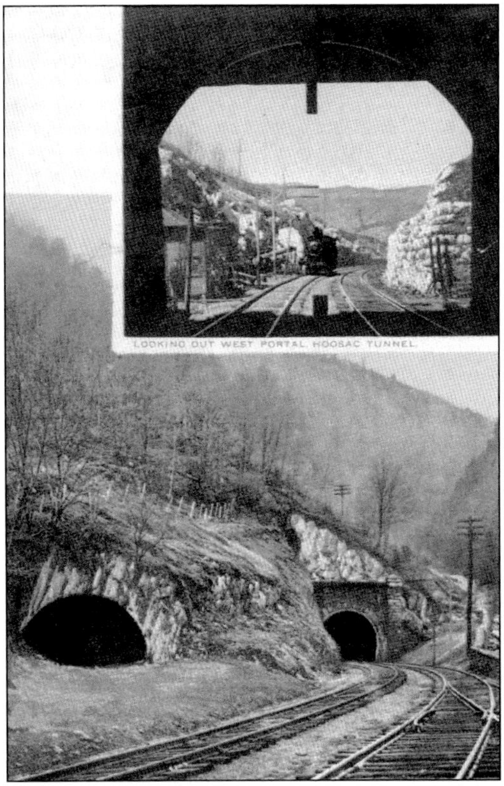

THE HOOSAC TUNNEL, EAST PORTAL. The Hoosac Tunnel, begun in 1851, was completed in 1875. With a total length of 4.5 miles, it was considered the longest tunnel in the United States. The amount of rock excavated totaled 1.9 million tons. Men employed during construction numbered to about 900 with 192 lives lost. The tunnel was 24 feet high and 20 feet wide. In 1911, it was equipped with electrical service.

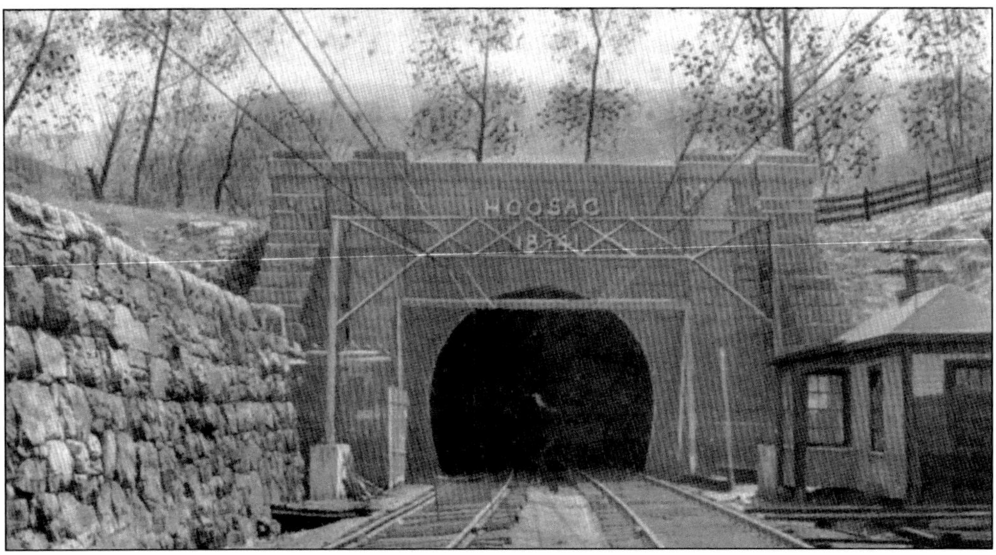

THE HOOSAC TUNNEL, WEST PORTAL, NORTH ADAMS, MASSACHUSETTS. A company of men took up the Hoosac Tunnel project, which had been agitated periodically since 1825, when it was proposed to bore through the range for a canal. The Troy and Greenfield Railroad was the corporate name of the tunnel road. From 1848 until 1887, there was hardly a session of the Massachusetts legislature that did not consider some action affecting this road. In 1862, the stockholders of the Troy and Greenfield finally gave up the task and abandoned the road; the Commonwealth of Massachusetts, which had advanced $778,695, then took possession.

THE HOOSAC TUNNEL UNDER CONSTRUCTION, 1871. By 1862, the road had almost been constructed from Greenfield to the east entrance of the tunnel and from the west side of the Hoosac mountain to the Vermont state line. In 1868, the Shanlys, a Montreal contracting firm, undertook the completion of the tunnel. On November 27, 1873, daylight penetrated through the hole in the mountain. About a year later, the tunnel was ready for trains. A state manager, Jeremiah Prescott, formerly superintendent of the Eastern Railroad, was assigned "to maintain the property and handle its movement of trains namely: the Fitchburg, Troy and Boston, Boston, Hoosac Tunnel and Western." The New Haven and Northampton Railroads paid tolls sufficient to meet expenses, interest, and the debt of nearly $14 million that the state had incurred.

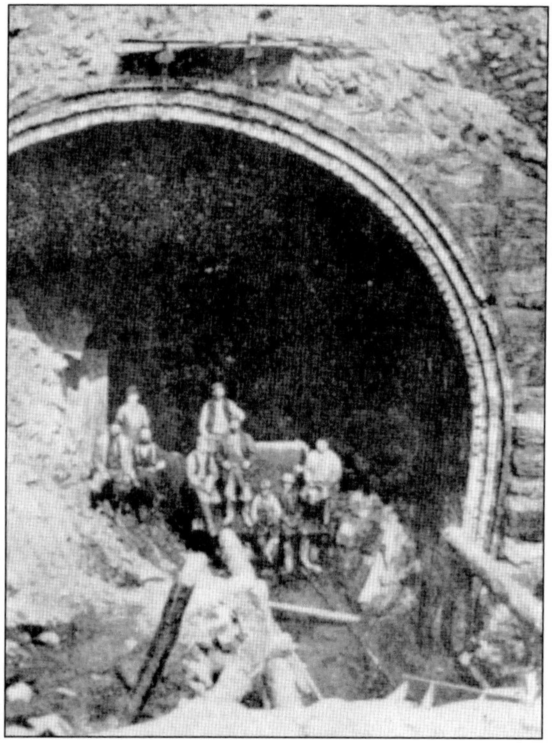

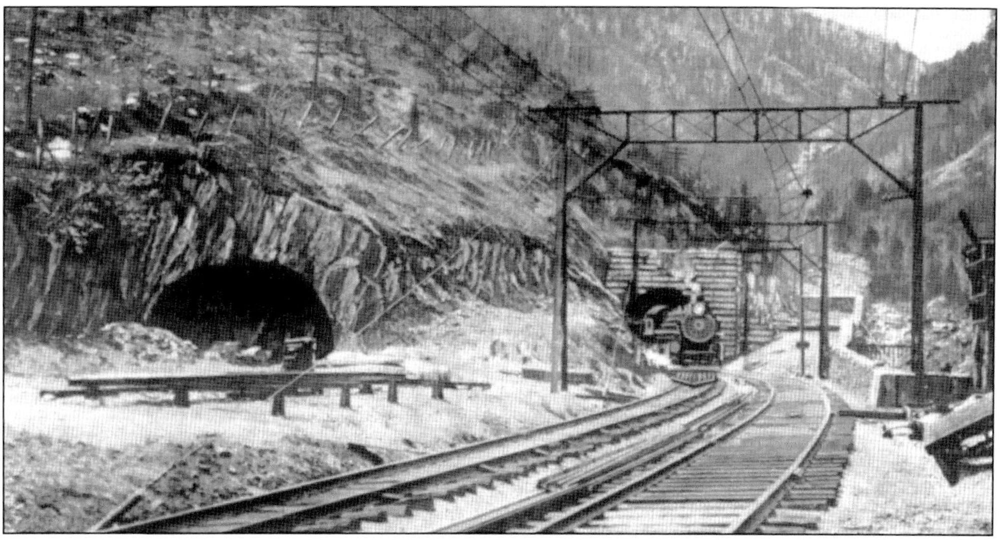

THE HOOSAC TUNNEL, EAST PORTAL WITH AN ABANDONED TUNNEL ON THE LEFT. The Commonwealth of Massachusetts ran the road in this fashion until 1887, when the Fitchburg Railroad absorbed the Boston, Hoosac Tunnel and Western (whose road ran from Rotterdam Junction, New York, to the Vermont and Massachusetts line), the Troy and Boston, and the state-owned Troy and Greenfield. The Fitchburg Railroad, in payment for the Troy and Greenfield and the Hoosac Tunnel, issued to the state $5 million in 50-year bonds and $5 million in common stock, which later paid no dividends. In 1900, upon the lease of the Fitchburg, the Boston & Maine bought the common stock from the state, and the Commonwealth of Massachusetts then became only a bondholder.

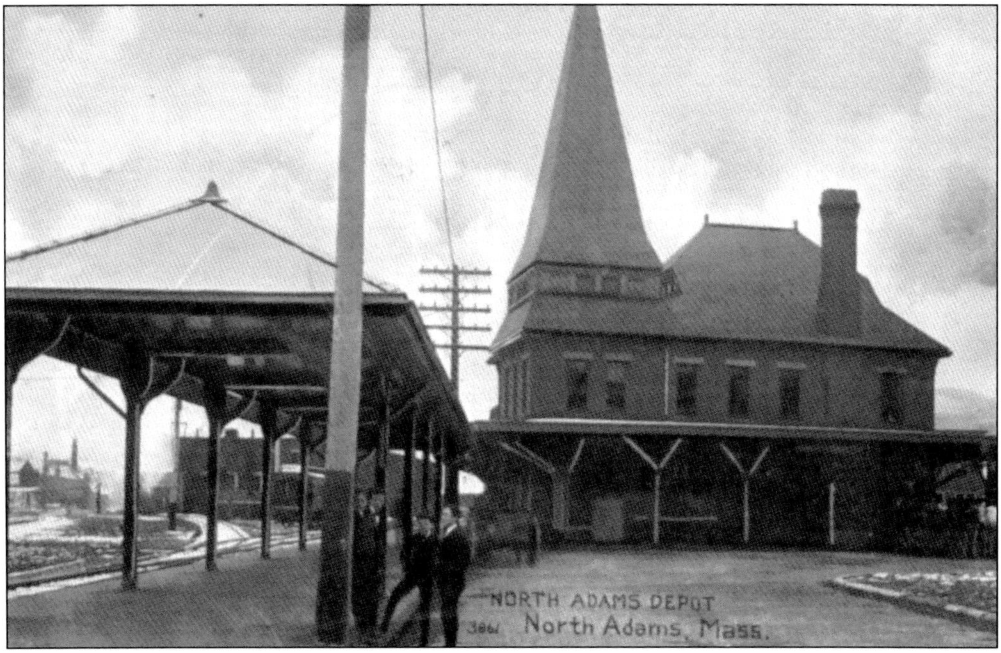

THE NORTH ADAMS DEPOT, NORTH ADAMS, MASSACHUSETTS. The building of the Hoosac Tunnel, with its northern terminal at North Adams, was a very important element in the development of the town. This was an active terminal for both the Boston & Maine and the Boston & Albany lines.

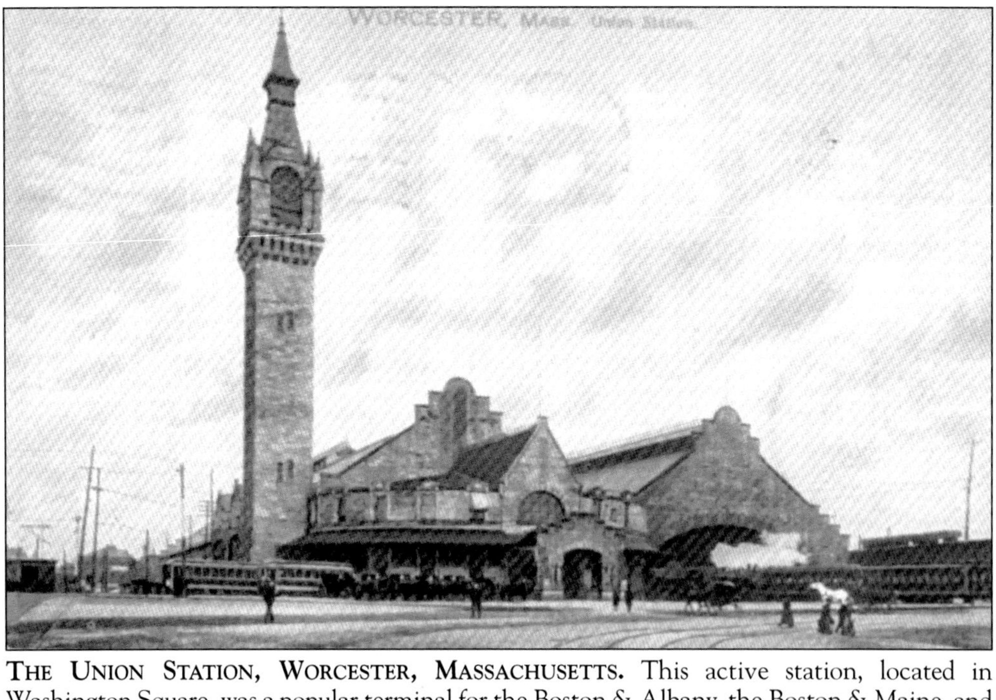

THE UNION STATION, WORCESTER, MASSACHUSETTS. This active station, located in Washington Square, was a popular terminal for the Boston & Albany, the Boston & Maine, and the New York, New Haven & Hartford lines.

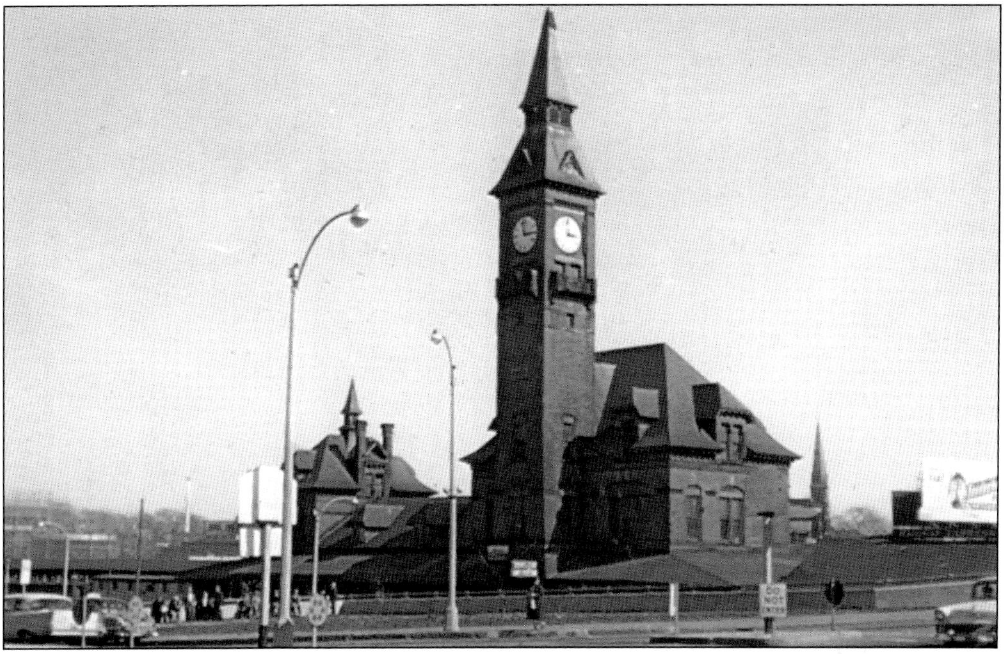

THE DEPOT SQUARE AND MAIN STREET, FITCHBURG, MASSACHUSETTS. Union Station was located at 264 Main Street in Fitchburg, Massachusetts. The opening of the Boston and Fitchburg Railroad in 1845 insured rapid transportation facilities and attracted new industries to the community. In the late 1800s, this terminal was used daily by both the Boston & Maine and the New York, New Haven & Hartford lines.

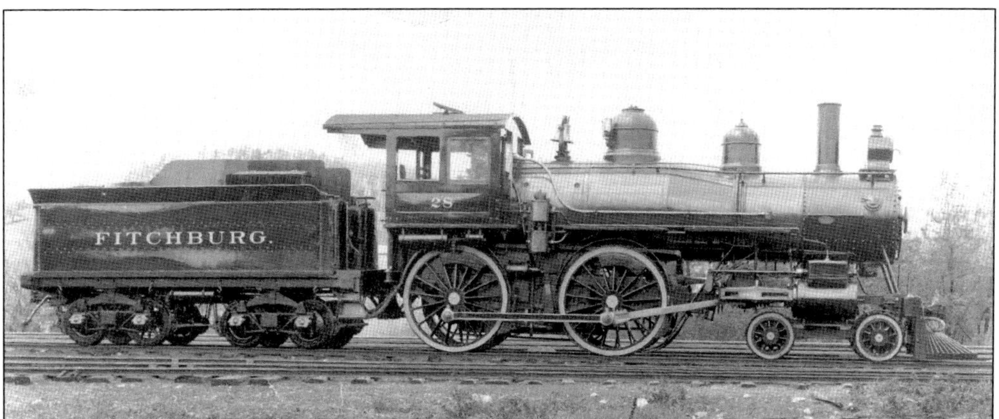

FITCHBURG RAILROAD NO. 28 (4-4-0). This locomotive was build by the Manchester Locomotive Works in 1895 with shop No. 1701. It had 18- by 24-inch cylinders. In 1899, it was redesignated No. 162. In 1900, the Boston & Maine named it No. 962 and in 1911 renumbered it as No. 940.

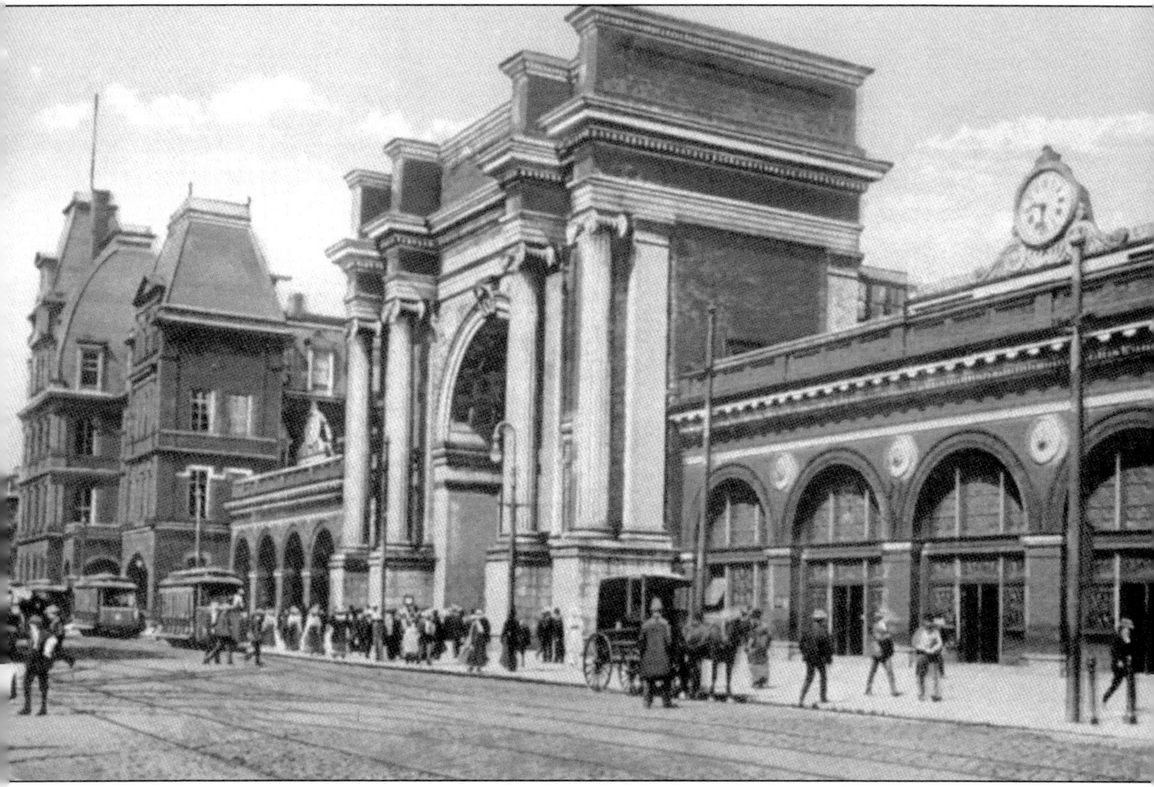

THE NORTH UNION STATION, BOSTON, MASSACHUSETTS, 1894. The North Union Station was jointly operated by the Boston & Maine and the Fitchburg Railroads. In 1895, the Concord & Montreal system was leased. In June 1900, the Boston & Maine leased the entire Fitchburg system for 99 years. Before this time, the Boston & Maine also acquired 51 percent of the capital stock of the Maine Central Railroad. This brought under Boston & Maine's control 1,122 of the 1,174 miles of railroad in New Hampshire. This fact had a profound influence on the future development of the Causeway Street area of Boston.

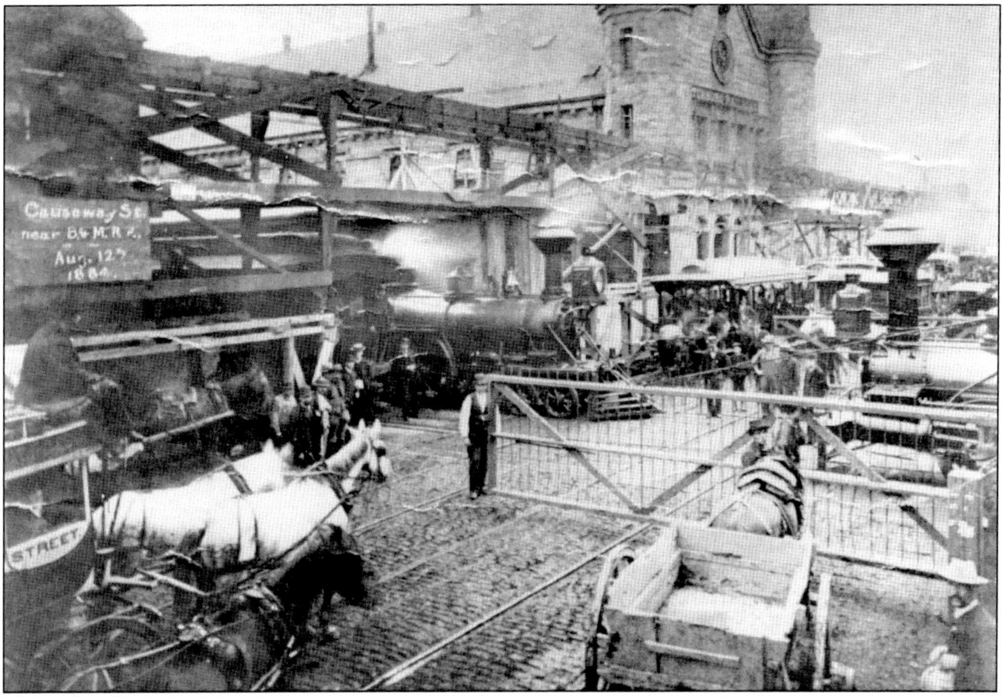

THE NORTH STATION, BOSTON, MASSACHUSETTS, 1894. Shown is a traffic jam on Causeway Street. The Boston & Maine crossed this street to reach its station at Haymarket Square. The next step was to consolidate all the railroads into one station. The Eastern Railroad's depot on Causeway Street and the Boston & Maine's own Haymarket Square depot were eliminated. On February 13, 1893, ground was broken for the new North Station. Tracks were being laid on May 15, 1893. The Fitchburg's "Castle," as seen at the eastern end of Causeway Street, continued to house the company offices until 1927, when it was dismantled to make way for the next station, to be known as the North Station terminal, and Boston Garden facility.

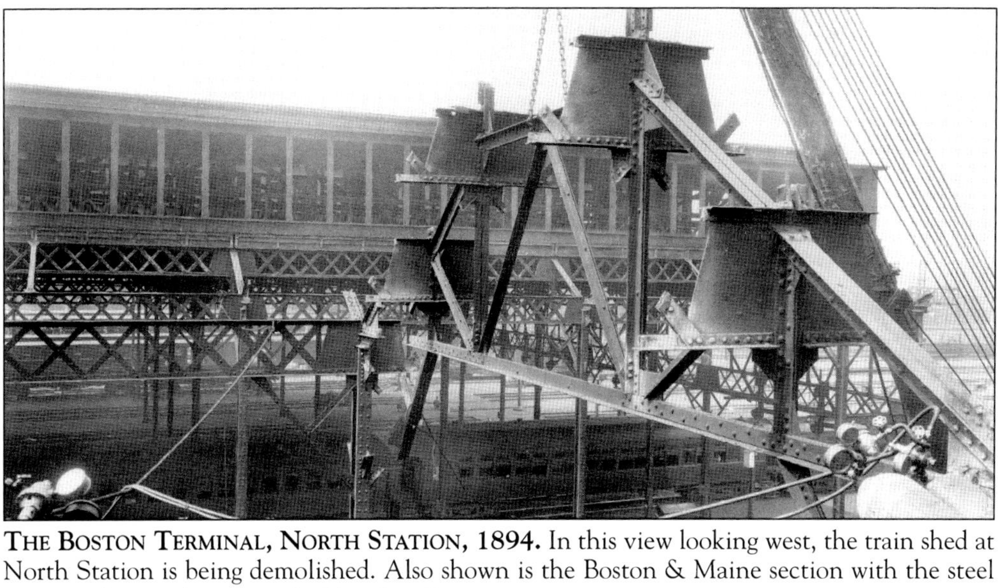

THE BOSTON TERMINAL, NORTH STATION, 1894. In this view looking west, the train shed at North Station is being demolished. Also shown is the Boston & Maine section with the steel construction work over tracks Nos. 1 to 5.

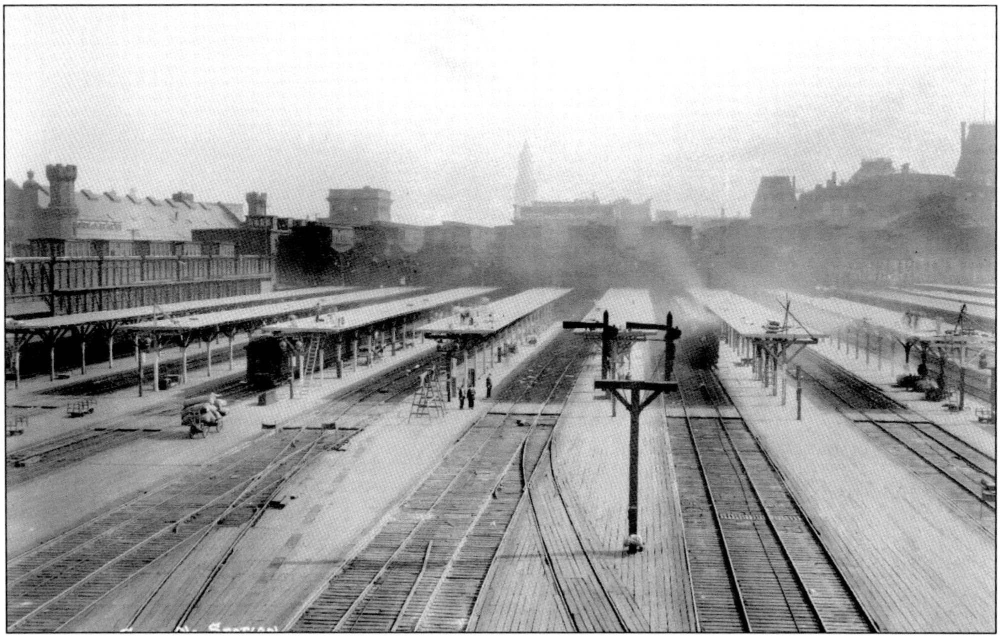

THE BOSTON TERMINAL, NORTH STATION, 1894. This view shows the Boston & Maine and Boston & Lowell sections, track Nos. 1 to 20. The Boston & Lowell's third station remained intact at this location until 1927, when the old building was replaced by the new North Station and the Boston Garden complex. The Boston & Lowell had the honor of being the last to go into memory.

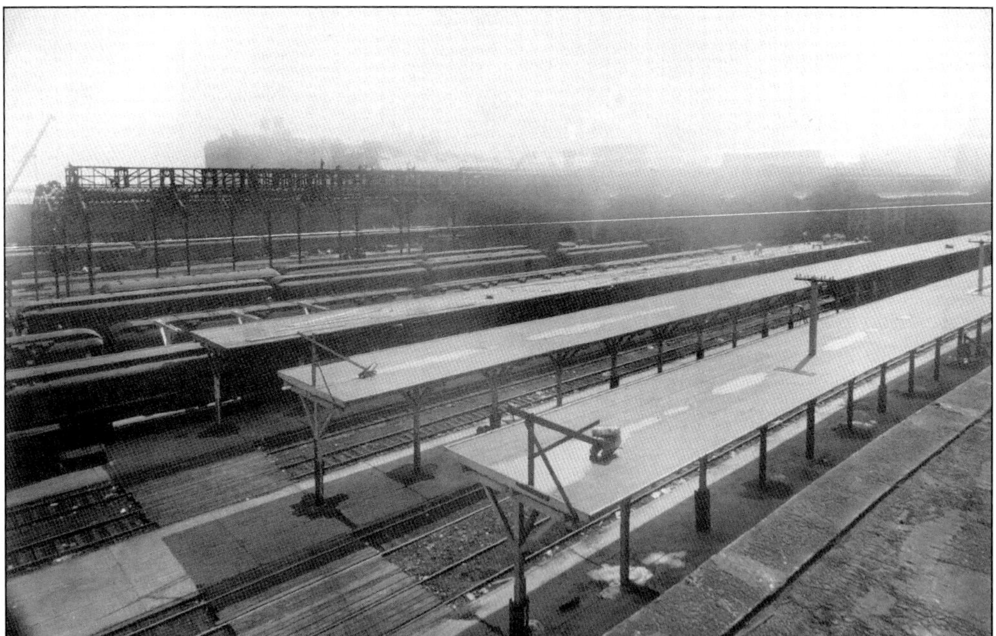

THE BOSTON TERMINAL, NORTH STATION, 1894. This bird's-eye view of the terminal looks east. In the background is the steelwork being done in the new North Station and Boston Garden complex on September 8, 1920.

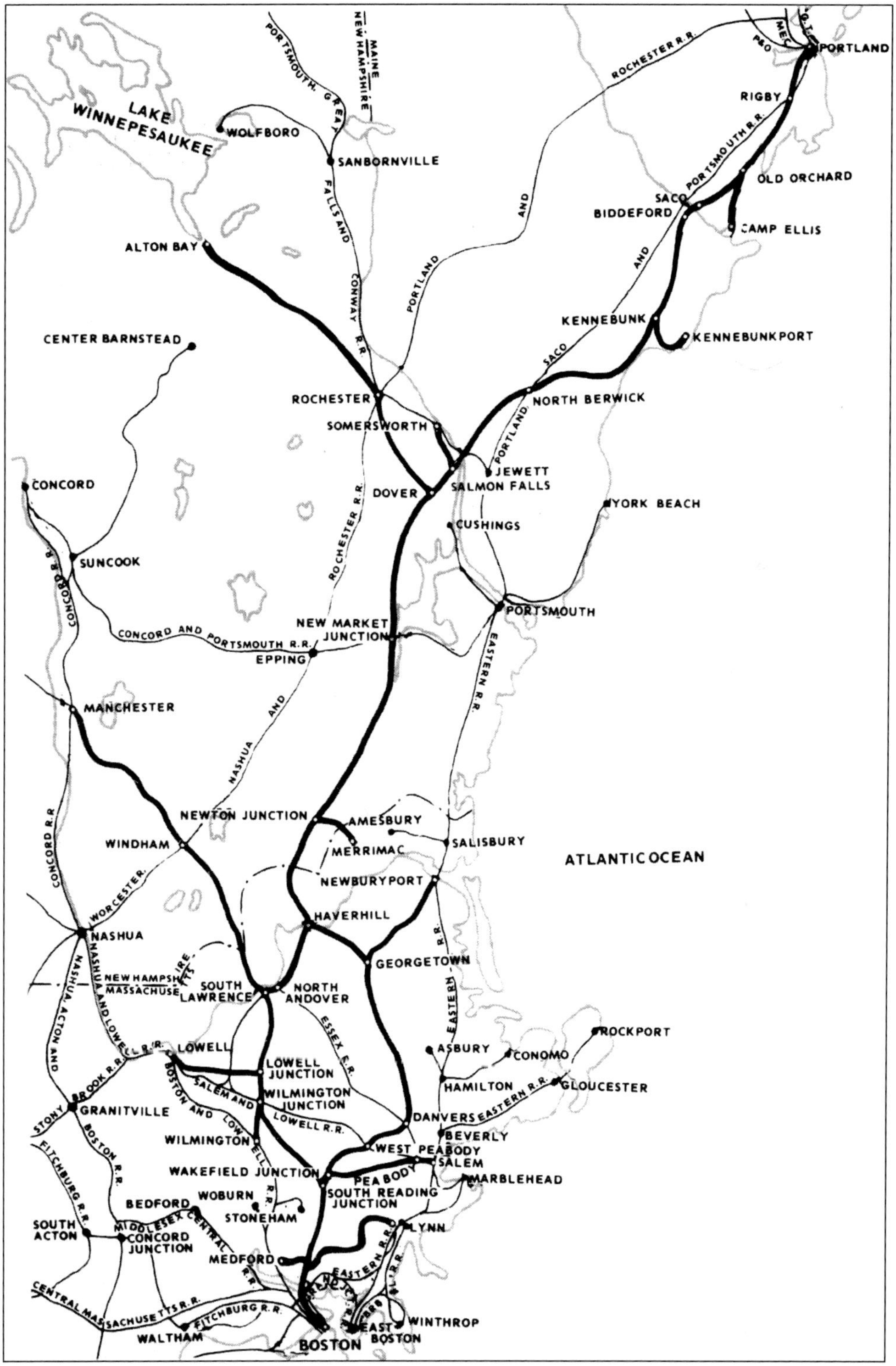

A Map of the Boston & Maine and Connections. Shown are the major routes of the Boston & Maine and its principal connections in Massachusetts, New Hampshire, and Maine.

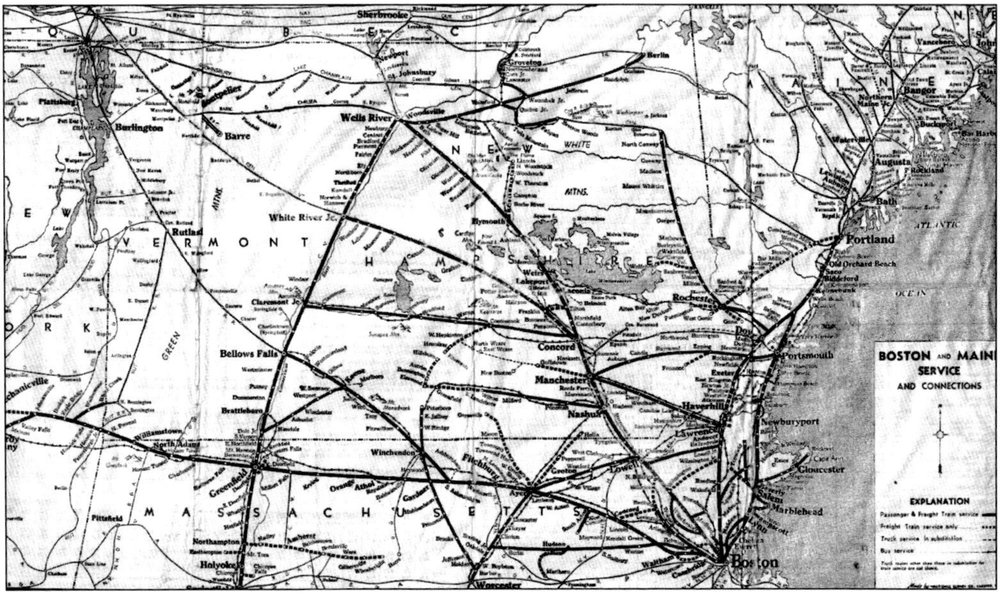

A MAP OF THE BOSTON & MAINE SYSTEM IN NEW ENGLAND. With the acquisition of the Boston & Lowell system, the Boston & Maine fell heir to the political contest in New Hampshire, with the Concord & Montreal Railroad as an opponent. Finally, however, the latter succumbed and was leased in 1895 to the Boston & Maine for 99 years.

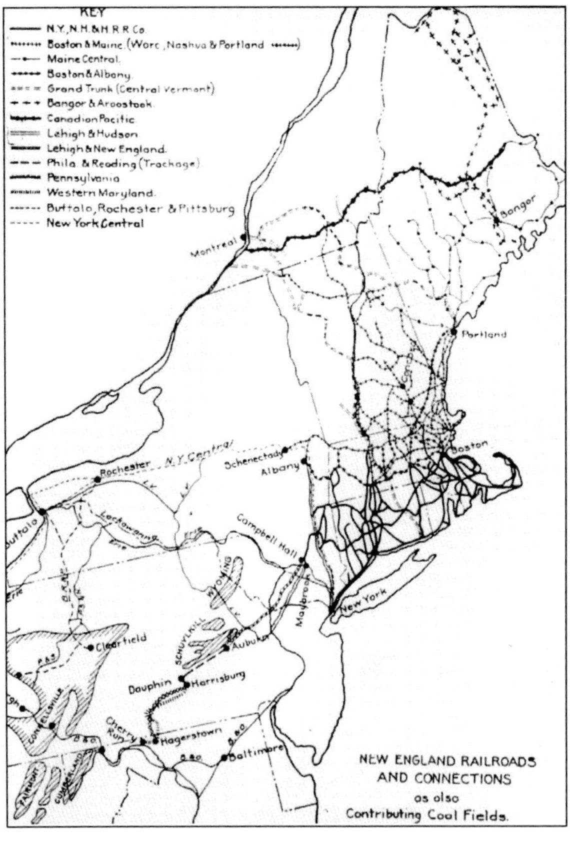

A MAP OF THE NEW ENGLAND RAILROADS, C. 1900. The importance of New England's railroads cannot be overestimated. Its roads and their connections are shown here. Many passengers traveled these routes for a summer's vacation to the grand resorts, and raw materials and finished products came to us over these lines.

Appendix A

TYPE AND CLASS OF BOSTON & MAINE LOCOMOTIVES

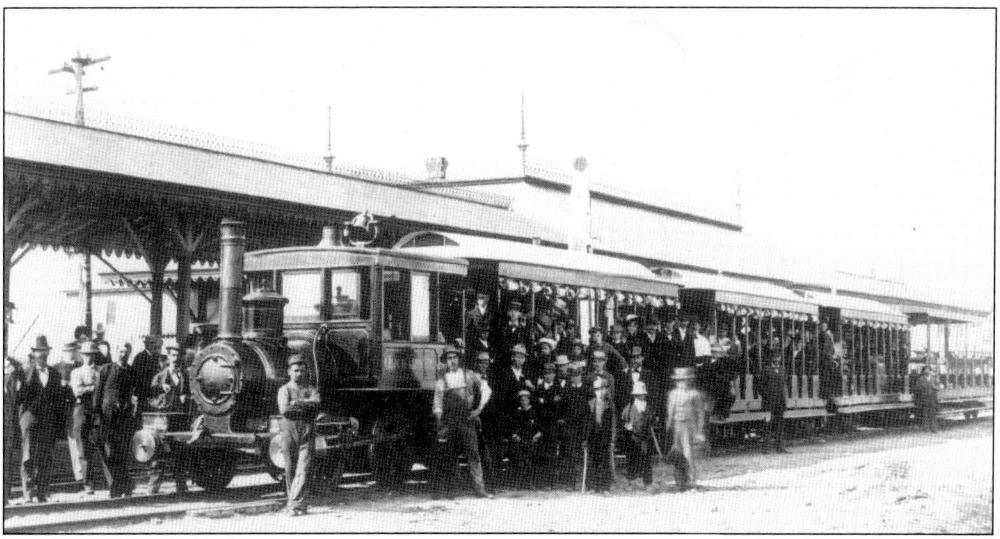

B & M "ORCHARD BEACH" (0-4-0), OLD ORCHARD, MAINE. The early locomotives presented a fascinating variety. In 1851, the New England Association of Railroad Superintendents and the Middlesex Mechanics Association put some engines on view, providing a chance to appraise them for those interested.

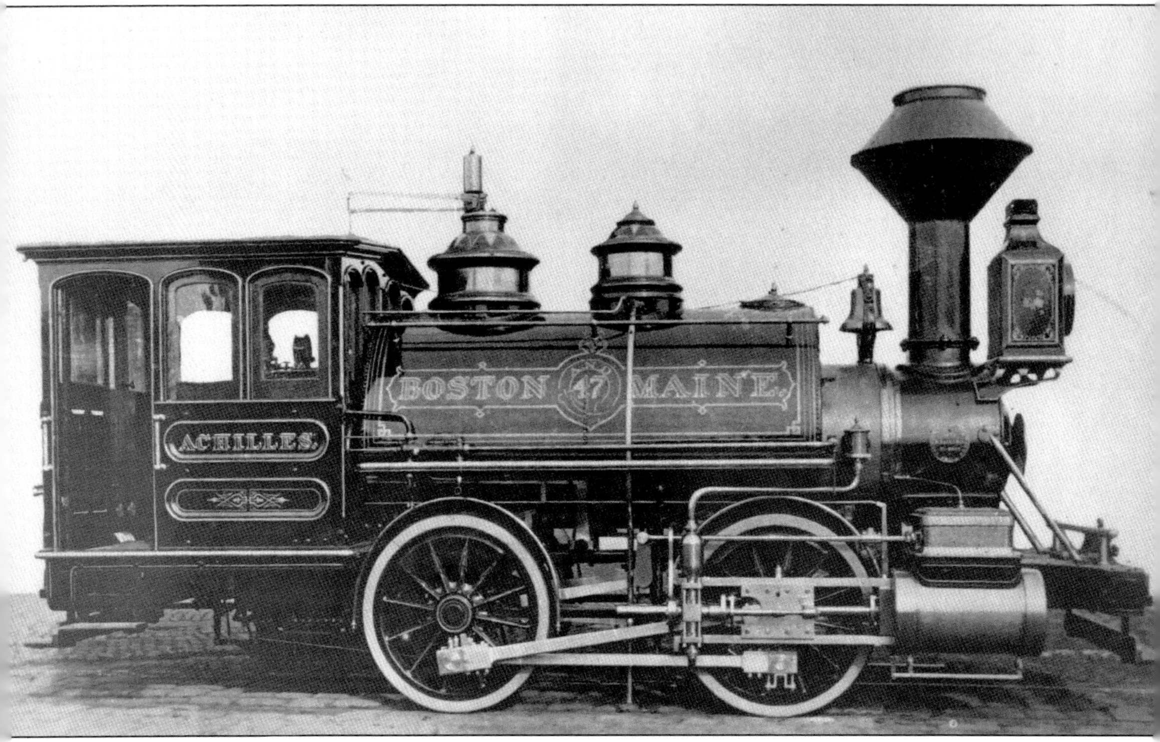

B & M No. 47, "Achilles," (0-4-0). All the early locomotives were named and more or less ornamented. The Boston & Maine was one of the last of the New England railroads to keep up the practice of naming engines.

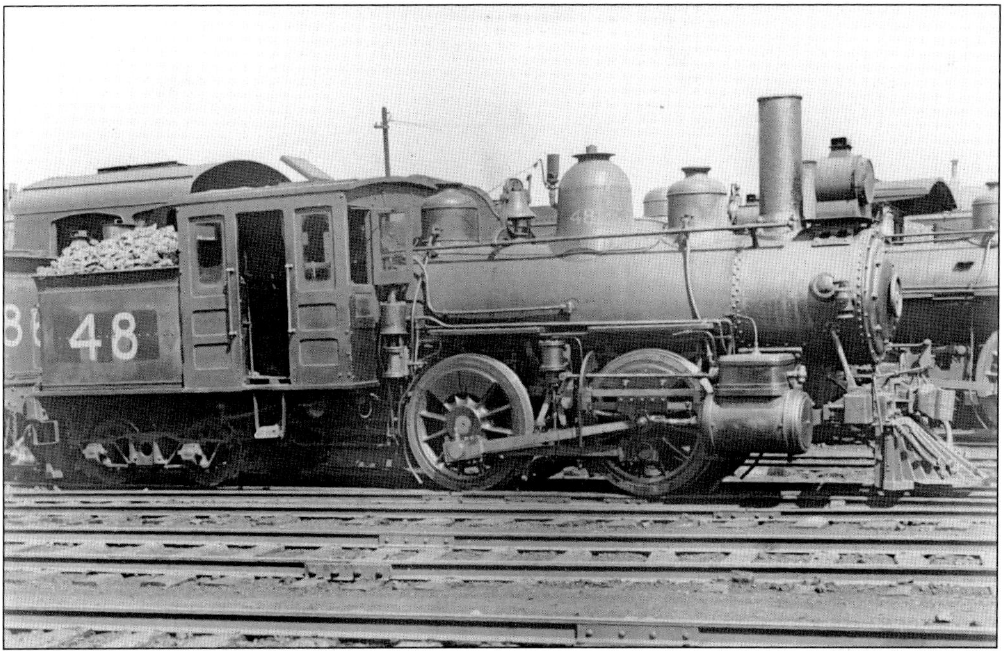

B & M No. 48, "Governor Carver" (0-4-0). The "Governor Carver" was built in Rhode Island in 1891.

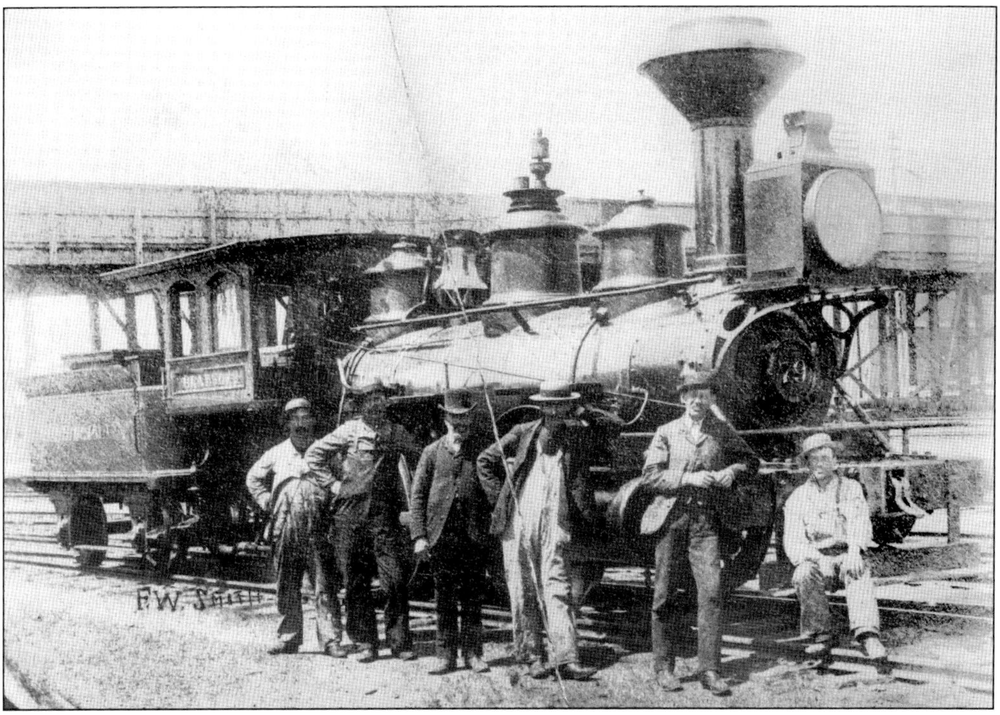

B & M No. 79, "Bradford" (0-4-0). This locomotive was built by the Manchester Locomotive Works in 1879.

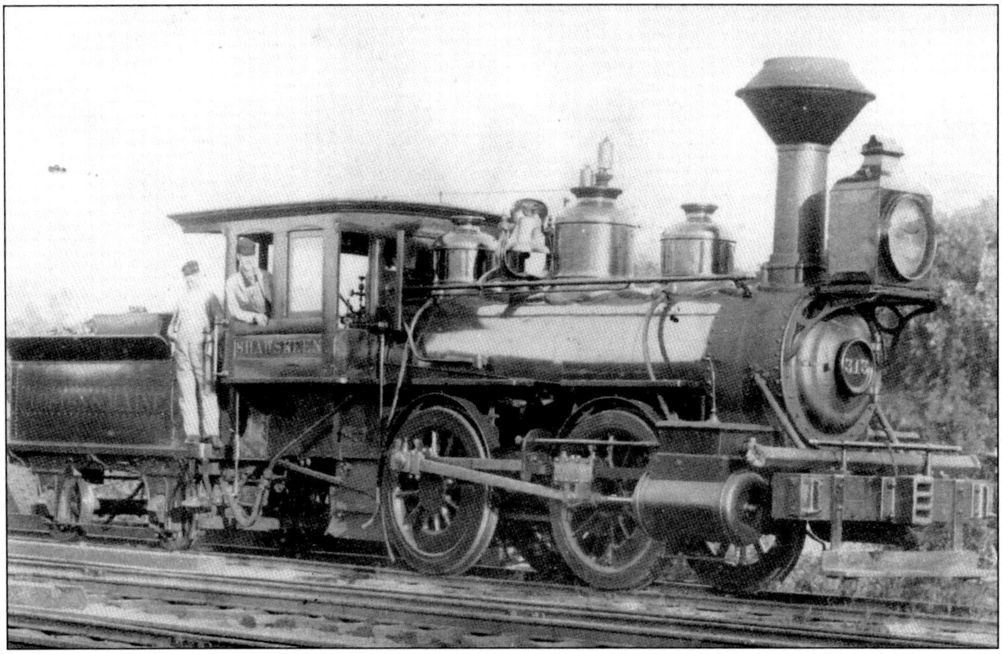

B & M No. 313, "Shawsheen" (0-4-0). The Hinkley Locomotive Works built this engine in 1873.

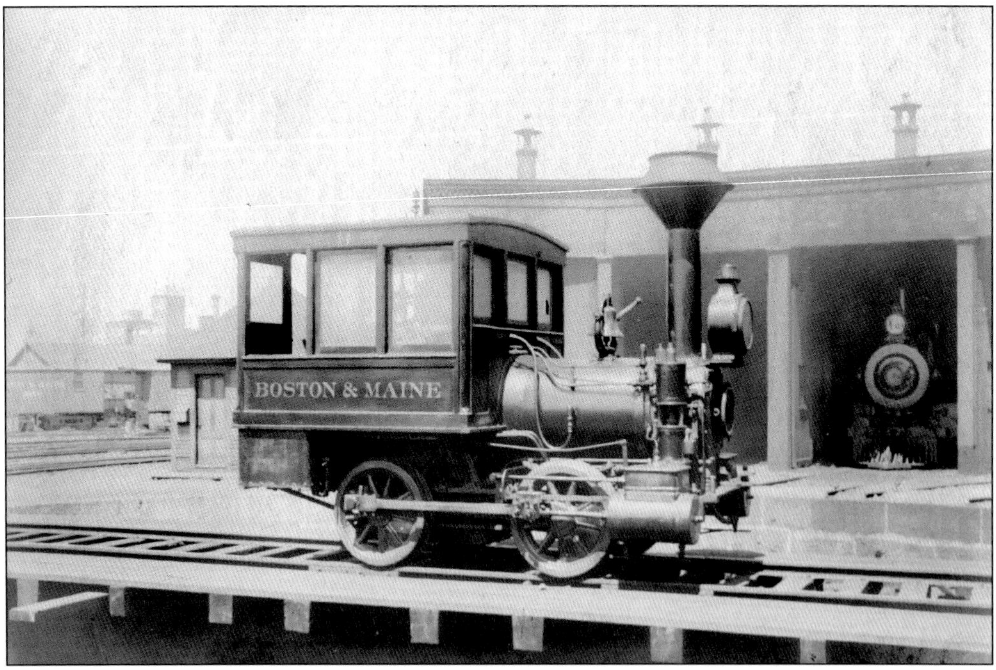

B & M No. 9 (0-4-0). Built by Grant Locomotive Works in 1878, this locomotive had 9- by 14-inch cylinders.

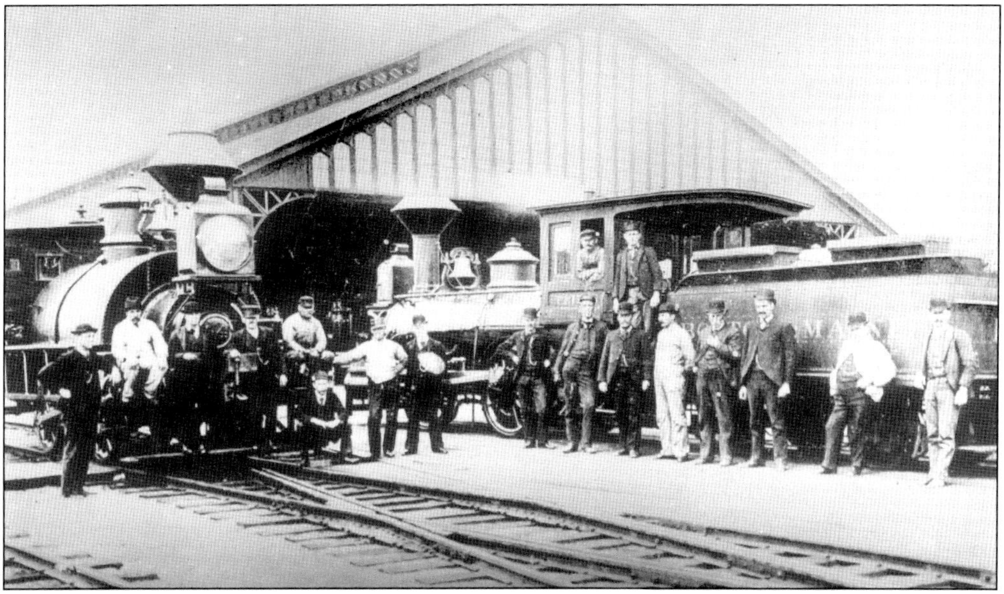

B & M No. 63, "Pride" (0-4-0). B & M No. 63 was built in Concord, New Hampshire, in 1872 with 13- by 20-inch cylinders.

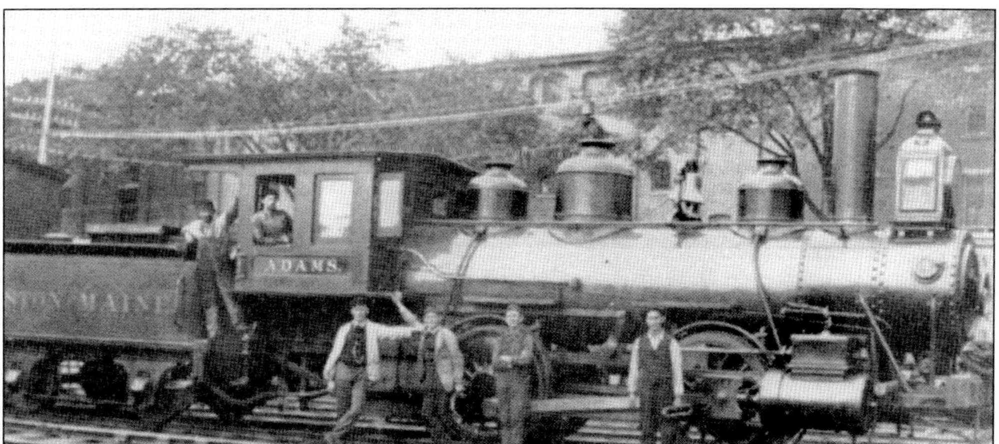

B & M No. 456, "Adams" (0-4-0). Built by the Manchester Locomotive Works in 1890, this engine was renumbered as No. 87 in 1911.

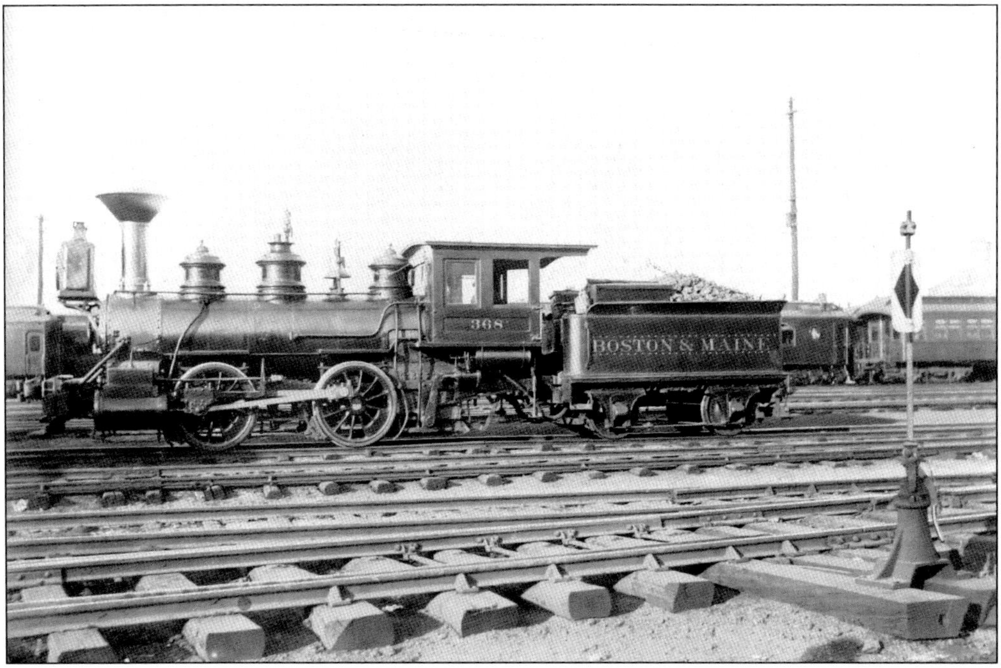

B & M No. 368, (0-4-0). Equipped with 15- by 22-inch cylinders, B & M No. 368 was built by the Hinkley Locomotive Works in 1878.

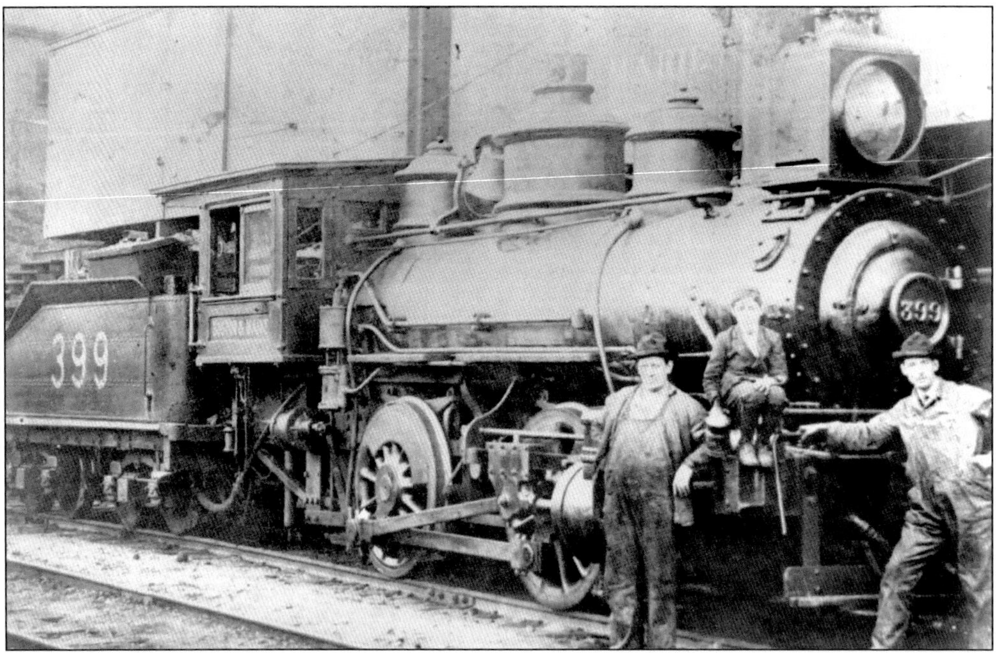

B & M No. 399 (0-4-0). Taken in Lowell, Massachusetts, this picture shows Arthur Huntley, engineer, and Ben Roper, the slim fireman on the far right.

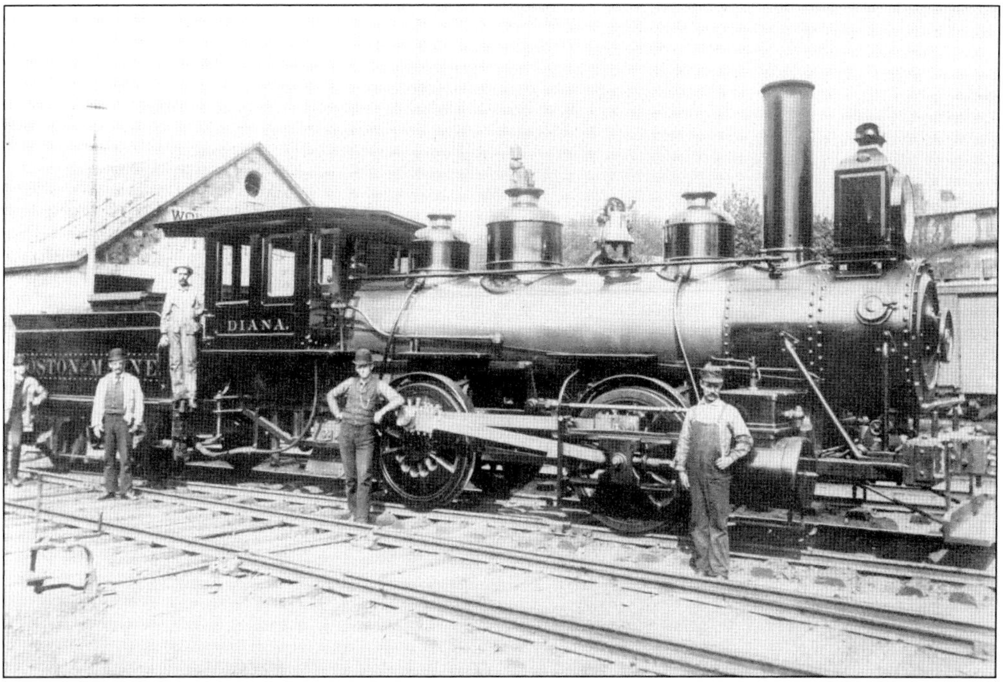

B & M No. 461, "Diana" (0-4-0). The locomotive "Diana," with 16- by 24-inch cylinders, was built by the Manchester Locomotive Works in 1891.

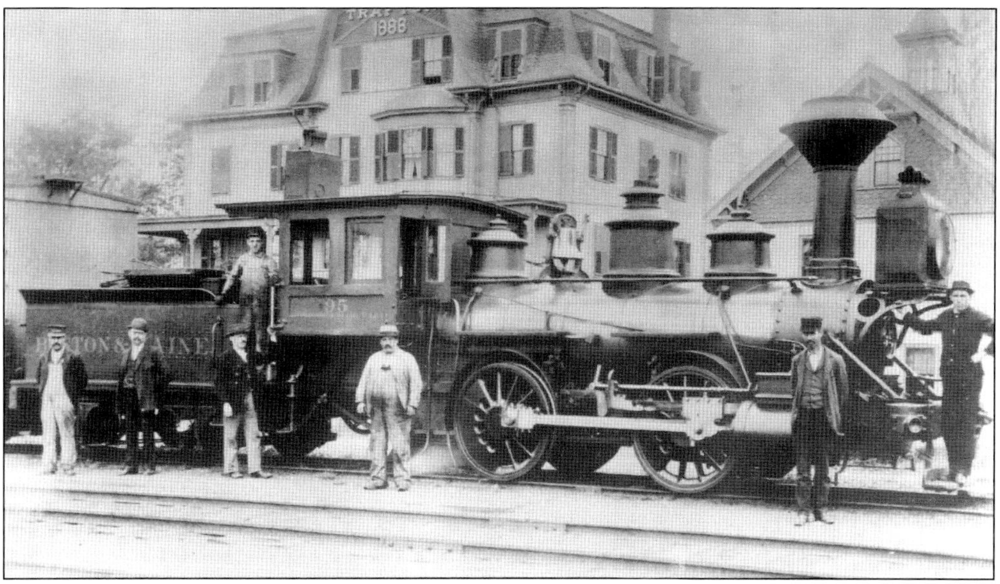

B & M No. 95, "Huron" (0-4-0). The crew members of each Boston & Maine locomotive took a great deal of pride in their engine. The bells and whistles were shined and the oil cups and other parts were kept polished. This work consumed as much as two or three hours of a fireman's work each day.

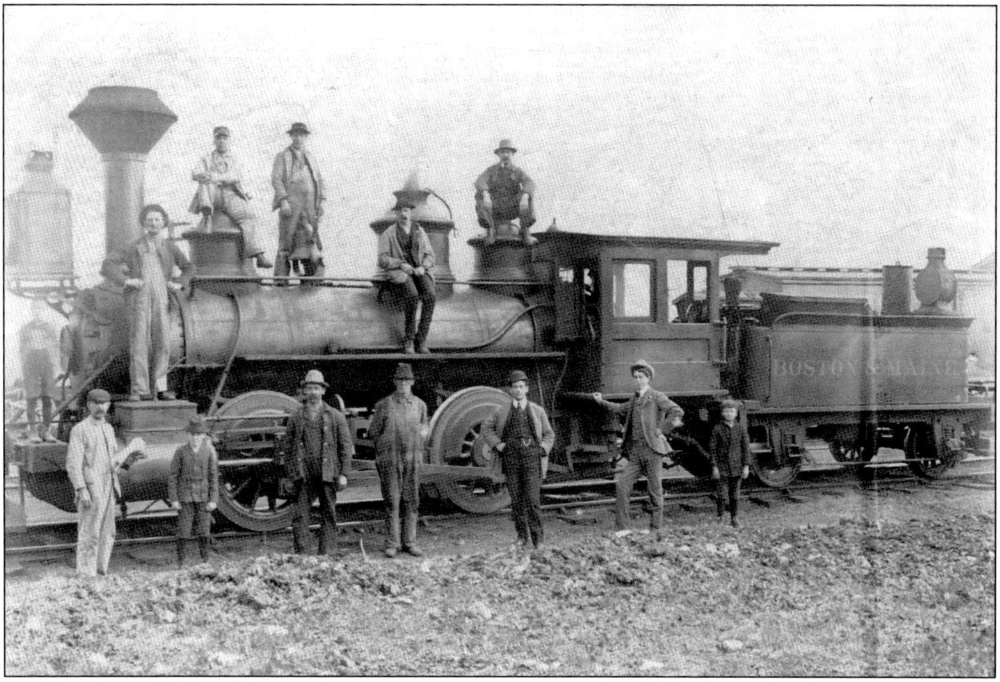

B & M No. 1097 (0-4-0). This engine was built in 1879 for the Troy & Boston Railroad and was designated No. 13. It had 16- by 22-inch cylinders. After the Fitchburg Railroad took control, it became No. 139 in 1895, then No. 342, and No. 603 in 1899. When the Boston & Maine leased the Fitchburg Railroad, it became No. 1097. The engine was retired in 1908.

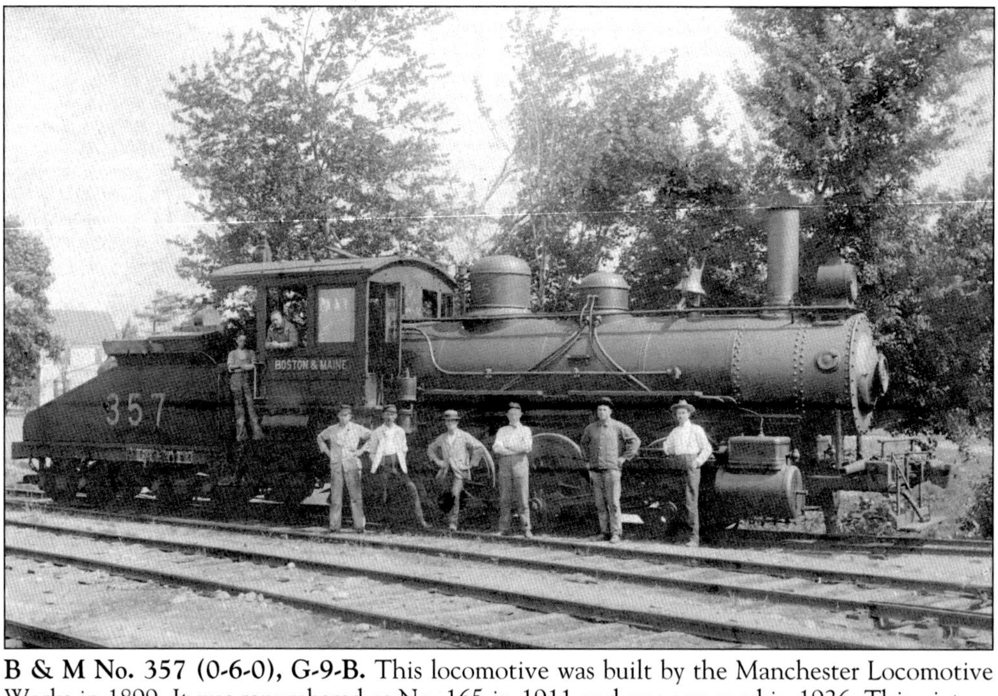

B & M No. 357 (0-6-0), G-9-B. This locomotive was built by the Manchester Locomotive Works in 1899. It was renumbered as No. 165 in 1911 and was scrapped in 1926. This picture was taken in Lowell, Massachusetts, near the Russell Lumber Company.

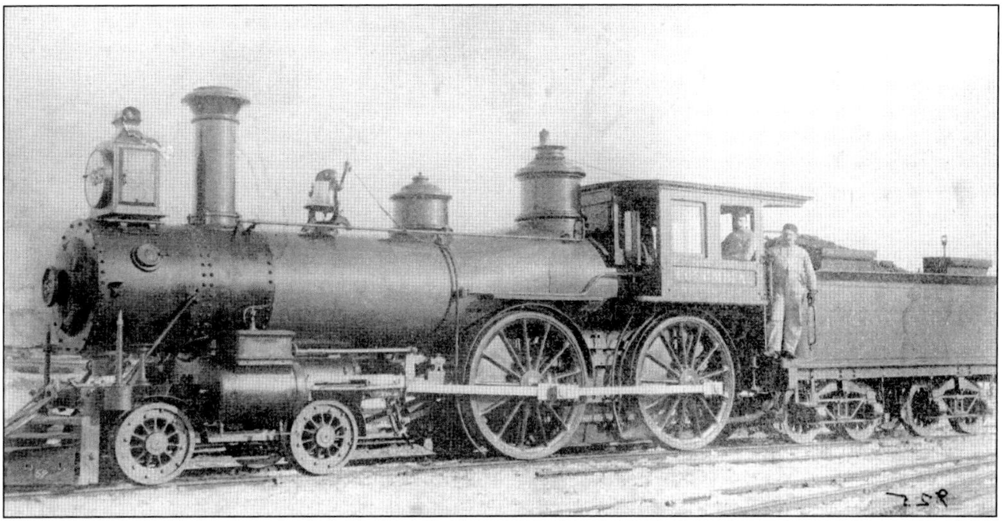

B & M No. 59, "Columbia" (4-4-0). The locomotive "Columbia," built by the Manchester Locomotive Works in 1872, had 17- by 22-inch cylinders. It was rebuilt in 1886.

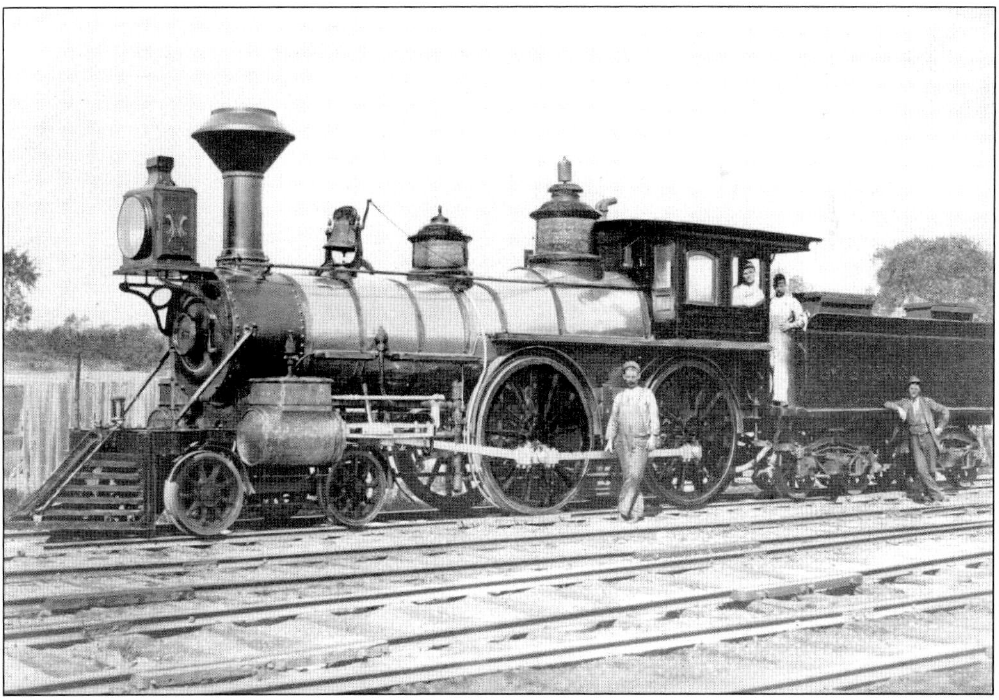

B & M No. 58, "William Merritt" (4-4-0). This locomotive was built in 1872 by the Manchester Locomotive Works. It had 17- by 22-inch cylinders. Rebuilt by the Boston & Maine in 1883, it was redesignated as No. 645 in 1911.

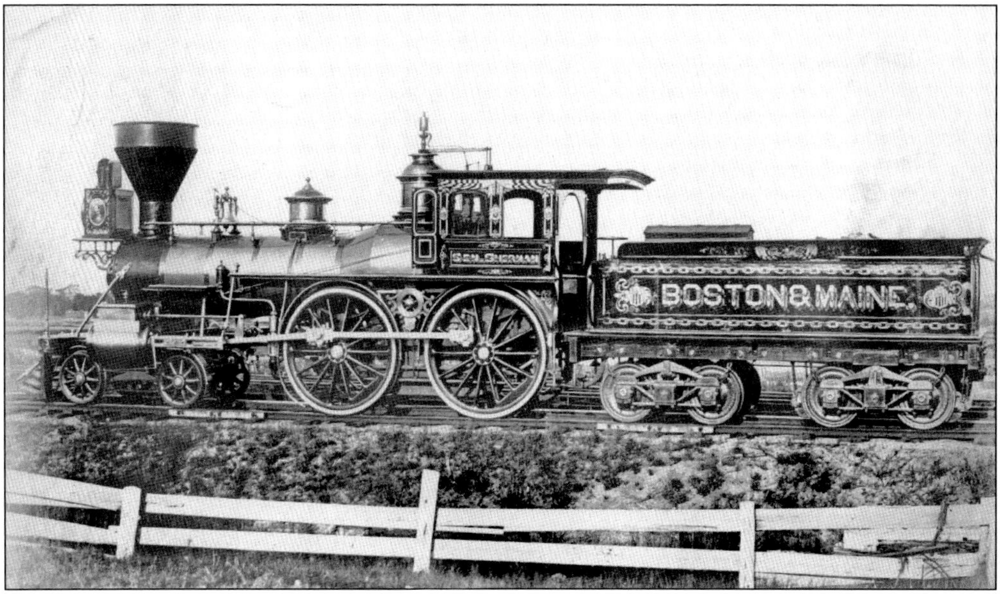

B & M No. 42, "General Sherman" (4-4-0). Built by Hinkley Locomotive Works in 1867, the "General Sherman" had 16- by 24-inch cylinders and was scrapped in 1908.

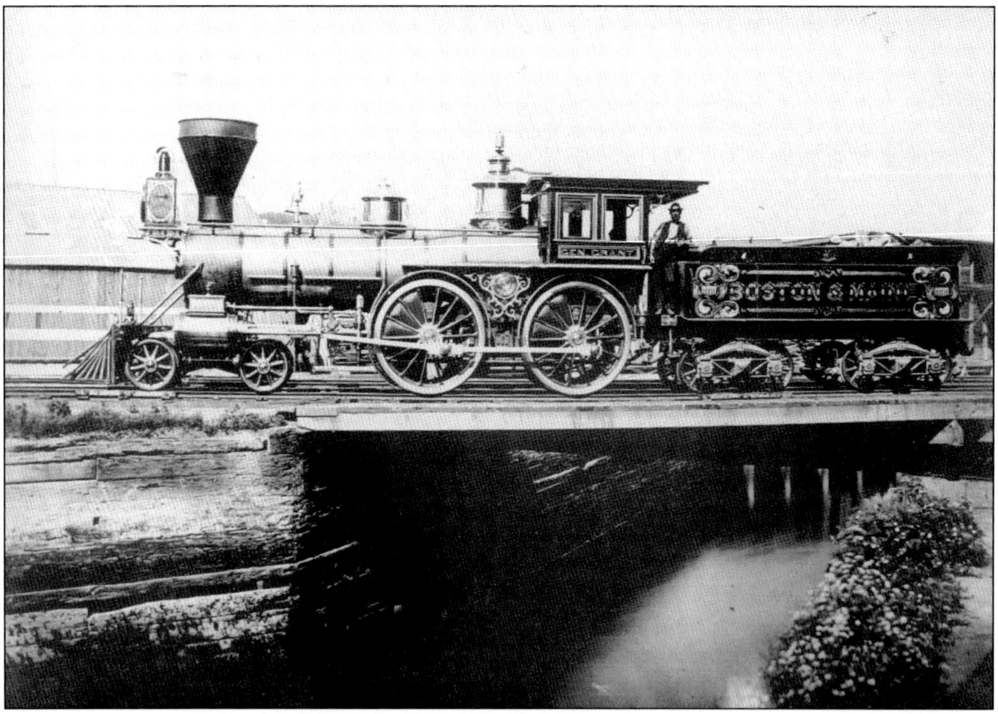

B & M No. 41, "General Grant" (4-4-0). The Manchester Locomotive Works built this engine in 1867. It had 16- by 24-inch cylinders and was scrapped in 1908.

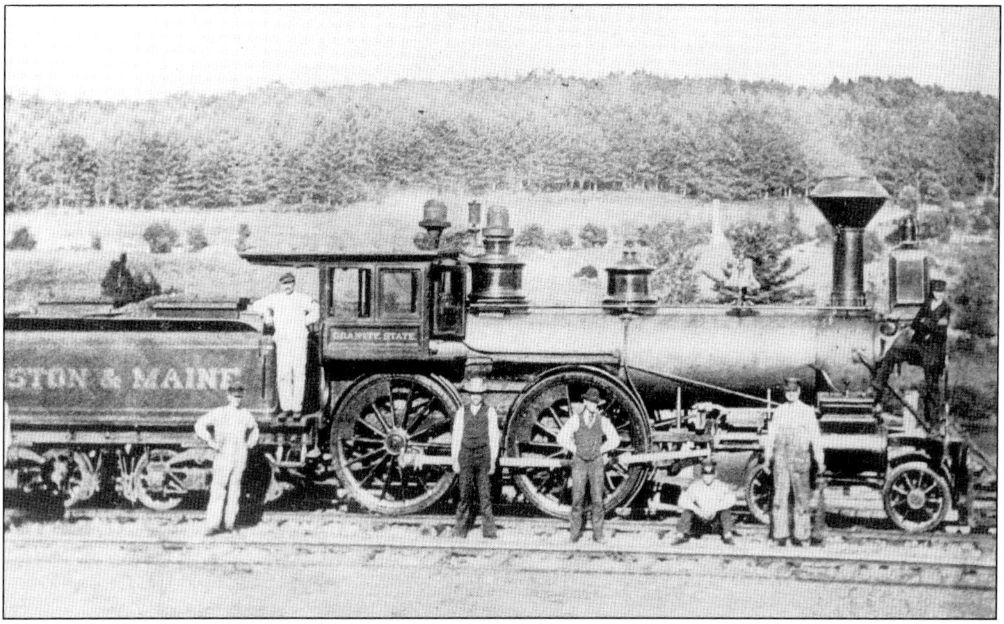

B & M NO. 18, "GRANITE STATE" (4-4-0). This locomotive, which had 14.75- by 20-inch cylinders, was built by Hinkley Drury. The first engine to burn coal, it ran the Dover–Alton Bay route and was finally scrapped in 1887.

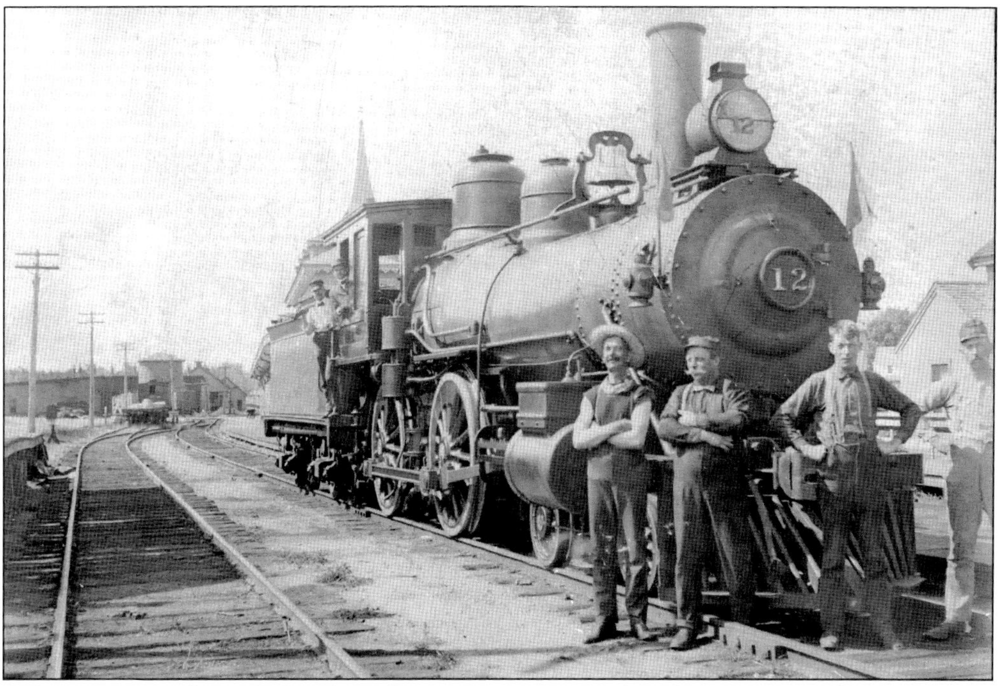

B & M NO. 12 (4-4-0). In 1911, this engine was renumbered as No. 862. This picture was taken at the Sanbornville Station in front of the engine house car shop. Standing in front of the locomotive are, from left to right, Winthrop Pike (engineer), Clarence Brook (conductor), Cenrille Abbott (brakeman), and Ernest Campbell (brakeman). In the cab are Frank Grans (manager for the Armstrong Restaurant) and Forrest L. Bracket (baggagemaster).

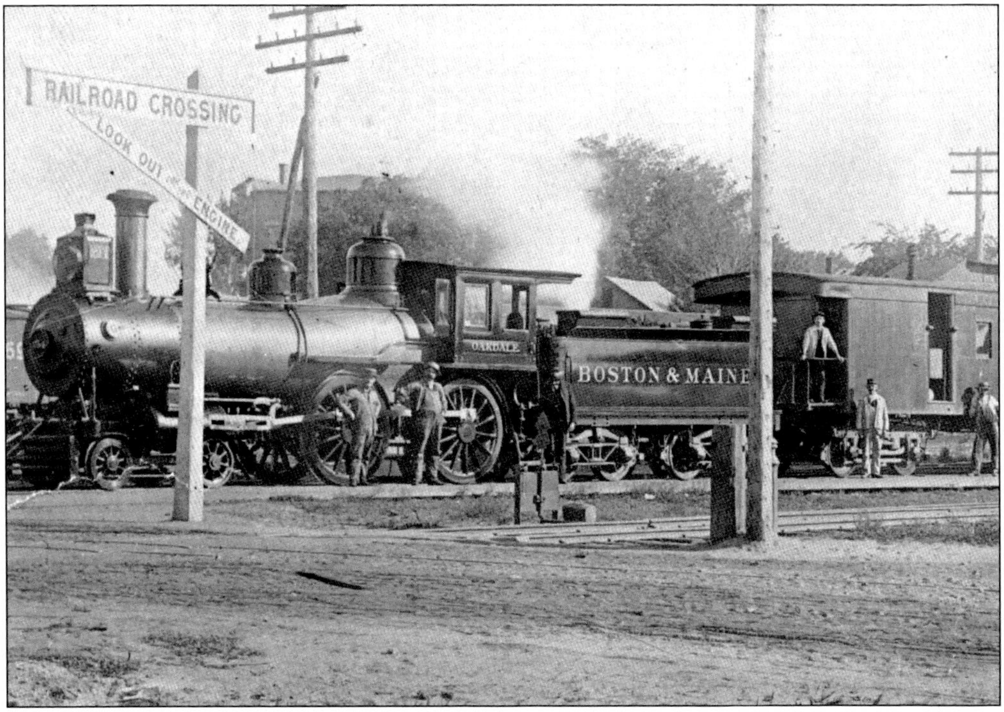

B & M No. 234, "Oakdale" (4-4-0). This engine was built in 1874 by the Manchester Locomotive Works for the Worcester, Nashua & Rochester Railroad. It had 16- by 22-inch cylinders and was originally designated No. 19, the "Portland." In 1886, the Boston & Maine leased this road, rebuilt the engine, and renumbered it as No. 234, the "Oakdale." In 1911, it became No. 750 and was retired shorty after in 1912.

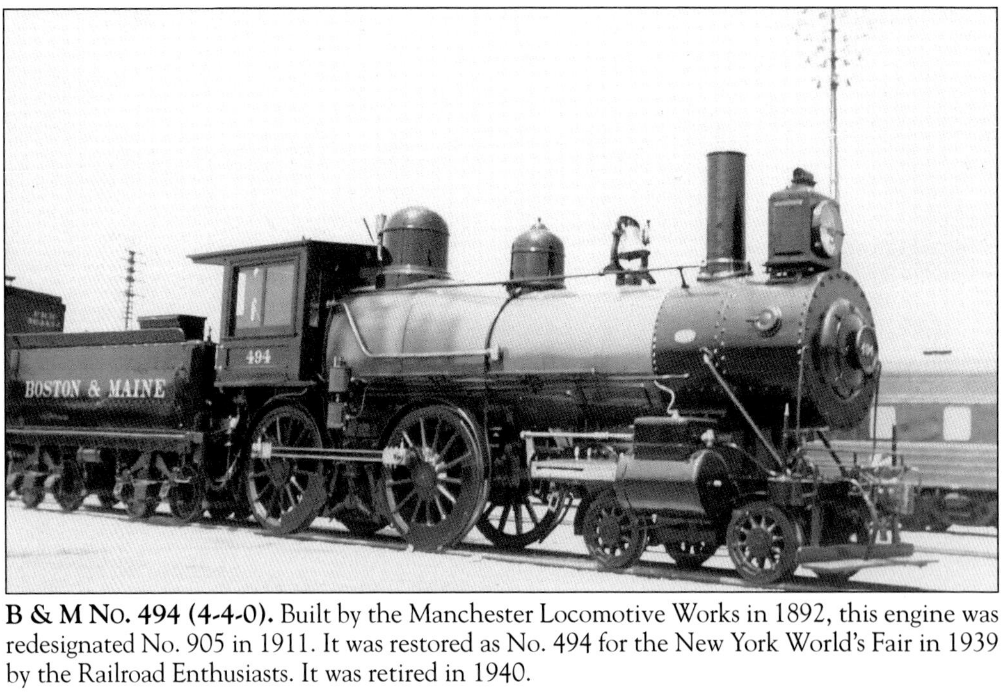

B & M No. 494 (4-4-0). Built by the Manchester Locomotive Works in 1892, this engine was redesignated No. 905 in 1911. It was restored as No. 494 for the New York World's Fair in 1939 by the Railroad Enthusiasts. It was retired in 1940.

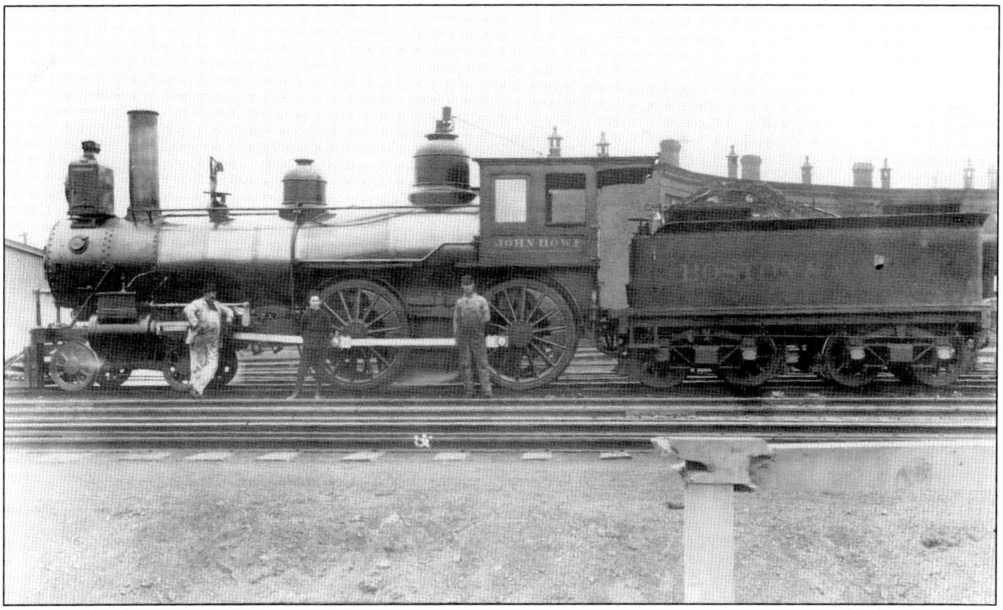

B & M NO. 634 (EASTERN RAILROAD), "JOHN HOWE" (4-4-0). Built with 17- by 22-inch cylinders, this engine was renumbered as No. 634. It was finally scrapped by the Boston & Maine in 1889.

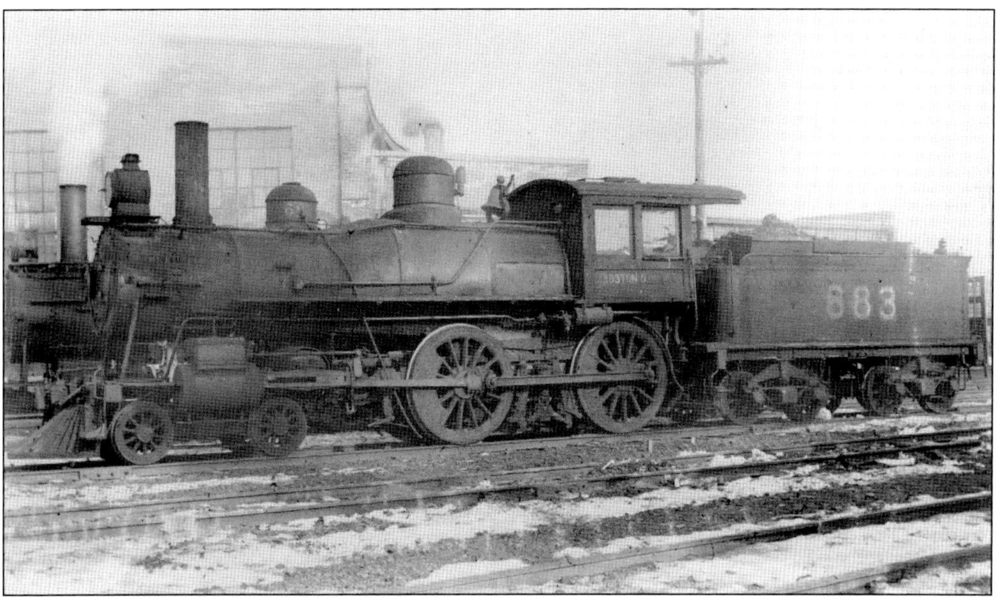

B & M NO. 683 (4-4-0). This locomotive originally belonged to the Massachusetts Central and then the Boston & Lowell as No. 65. Finally, in 1887, it became No. 365 of the Boston & Maine.

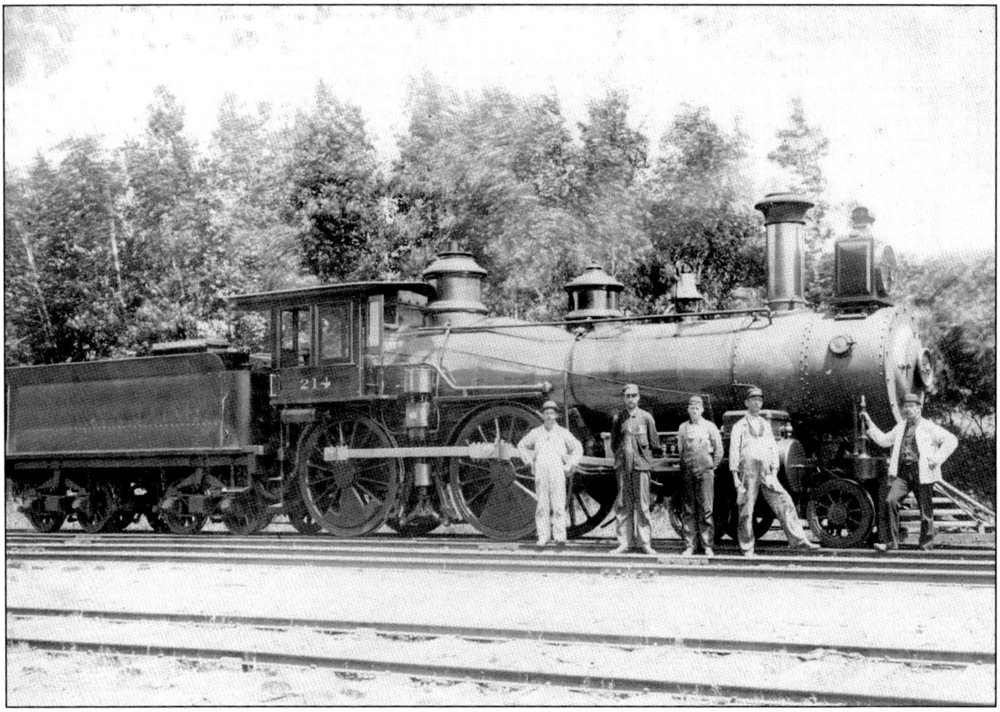

B & M No. 214 (4-4-0). In 1911, this engine became No. 841. This 1895 picture was taken in the Sanbornville yard in New Hampshire.

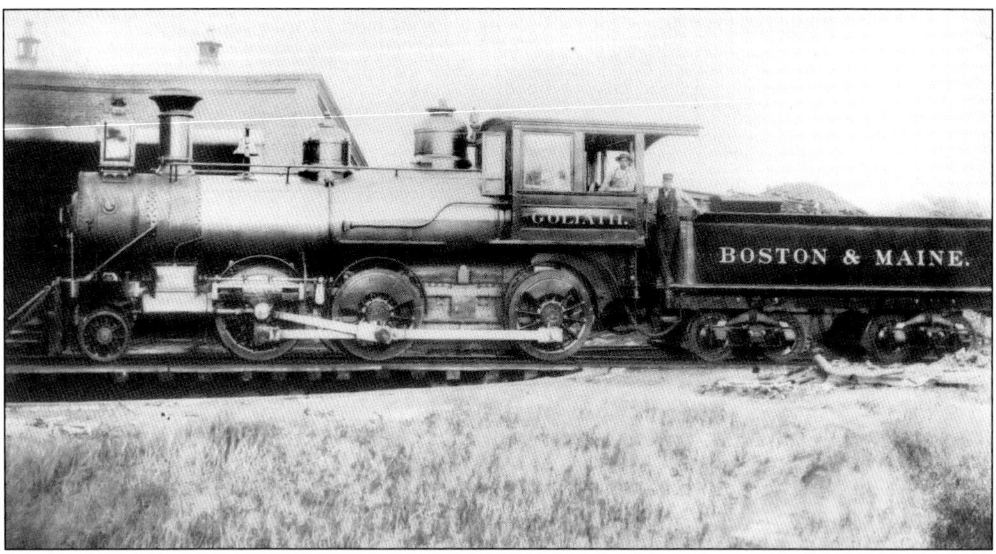

B & M No. 245, "Goliath" (2-4-0). The locomotive "Goliath" was built in 1885 by the Hinkley Locomotive Works with shop No. 1529. It had 18- by 24-inch cylinders and was renumbered as No. 1301 in 1911.

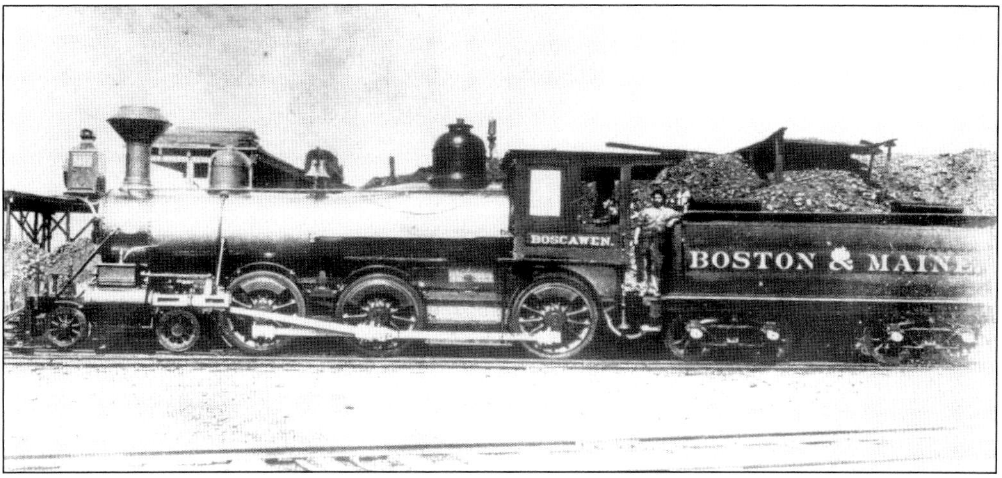

B & M No. 258, "Boscawen" (4-6-0). Built by the Manchester Locomotive Works in 1888, the "Boscawen" had 17- by 24-inch cylinders. It hauled freight trains through Oakdale, Massachusetts, in 1892.

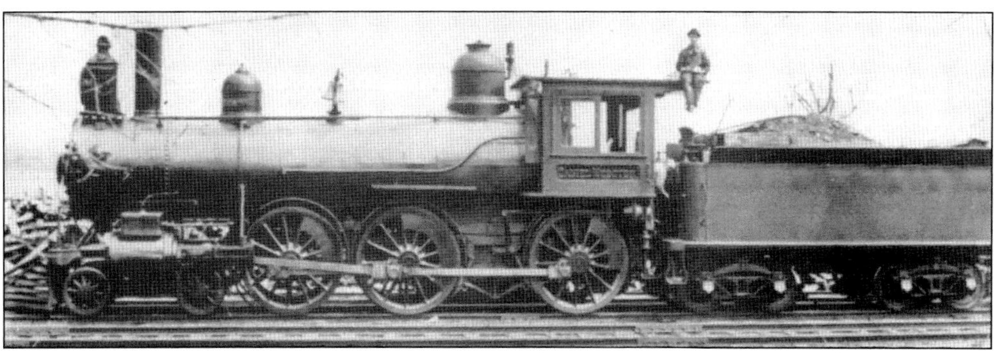

B & M No. 759, "Daniel Webster" (4-6-0). This locomotive was built by the Manchester Locomotive Works for the old Concord & Montreal Railroad as No. 59 in 1890. It was used years ago in hauling heavy summer passenger trains between White River Junction and Bretton Woods, New Hampshire.

APPENDIX B
COMPONENT RAILROAD LINES FORMING THE BOSTON AND MAINE SYSTEM
Corporate Name

East Barre and Chelsea Railroad Company
Eastern Rail-road Company
Eastern Railroad in New Hampshire
Essex Rail-road Company
Essex Branch Railroad Company
Essex County Railroad Company
Fitchburg Rail-road Company
Franklin and Bristol Railroad
Franklin & Tilton Railroad
Georgetown Branch Rail-road Company
Great Falls and Conway Railroad
Great Falls and South Berwick Branch Rail-road Company
Greenfield and Fitchburg Railroad Company
Greenfield and Northampton Railroad Company
Groton and Nashua Railroad Corporation
Hoosac Tunnel anad Saratoga Railraod
Kennebunk and Kennebunkport Railroad
Lake Shore Railroad
Lamoille Valley Railroad
Lancaster and Sterling Branch Rail-road Company
Lexington and Arlington Railroad Company
Lexington and West Cambridge Rail-road Company
Lowell and Andover Rail-road Company
Lowell and Andover Railroad Company
Lowell and Lawrence Railroad Company
Manchester and Keene Railroad
Manchester and Lawrence Railroad
Manchester and North Weare Railroad
Marblehead and Lynn Railroad Company
Marlborough Branch Railroad Company
Marlborough and Feltonville Branch Railroad Company
Massachusetts Central Railroad Company
Massawippi Valley Railroad Company
Medford Branch Rail-Road Company
Merrimack and Connecticut River Railroad
Middlesex Central Railroad Company
Missisquoi and Clyde Rivers Railroad Company
Monadnock Railroad Company (Cons.)
Monadnock Railroad Company (NH)
Monadock Railroad Company (MA)
Montpelier and Wells River Railroad
Montpelier and St. Johnsbury Railroad Company
Mount Tom and Eassthampton Railroad Company
Mount Washington Railroad Company
Mystic River Railroad
Nashua & Acton Railroad
Nashua, Acton and Boston Railroad Company
Nashua and Epping Railroad Company
Nashua and Lowell Railroad Corporation (Cons.)
Nashua and Lowell Railroad Corporation (NH)
Nashua and Lowell Railroad Corporation (MA)
New Boston Railroad Company
Newburyport Railroad Company
Newburyport Rail-road Company
Newburyport City Railroad Company
New Hampshire Central Railroad Company
New Hampshire (Central) Railroad Company
Newport and Richford Railroad Company
Northampton and Springfield Rail-road Corporation
Northern Railroad
Ocean Terminal Railroad Company
Old Colony Railroad
Orchard Brance Railroad Company
Pemigewasset Valley Railroad
Peterborough and Shirley Rail-road Company
Peterborough and Shirley Railroad Company
Portland and Rochester Railroad
Portland and Rochester Railroad Company
Portland, Saco and Portsmouth Rail Road Company
Portsmouth and Concord Railroad
Portsmouth and Dover Railroad
Portsmouth, Great Falls and Company Railroad
Portsmouth Horse Railroad Company
Portsmouth, New Market and Concord Railroad
Portsmouth, New Market and EXeter Railroad
Profile and Franconia Notch Railroad
Proprietors of Connecticut River Bridge
Proprietors of Wells River Bridge
Rockport Railroad Company
Salem and Lowell Railroad Company
Salisbury Branch Rail-road Company
Saratoga Lake Railway Company
Saugus Branch Railroad Company
Southern Vermont Rail Road Company
South Reading Branch Railroad
Stoneham Branch Railroad Company
Stony Brook Rail-road Corporation
Sugar River Railroad
Sullivan Railroad Company
Suncook Valley Company
Suncook Valley Extension Railroad
The Ashburnham Railroad Company
The Boston, Hoosac Tunnel and Western Railway Company (Cons.)
The Boston, Hoosac Tunnel and Western Railway Company (Vt)
The Concord & Montreal Railroad
The Concord Street Railway
The Connecticut & Passumpsic Rivers Railroad Company
The Maine, New Hampshire & Massachusettts Railroad Corporation
The Nashua & Rochester Railroad
The Peterborough & Hillsborough Railroad
The Peterborough and Shirley Railroad Company
The Proprietors of Portsmouth Bridge
The St. Johnsbury and Lake Champlain Railroad Company
The Sullivan County Railroad
The Vermont Valley Rail Road Company of 1871
The Wolfeborough Railroad
Tilton & Belmont Railroad
Trackage Rights
Troy and Bennington Rail Road Company
Troy and Boston Railroad Company
Troy and Greenfield Railroad Company
Troy, Saratoga and Northern Railroad
Turner's Falls Branch Railroad Company
Vermont and Massachusetts Rail-road Company
Vermont Valley Railroad
Vermont Valley Railroad Company
Waltham and Watertown Branch Railroad Company
Watertown Branch Rail-road Company
Wayland and Sudbury Branch Railroad Company
West Amsbury Branch Railroad Company (Cons.)
West Amsbury Branch Railroad Company
West Amsbury Branch Railroad
Whitefield and Jefferson Railroad
White Mountains Railroad
White Mountain (NH) Railroad
Wilton Railroad Company
Winchendon Rail-road Company
Woburn Branch Extension Rail-road Company
Worcester Branch Rail-road Company
Worcester and Nashua Rail-road Company (Cons.)
Worcester and Nashua Rail-road Company (MA)
Worcester, Nashua and Rochester Railroad Company
York and Cumberland Railroad Company
York Harbor and Beach Railroad Company

COMPONENT RAILROAD LINES FORMING THE BOSTON & MAINE SYSTEM. Shown is a complete listing of all the independent railroad lines that were either leased or bought out by the Boston and Maine Rail Road Company.